Psychotherapy and Spirituality

of related interest

Spiritual Dimensions of Pastoral Care
Practical Theology in a Multidisciplinary Context
Edited by David Willows and John Swinton
ISBN 1 85302 892 4

Spirituality and Art Therapy
Living the Connection
Edited by Mimi Farrelly-Hansen
ISBN 1 85302 952 1

Spirituality in Mental Health Care
John Swinton
ISBN 1 85302 804 5

Spirituality, Healing and Medicine
Return to the Silence
David Aldridge
ISBN 1 85302 554 2

Circular Reflections
Selected Papers on Group Analysis and Psychoanalysis
Malcolm Pines
ISBN 1 85302 492 9

Psychotherapy and Spirituality
Integrating the spiritual dimension into therapeutic practice

Agneta Schreurs

Jessica Kingsley Publishers
London and Philadelphia

First published in the United Kingdom in 2002 by
Jessica Kingsley Publishers Ltd
116 Pentonville Road
London N1 9JB, England
and
325 Chestnut Street
Philadelphia, PA 19106, USA

www.jkp.com

Cover illustration: 'The Golden Bird' (1983), Jaap Schreurs (1913–1983)
Cover design: Nelleke Oosten

Library of Congress Cataloging in Publication Data
A CIP catalog record for this book is available from the Library of Congress

British Library Cataloguing in Publication Data
A CIP catalogue record for this book is available from the British Library

ISBN 1 85302 975 0

Printed and Bound in Great Britain by
Athenaeum Press, Gateshead, Tyne and Wear

To my son Hans

Contents

Acknowledgements

This book would not have been written had not Dr Malcolm Pines, at that time President of the Group Analytic Society, welcomed a visitor from the Netherlands who told him that she wanted to write a book about spiritual issues in psychotherapy. He went much further than just giving me some of his valuable time. He promised to act as editor, put me in contact with the publisher, and encouraged me again and again during the writing process. Therefore my first thanks go to Malcolm Pines, without whom this book would never have come into existence.

I want to thank Revd Canon Beaumont Stevenson, Anglican priest and group analyst at Oxford. We have spent many summer holidays writing, reading and exchanging ideas about spiritual direction and psychotherapy. In particular the chapters of Part 1 have profited considerably from our discussions. I have to thank him for the wonderful atmosphere of creativity and spiritual depth he brought into our meetings, for his suggestions, examples and inspiring ideas, and above all for his friendship. The book he is now preparing, entitled *We as Me: Spirituality and Group Analysis,* provides an in-depth discussion of themes (e.g. guilt, suffering) which are discussed only briefly in my book.

I am especially appreciative of the guidance and encouragement of many years' standing of Dr Rob Gras. During my studies at the University of Amsterdam, he was my lecturer and trainer in group methodology. He did much more than just teach his students group theory and technique: he first of all taught us to be authentic and compassionate human beings. That was the foundation upon which technique and theory were built up as an enrichment and professionalisation of what was already there by nature. Many years later, he was the supervisor of my dissertation. Still later, when I started working on this book, he volunteered to read and comment on my texts, so I have profited from his expertise all through the years of its germination. His way of criticising and commenting was again one of uncovering and building upon what was already there.

Another teacher I want to thank is Professor Vincent Brümmer, professor in philosophy at the theological faculty of the University of Utrecht. I was 40 years young, already conducting groups for many years, when I decided to start the study of theology. Vincent's contagious enthusiasm made me overcome my initial hesitation, and I ended up taking philosophy as a main subject and working as his assistant for four unforgettable years. He was not directly involved in the production of this book, but I could never have written it without the thorough training in systematic and analytic thinking he has put me through in the past. As the last chapters of this book witness, I am also much indebted to his seminal books on love, prayer and personhood.

I also want to thank Drs Arthur Hegger of the Dutch Reformed Institute for Ambulant Mental Health Care (Eleos), Mr Tony Earl from the University of Utrecht, and my colleagues of the research project on spirituality at the Free University of Amsterdam, Drs Gerben Groenewoud, Dr Wim de Haas, Professor Evert van Olst, Drs Jan van Os and Dr Bart Voorsluis, for their invaluable and substantial help and many inspiring discussions.

It would have been impossible for me to undertake this work without the wholehearted support of many other friends and of my family. I cannot possibly mention everyone, so I say to all of you: thank you for your invaluable help, thank you for your encouragement, thank you for your faith in me.

Agneta Schreurs
November 2001

Foreword

This is a very important book: Agneta Schreurs skilfully interweaves the outlooks and insights of the Western tradition of psychotherapy, religion and spirituality. She does this clearly, sympathetically and persuasively. Readers will gain greatly from her understanding of the Foundation Matrix of our society and how, invisibly, as characterises the Foundation Matrix, our psyches are permeated by this inherited tradition. Her book is firmly rooted in a well understood and presented group analytic dynamic matrix.

This deep, fascinating monograph is written by a person who combines rarely found qualities: deep learning in theology; psychotherapeutic knowledge and experience; a sure grasp of the historical development of western society, who writes both clearly and persuasively. Agneta Schreurs addresses the reader and draws her/him along in her discussion of the deep human values addressed by theology, religion, spirituality and psychotherapy: sadness, (un)forgiveness, guilt, shame, remorse, revenge, loss of meaning in life. She shows us that a patient's spirituality can, when recognised, play a positive role in therapy. She skilfully disentangles the complex weave of psycho-pathology and religious issues in ways that illuminate these dark areas. She educates us and points to the further readings that will take us further along these paths.

Agneta Schreurs is Dutch and comes from a culture where theology and religion remain salient, a country where Protestantism and Catholicism are living cultural forces. We benefit from her immersion in that rich Northern European Foundation Matrix.

For over two decades group analysts from several European countries have met in a transcultural context in efforts to identify and to articulate 'hidden dimensions' of language, culture, history in our source countries. (One contribution from this work by L. Michel is referred to in this book). In one workshop when we asked participants to form themselves into groups of their religious education – Catholic, Protestant, Jewish, Muslem, Zoroastrian, Atheist, – the alarm was considerable, the outcome productive. For the most part we psycho-therapists put aside, so we believe, our religious and spiritual roots and therefore pay insufficient attention to the religious and spiritual issues in our patients. Robin Skynner, Murray Cox, Ronald Sandison, and Beaumont Stevenson stand out as exceptions; surprisingly, though we muster several clerics amongst the membership of the Institute of Group Analysis London, they have not yet contributed to our literature as much as they might. I hope that they, and those elsewhere, will be stimulated by their reading of this book and be persuaded by it to share their invaluable experience and insights into the role of spirituality in the psychotherapeutic process. Such would be a very welcome input to the Institute's literature.

Interest in the spiritual dimension of psychiatry is growing. The Royal College of Psychiatrists in Britain now has a special interest group in spirituality which is active, well-supported and was founded by a group analyst, Dr Andrew Powell. The rich bibliography in this book whets the reader's appetite for more.

I find the description of root metaphors and primary narrative structures illuminating and the warning about the danger of authoritarian ideology reminds me of the distinction Mikhail Bakhtin draws between the authoritarian voice that allows no dialogue and the persuasive voice that welcomes it. I hope that psychotherapists speak with the latter.

This book has grown through a long gestation and it could not have been otherwise. It is a product of a fine mind that has explored the illumination and also the dark night of the human spirit. We will all benefit through reading it attentively.

Malcolm Pines

Introduction

A woman in therapy is convinced that the death of her child is God's punishment for her sin of adultery... In a therapy group, a priest expresses his joy at his impending death... At the intake procedure, a religious patient expresses his fear that his faith will be 'explained away' in psychotherapy.

The purpose of writing this book is to introduce professionally trained psycho-therapists and mental health counsellors to the subject of spirituality and the influence it has – for better or worse – on therapeutic progress. It introduces this notoriously complex field in a way that is adapted to the needs of therapists who have to deal with the entanglement of psychological and spiritual problems. The book is about 'ordinary' spirituality, that is to say, the phenomena that are inherent in the change processes of spiritual awakening and a subsequent spiritual development. Nearly everybody who discovers his own spiritual longing and chooses to re-orient his life accordingly – patients and their therapists being no exception – is likely to be confronted with these phenomena and challenges. In this book the focus is in particular on the ways in which patients and therapists respond to spirituality *in a therapeutic setting*. It is *not* about extreme phenomena such as for example the hyper-religiosity of many psychotic patients. There is already much literature available on that subject.[1] It is addressed primarily to psychotherapists and mental health coun-sellors practising in general mental health residential units and day-to-day consultation clinics. The book presupposes no religious background of its readers, nor anything more than a general knowledge of religious beliefs, disci-plines and modes of spiritual development. Experience suggests, however, that the material presented can also be useful for religious therapists, pastoral psy-chotherapists, pastoral counsellors and the clergy.

The motivation in writing this book is that in many discussions my non-religious (secular-oriented) colleagues indicated that they felt uncomfort-able whenever their patients raised spiritual concerns. Coming from an agnostic or atheistic family background, often even third or fourth generation, they expressed the need for information that could help them understand what it means for their patients to be involved and motivated by a spiritual life. Their formal education, they claimed, had not helped them either in this area. Neither their university faculties nor their professional training institutes had taught them the subject of psychology of religion. And few (if any) of their teachers and trainers had ever helped them to understand spiritual people and what difference their religiosity makes in the way they relate to life. Yet this is the kind of knowledge therapists need for understanding these patients and for helping them sort out the role their spirituality plays in their problems. Moreover, most courses do not include a training aimed at working through therapists' own personal (non-, anti-) religious history, in order to help them recognise their countertransference in this area.

The literature on this subject shows that my colleagues were no exception. One example is an article on the new category 'Religious or Spiritual Problem' in DSM-IV (Code V 62.89). In this article, Lukoff, Lu and Turner write about the American situation that, in a survey of Association of Psychology Internship Centers training directors, 83 per cent of the respondents reported that discussions of religious and spiritual issues in training occurred rarely or never, and that one hundred per cent indicated that they had received no education or training in religious or spiritual issues during their formal internships. They also mention that a national study of APA-member psychologists found that 85 per cent reported rarely or never having discussed religion and spiritual issues during their own training. Other surveys also suggest that this lack of training is the norm throughout the mental health professions. Still other studies report that most psychotherapists either avoid the theme of religion, or handle it with insufficient professionalism.[2] Many are not aware of their specific countertransference with respect to religion and spirituality. Yet research has convincingly shown how necessary it is that therapists recognise their countertransference when treating religious patients.[3]

In view of this situation, this book is meant to contribute to the development of professional know-how in this field. It offers a general framework, which the reader can fill in later on with more detailed information and insights gained from further studies. It presents selected information meant to enable therapists to empathise with their patients and to see in what respects the goals and aims of spiritual life diverge from and converge with those implied in most therapeutic theory and practice. Vagueness about such divergences is often at the background of misinterpreting people's behaviour and expressions, whereas areas of convergence may strongly support therapeutic effort. It also tries to enable therapists to locate some of the most common difficulties and tensions inherent in the very enterprise of engaging in spiritual life, which may interact with psychological problems in unexpected ways.

In short, this book focuses on an exploration of the interface between psycho-therapy and spirituality. This not surprisingly raises a major problem, i.e. there are so many different methodologies, philosophies and theoretical conceptualisations championed by the various therapeutic schools and by worldwide spiritual traditions, that the book would become much too compli-cated and cluttered if I tried to take all of these into account. I have decided therefore that the readers are much better served by explaining, as clearly and systematically as I can, the main connections between *one* therapeutic school and *one* spiritual tradition. Understanding the implications of these then enables the readers to think through how they would apply what I write about this one therapy and this one spiritual tradition to other therapies and other spiritualities. The material in this book is therefore mainly restricted – with a few exceptions – to the therapeutic school of *group analysis* and the spiritual tradition of mainstream Western *Christianity*. (The term 'tradition' in spirituality is the equivalent of the term 'school' in therapeutic language use. It does not imply that spiritual traditions are traditional in the sense of conservative – actually many spiritual traditions are quite open to new insights and practices.)

It should be kept in mind, however, that group analysis and the concepts and recommendations I attach to it can serve as a *template* for their use in ap-proaches involving other therapeutic methodology such as, for example, the other insight-oriented psychotherapies. I have consequently tried to write in such a way that therapists of other schools can think the material through and adapt it to their own practice. The book, it must also be said, does not require specific foreknowledge of group analytic concepts *per se*. In so far as the ones I have used are not self-evident, I explain them and refer to key literature.

Mainstream Christian spirituality, it must be recognised, can serve only as an insight into the spirituality of other Christian denominations, other religions and movements such as New Age in a limited way. This choice of Christian spirituality as the book's focus of attention in no way implies a lack of value or respect for other spiritual traditions. Many aspects of spirituality are shared by these. Neither do I ignore the fact that some spiritual phenomena and techniques seem to be rather universal. However, understanding the con-nections between your own profession and *one* spiritual tradition will enable you to know at least which questions you need to ask in order to find similar connections with other forms of spiritual life. If you however decide to go more deeply into other forms of spirituality, this book offers a good starting point and references to help you.

Let me now present an overview of the contents of the four parts of this book.

Part 1 is intended as an introduction to the subject matter. With this intention in mind, the chapters are kept rather short. Each chapter presents one or two vignettes, which together illustrate various ways in which spiritual concerns may come up in the context of psychotherapy. Each one is then briefly commented upon from the viewpoint of a professional spiritual director. This is to make the readers familiar with the spiritual perspective in a concrete way, while simultaneously showing where and how it differs in emphasis from the psychological perspective. Occasionally, I have inserted questions into the text directly addressed to the readers. These are to make them notice and reflect on their personal response to what is being presented. The concluding text of Part 1 ends with inviting readers to use these responses as a first exploration of their own possible countertransference in relation to spiritual matters that have been raised in the preceding chapters.

Part 2 focuses on therapists *and* patients as they relate to and communicate with each other *in* the institutionalised practice of psychotherapy, which largely determines the rules and goals of their interaction, and which is itself in its turn largely determined by non-religious Western culture and its ideologies. The difficulties and differences in interpretation shown in the vignettes of the chapters of Part 1 are in part the result of the fact that our culture is split up into (at least) two partly overlapping, partly conflicting subcultures, the religious and the secular one. This break-up in our culture influences the therapeutic communication more deeply than we tend to realise. This is why Chapter 7 explores the cultural background of this underlying discrepancy. Chapter 8 connects it to phenomena such as metatransference and metacounter-transference, whereas Chapters 9 and 10 connect it with metaphors which function as organising principles of thought, perception and experience, and as such largely determine the deep structure of how we construct 'meaning' in our lives. Chapter 11 shows how for many *non*-religious individuals and communities, spiritual metaphors still tend to act as an unconscious 'grammar' for structuring *their* ways of thinking, perceiving and relating to life. More significantly (in the context of psychotherapy), these underlying organising principles also often determine the nature of their problems and conflicts.

In Part 3 I take yet another point of view. I now turn to the individual who seeks an ever-deepening personal relationship with God. I treat that as a normal, often deep-rooted and passionate, human desire with as much a curative as a disruptive potential in the therapeutic process. My approach in these chapters is to look at spirituality as a change process that is connected with the quality of the personal relationship between a person and God. It is rather unusual to include the dynamics of communication with a *real* divine being. Some readers may feel uncomfortable with my slipping such a theological notion into this book, so let me justify why I do so.

Ever since the famous controversy between Freud and Jung, most influential psychotherapeutic theories have had a negative view of religion. This is changing rapidly, however. An increasing number of theorists and researchers take a much more positive attitude towards the reality of the relationship between psychological and religious processes, as also about the therapeutic elements in many religions. Object relations theory in particular has bridged the gap to a considerable extent. It provides a sophisticated conceptual framework, as well as evidence for its validity, for describing the gradual development of a representation or concept of a personal God, which in its turn enters into a relationship with, and promotes the development of the 'self'. Yet even these studies, just like the earlier ones, assume that religious experiences and religious object representations should ultimately be attributed to *only* mental activity. They are not concerned with any *real* relationship between humans and a divine 'object' that in fact exists independent of human perception and language.

Such methodological restriction to subjective issues like 'religious feelings' and 'mental representations of God' is obviously legitimate for research purposes. But for *therapeutic purposes* there are two serious objections against dealing with religious material as if there is ultimately nothing other than internal feelings and representations. First, the above assumption conflicts radically with the worldview of most religions and that fact alone already influences treatment. Second, the *inter*subjective aspects of spirituality are systematically kept out of the picture. Yet it is precisely this intersubjectivity, this person-to-person communication or 'communion' with the real God, which is at the heart of religion and at the heart of individual spiritual life.

In choosing to approach spirituality as a learning and change process that is connected with a personal relationship between a human being and God as a real Transcendent Other, I am in fact choosing to introduce insights and expertise from the field of *spiritual direction* into the field of psychotherapy in both a group and a dyad setting. 'Spiritual direction' is the technical term for guiding people's spiritual journey to a life in communion with God. It is a theological specialisation of much older origin than pastoral counselling and pastoral psychotherapy. It is universally present in all major world religions, as for example via the person of the guru in Hinduism and the Zen master in Buddhism. Chapter 12 makes a short excursion into this field of spiritual direction. It touches on three key concepts of a simple and rather universal systematisation of stages in spiritual development. These stages are identified as purification (or purgation), illumination and union (or communion). I then proceed to show how these key concepts can be used for characterising the dynamics of spiritual change and its subsequent potential to accelerate psychotherapeutic progress.

When looking at spirituality as primarily a personal *relationship* with a transcendent Being, we can look at this relationship from three interdependent viewpoints: the *subjective*, the *objective* and the *intersubjective* point of view. From the first, one concentrates on the 'subject' who involves himself in the relationship. From the second, one considers how such a subject experiences and gets to know the 'object', the other partner in the relationship. From the third, one looks at what is happening 'between' the two. Each viewpoint highlights a different aspect of the same relationship. These three aspects are inherent in any serious and personal involvement, be it with a transcendent reality or otherwise. Structuring spirituality in this way is an obvious choice, because most therapies approach people as 'persons-in-relation' who, it is hoped, will change in and through the therapeutic relationship. Religious people bring their relationship with their God with them into therapy, so this is the area where therapy and religion are most likely to overlap, and therefore where it is most relevant to be aware of the differences and to make use of the similarities. This approach allows me to make the convergences and divergences between therapy and spirituality visible. It also allows me to include the many people whose spirituality is nowadays less and less embedded in a particular religion.

Chapters 13 and 14 approach spirituality from the 'subjective' viewpoint and consider what I have called the *existential aspect*. Any personal relationship requires one's involvement with the other to be motivated at an authentic level of the personality. Otherwise it is not a personal relationship but something different. But we know from therapeutic experience that there are many people who are not at all clear who they really are and what they really want in their lives. Many need to go through quite a process of sorting out and 'purifying' (as they say in traditional spiritual terminology) their authentic motivations from the inauthentic, and then need a lot of support in finding the courage to start living authentically in response to these. The same is true for building a relationship with God.

Chapters 15 and 16 are concerned with the tricky problem of how to know the 'object', the divine partner in the relationship. I have called this the *cognitive aspect*. Any genuine personal relationship requires that we get rid of the projections and transferences that keep us from knowing the other partner, the 'object', as he really is. This is also true of the relationship between man and God, so spiritual people need to get rid of – 'purify' themselves from – the projections, transferences, other false images of God and their own self-deceit that stand in the way of knowing and communicating with God as he really is. In this respect the learning goals in therapy and spiritual direction run largely parallel. Indeed, the largest part of spiritual direction is and has always been removing such psychological obstacles. But a personal relationship also requires at least some *knowledge of the other partner*. We need such knowledge as a basis for a real and mutual relationship as contrasted to an imagined one. And this is also true of the relationship with God. God being transcendent and invisible, the cognitive processes involved here are obviously different from the ones in human relations. Therefore Chapter 15 explains the phenomenon of intuitive – 'illuminative' – spiritual cognition, while Chapter 16 discusses what is involved in spiritual persons' search for intellectual integrity.

Part 4 looks at what happens *between* two partners, which I have called the *relational aspect*. How can a relationship develop to such a depth that people describe it as 'communion', sometimes even as 'union'? Chapter 17 considers what relational capacities people need for achieving more spiritual depth and intimacy, and at what points these converge with and diverge from the relational qualities aimed at in therapy. Chapter 18 then explains the function of theology for implementing a spiritual relationship and discusses how some theologies may actually be obstacles to therapeutic progress. Chapters 19 to 22 put the relational aspect in context by exploring how people have used – and still continue to use – three different types of human relationships as a kind of model for implementing their relationship with God. Each of these three has its own potential for bringing about or supporting therapeutic change.

PART 1

Spirituality in the Therapeutic Session

Introducing Part 1

People feel deeply about religion and spirituality. If they are passionate in this area, their desire is at least as fervent as sexual desire. If they are afraid of it, they are haunted by intense and pervasive fears. If they are misunderstood or disrespected, it touches the very core of their personality. If they are troubled by spiritual doubt, their very existence can be at stake. This is why spiritual concerns are particularly relevant to psychotherapy, irrespective of whether they are explicitly approached as such.

The question is, however, *how* do spiritual concerns manifest themselves within psychotherapy? In various ways of course, just like any other vital concern. And how can the therapist deal with them adequately? That would also vary, depending on his methodology and his understanding of what is going on. (Throughout the book I use 'he', 'him' and 'his', where 'she or he', 'her or him' and 'her or his' would make for more correct but less fluent language.)

To illustrate and to introduce in a concrete way the variety of ways in which spirituality may interact with psychotherapy – sometimes positively, sometimes negatively – this first part consists of a series of short chapters presenting various examples. My intention in using them is to show how spiritual concerns may be present either explicitly and verbalised, or implicitly and even unconsciously. Each example will be commented on, not exhaustively but enough to give an idea how it could be looked upon from a spiritual point of view.

Some of the commentaries on these cases discuss methodological issues and offer some suggestions of how to deal with them. Just like the case histories, the latter are also meant as examples, and that goes for similar suggestions in the later chapters too. This is because this book is not meant to be some sort of handbook providing a specific methodology for religious or spiritual problems. The emphasis is on providing sufficient insight into the dynamics of such problems to enable therapists to approach them in a way that is compatible with the methodology they already use.

These same commentaries will also serve to describe some terms I want to use in this book. Spiritual terms are notoriously difficult, because they have been developed within specific historical contexts. Even such general words as 'soul' and 'spirit' and 'spirituality' are so varying in meaning and so laden with different metaphysical and anthropological theories that one has to make a study to find out what they mean in any specific text. Therefore I prefer to use as few technical terms as possible, and to describe these terms in the context of examples rather than use definitions. One important distinction I prefer to explain here at the beginning of this book, however, is the distinction I draw between 'religion' and 'spirituality'.

'*Religion*' is the broader concept, denoting how a whole religious community lives with God (or however they envisage the transcendent Being). In the course of its history such a community has developed its own teachings, sacraments, forms of worship, prayer and meditation, rituals, and so on. These are usually handed down from generation to generation. They are also developed further from generation to generation. The majority of such religious traditions provide for the *individual* member of the community a variety of opportunities to develop also a *personal* relationship with the tran-scendent Being. The latter is what '*spirituality*' refers to: the personal, relational aspect of religion. It is about an individual's inner life, his ideals, attitudes, thoughts, feelings and prayers towards the Divine, and about how he expresses these in his daily way of life.

Of these two concepts, it is 'spirituality' that is most relevant for psycho-therapy. Psychotherapy addresses the individual's personal relationships. This is so whether the individual's personal relationship with the Transcendent may be the central concern in his life or not, or whether he may have found a spiritual home in some religion or not. That is why personal spirituality rather than religion is given prominence in this book.

For people who exercise and develop their personal spiritual relationship *within* a religion, this distinction between 'religion' and 'spirituality' sounds rather artificial. For them, both are inextricably bound up with each other. There is nothing special about that. In much the same way, for example, in a marriage the nature and the quality of the affective relationship between the partners is also inextricably bound up with the way they raise their children, do their housekeeping, spend their holidays, and so on. If that personal relation-ship is warm, open and loving, then they will perform all everyday activities and also their birthdays and other special family rituals differently than if their relationship is a cold one. In the same way one's participation in religious rituals and other activities will become empty routine if one is not personally, that is, spiritually, involved in them.

In short, religion with its teachings and public worship is of enormous significance in nurturing spirituality so that it grows and develops ideally in a healthy and balanced way. But there are two things which in a therapeutic setting we must not forget:

First, not all religious communities realise this ideal. And if the religious community concerned does not fulfil that ideal, that, too, will have consequences for one's personal spiritual life. Generally religious patients will view and experience their own spirituality as an integral part of the whole of their religion. But if they have problems with their community, or if their community restricts their personal spiritual development, then they may tend to seek other spiritual pathways, ones that are at odds (sometimes dangerously) with their religion.

Second, in the world we live in, in contrast to earlier times, spirituality is not exclusive to a religion. It exists outside formal religion too, and in a way that is relevant for therapy. There are now also large numbers of people who from youth on never have had any connection with a religion. Yet many of them know a deep and sincere spiritual longing and are therefore seeking some form of spiritual life – often in a way that is therapeutically relevant.

I draw this distinction between 'religion' and 'spirituality' because in this book I want to talk about spirituality occurring both *within* religion and also, equally important, *outside* of it. I also draw this distinction because I want to refer to religion as the social-cultural and religious *context* of spirituality, especially because religious patients' spirituality is largely determined by it.

CHAPTER 1

Flight, Fright or Faith?

Vignette 1

The group had less than three more months to run. One of the members, a priest, told the group that he had just been told that he had about as many months to live. The group was stunned. 'How did he feel?' 'Excited,' he replied, 'three months from now I will know for sure what I have been wondering about for most of my life.' The group picked up that theme and balanced his excitement with their sadness at losing him and their fear of death.

Before reading on, please think about this example for a moment, and ask yourself: How would I, as a therapist, respond to this patient's enthusiasm?

When this incident occurred, the therapist was faced with a group situation in which he could choose to respond in three different ways. He could interpret the patient's excitement as his running away from facing the reality of his impending death. Or he could interpret his telling of this fact at this particular moment in this particular group as an indirect expression of the group's fear of the approaching end of the group. Or he could choose not to interpret, but instead to allow this to be a serious communication of joy about the prospect of the experience of death and resurrection as the pinnacle of the priest's spiritual journey.[1]

This communication could in fact be *all* these things: it could be a manic flight *as well as* a mouthpiece for the group talking about their own imminent group break-up/death, *and also* a straightforward spiritual communication. The therapist's decision will determine the course of the group's subsequent learning.

In this case the therapist took the third option. It led to an intense exchange of religious views and religious experiences, which was useful both for the individual members and for the group as a whole because a new area of openness was introduced. In areas that matter deeply to people, authentic communication facilitates their expression on other sensitive issues. The whole group climate may change towards more depth and honesty. Moreover, as this happened in a late phase of the group process, there was sufficient reason for the therapist to expect the group to resonate on this deeper level.

It would have been perfectly legitimate to stay out of the spiritual, and take one of the first two options. At first sight there is no reason whatsoever not to respond on the basis of either the supposed fear of physical death nor on the supposed fear of the group's 'death'. On second reflection, however, choosing one of these alternative responses not only may block the opportunity for exploring the spiritual area that was presenting itself, but also may block the expression of such concerns by individual members of the group in the later sessions. People tend to be sensitive about expressing religious feelings outside their trusted circle of co-religionists, so they will easily feel their expression is being 'explained away' even though this may not be the therapist's intention. Other group members may also pick up the idea that straightforward communication of faith is 'not done' in therapy. As a result patients may not feel completely listened to and what is most central in their lives may remain unexplored. This creates the risk that these central concerns will become split off from the rest of the person's life. If the therapist is at least conversant in this area, patients may feel relieved to have the concerns acknowledged whenever they emerge. This can be so whether or not these concerns are worked on in their therapy group. As a result focus in a therapy session on such matters which may be concerning them intimately, or disturbing them deeply, is made legitimate.

CHAPTER 2

Groundless or Reasonable Fear?

Vignette 2

In a case conference I was once asked (as the therapeutic consultant present) for advice by a group psychotherapist who was confronted with a problem. His patient, a member of a strict Protestant denomination, during the intake interview indicated that he was afraid his religion would not be respected in therapy.

This vignette presents in a nutshell one of the key problems this book tries to approach, i.e. that non-religious therapists and religious patients already have a problem *with each other* well before they engage in psychotherapy. I have already touched on this in the introduction to this book, and I shall return to this 'pre-existing problem' extensively in the chapters of Part 2. In this chapter I would like to use this rather simple example, first to help the reader reflect on his own ideas about what to do in such a case, and second to give some short comments on the background of this patient's fear and on the strategy the consultant suggested to the therapist.

Before we meet the essentials of the advice the consultant gave, I invite you, as the reader, to put yourself in the role of the consultant and reflect for a few moments on what *your* advice might be or on what *you* think the consultant's advice might have been: How would you suggest the therapist can best respond to the patient's anxiety? *Before* the patient joined the therapy group? At the *start* of the patient's therapy? *During* the patient's therapy?

I would first like to make some general comments on the reasonableness of such a religious minded patient. He *may* use his religious fear to hide his resistance to psychotherapy of course, but even if he does so, his fear of disrespect is a reasonable fear and should be approached as such. First of all, he belongs to a community that is only too often not understood and sometimes not respected. Many converts, for example, have found that conversion often means loss of former friends. Many religious people, in particular members of strict churches, are labelled as 'fundamentalists' and treated as if they were narrow-minded fanatics. And yet faithful observance of orthodox teachings, be they Jewish, Christian or Islamic, is not in the least identical with fundamentalism or fanaticism.

One example of how widespread the ignorance about the particular sensitivities of this part of the population is can be found in an article in a Dutch weekly.[1] It reports with some uneasiness on an incident that happened when a mother brought her daughter to a regional mental health institute. During the intake interview the mother is asked whether other professional helpers are or would be involved. The woman answered, 'Yes, the Church minister,' whereupon the therapist responded with, 'The minister is not a professional helper.' The article goes on to tell its readers of the mother's reaction. It reports that during the rest of the intake interview the mother remains polite but afterwards she phones in to cancel the next appointment, saying that after all her daughter is not too bad. However, this is not the real reason for cutting off the contact. The mother reasoned: 'They do not accept my faith because they do not accept the minister. Therefore I cannot trust them with my daughter.'

This was not an isolated incident of a lack of perception which can be met in psychotherapy concerning religious aspects and is proved to be (unwittingly) hurtful to the patient and unhelpful to the therapeutic process that may be under way. How understandable the mother's withdrawal of her child from therapy on religious grounds as reported above could have been is illustrated in a further story. This is an actual happening concerning religious vulnerability and lack of religious awareness told by a psychotherapist working in the child psychiatry ward at a large hospital. One of their patients was a 9-year-old girl from a part of the Netherlands where the population is of a traditional Christian faith. After about half a year a new young psychiatrist was added to the staff. At a staff meeting she described how this girl had a problem with the other children in the hospital school, with the nurses, with her therapists, and with her psychiatrist. The problem was that they were continually swearing. There is indeed a kind of urban subculture where people have a habit of swearing without recognising that their swear words could offend another's religious sensibility and thereby hurt them deeply. This child had been raised in a culture where swearing is not only uncivilised and insulting, but also a *sin*. During the staff meeting it appeared that the child had once brought this subject up with her psychiatrist, but that he had treated it as *her* problem. As a result she had never brought the subject up again. It took the sensitivity of the new psychiatrist, who was the daughter of a Dutch Reformed minister, to see that it was the *hospital's* problem.

Thus we can see it as fair comment to say that religious patients do indeed have reason to anticipate incomprehension or even unintended disrespect. Some will ask for a therapist of the same faith but these are not always available. Some decide not to enter therapy at all. Some drop out after encountering what they consider to be the first sign of disrespect.

Now let us extrapolate a little further from these general comments and return to the therapist's dilemma in vignette 2 and the advice the consultant gave him. We will do this under the title of a sequel using the consultant's own account of his advice.

Sequel to vignette 2

I (the consultant) suggested that the therapist should ask the patient to tell in the very first group session what his central beliefs were that he wanted to be respected and to be very clear about them, so that he (the therapist) and the other group members would not trample on these beliefs. After that he could ask the patient to state what he wanted changed or what his unhappiness was about, and to make clear to the therapist and the others, that this would be the area they would work on in therapy. Whenever there were signs of a conflict occurring between that and his faith, the therapist should first help the patient to clarify what the conflict was, while respecting the patient's faith. Thereafter he should allow the patient to make his own choice about what he wanted to work at in therapy and what not.

I invite you, as the reader, again to reflect for a few moments:

What do you as the reader think about this suggestion? Do you think *you* could manage the patient's problem in the way this consultant suggests? Do you think the average patient would be able to verbalise his faith that well? That he would be able to assert himself when such a situation occurs, in a group culture which is alienated from religious faith, or against members who themselves have suffered rejection by their church, or if no subgrouping has developed around this issue? Do you think the strategy advised for the patient would be accepted by the group? Do you think the area to be worked on in therapy can indeed be partitioned off from a patient's faith? In short, do you think the consultant's advice is built around a *feasible* strategy – for therapist, patient and the group?

Let us take a closer look at this consultant's advice. It is quite clear that *any* therapist should try to protect *every* patient from *any* kind of disrespect.

However, in this case it was not sufficient for the therapist to state this as a general principle. At the intake the patient needed more reassurance, and this particular therapist himself obviously needed some reassurance too – otherwise he would not have asked for advice. The consultant suggested that the therapist should give the patient such reassurance, namely that he should tell the patient what the therapist would do to protect him. The consultant also suggested how the therapist involved should also reassure himself. He advised the therapist to emphasise to his patient how important it was for the patient himself to be open about things which troubled him on religious grounds if unintentional hurt was to be avoided.

The consultant also suggested that the therapist should tell the patient what he, the therapist, would do when the conflict was not between the patient and the others, but within the patient himself. By clarifying the inner conflict the therapist would give the patient the means to make a clear decision which is impossible as long as he feels confused and threatened. By differentiating the psychological from the religious, the therapist will reassure both himself and the patient that, although religious concerns may be freely shared, the issues that will actually be worked on will be those the therapist is qualified and contracted to treat. At the same time the therapist acknowledges the patient's inner conflict as a real one which will not be 'explained away' in therapy.

My own personal reaction to the advice, its strategy and its feasibility may be helpful here. Reflecting on it, I must say that I personally agree with the basic principles behind the consultant's suggestions. Yet I have two reservations. The first one is about the *feasibility* of having a patient clearly state his central beliefs and differentiate these from his psychological problems right at his entrance into a therapy group. Many people are very shy about saying what their religion really means to them. They will express their personal spiritual feelings only after they have learned to trust the others. Second, though I agree that a therapist should restrict himself to what he is qualified to do, I also doubt that the patient or the therapist can make a neat and tidy *division of tasks between the psychological and the spiritual.* In the rest of this book it will become clear that to a person who is authentically committed to spiritual life there simply are no 'pure' psychological problems. In the other parts of this book I hope to demonstrate that nevertheless a psychotherapist can provide valuable help and yet stay within his own psychotherapeutic territory and responsibility.

What strikes me in this vignette is that neither the consultant nor the therapist came up with the idea that in such a case it could be helpful to work with the patient's minister or another spiritual counsellor. I personally would think it worthwhile to advise the patient to seek spiritual counselling as well, offering to co-operate personally with the pastor or spiritual counsellor if needed. Faith is not a static quality. Whenever there is a conflict between psychotherapy and religion, the conflict is quite probably with childish, rigid, egocentric, or manipulative traits in the person's religion. Then, the crisis is in fact a sign that the person apparently needs to shed both psychological *and* spiritual malfunctioning. If this is the case, then it may be possible to co-operate with the patient's spiritual counsellor in the same way one would do so with the patient's doctor.

If the patient agrees to that, the therapist himself could also profit from a contact with the patient's minister, who may very well know the patient from his early youth on, know his family and their problems if there were such, and who has probably also shared many social and religious events such as marriages, funerals and celebrations with them. Such therapist–minister/priest contact can also inform the therapist about sensitivities in his patient's religious culture he could not be aware of. The above incident of the hospitalised girl who worried about the personnel's and other children's swearing was an example of such an unrecognised sensitivity.

In respect to contact between therapists and religious counsellors, a Dutch questionnaire revealed some interesting data. The questionnaire was addressed to ministers and priests and to professional psychotherapists from the regional mental health services in the Netherlands. Each was asked about referral to the other. The outcome was that the ministers and priests rather often referred parishioners to psychotherapists. The therapists interviewed, on the contrary, never once referred a patient to a minister or priest.

CHAPTER 3

Psychological or Spiritual Trauma?

Vignette 3

A young student had got himself involved in a fringe religious sect and literally had to escape from it. He had been taken abroad. The sect had 'kept' his passport for him, so he had to escape without his passport and argue himself through passport controls in order to get back home. It took much therapy in order to work through the guilt and the psychological damage the sect's action and his own response to it caused. Also his spiritual seeking, which was a prominent feature of his personality, was almost permanently damaged. All that remained was a sense of altruism which was expressed through the occupation which he later took up.

As a therapist, how would you approach this student's problem?

The preceding examples (vignettes 1 and 2 and their commentaries) assumed that religion played a positive role in the life of these people. In contrast, the example above shows an individual damaged by his own religious community. Unfortunately, there are very many cases of damage done either by the established churches or by sects. They frequently involve people who are deeply and authentically religious, people who have participated intensely in a religious community which for some reason they have left or from which they have been excluded. Many will have devoted a lot of time, love, and money to spiritual activities and often charitable work. One can hardly overestimate the pain of these people. Some of them become alienated from their church but not from their faith. Others lose their faith, become disillusioned and cynical, and this of course has an impact on their psychological state. Such people may begin therapy with serious relational problems, for example. In due time the spiritual trauma lurking behind the relational problems can emerge. How does one (as a therapist) deal with such problems?

An obvious line to pursue would be to refer to a pastor, preferably from their own religious community. An example of this is a man who had once been a priest. He was angry that his church had 'not wanted to know' about him after he had recovered from a bout of mental illness. The incident had occurred some twenty years earlier. In the mean time he had become a valued minister in another denomination. However, he still felt so hurt by what had happened that he started to cry as he told the group about it. After this incident in the group he decided to confront a priest with his hurt and his anger. In the group session which followed this confrontation, the patient said that the priest had acknowledged that the church was guilty of having deeply harmed him. He went on to say that the priest then had knelt in front of him, and had formally asked him for forgiveness for 'his' (the institutional church's) wrongdoing – upon which the excluded priest tearfully gave it. This was a turning point in his therapy.

But how many of such people would be prepared to go to a pastor? Would they not be so hurt that they could not bear to have anything to do with any church? And for a therapist, would it really be a good idea to refer people like the young student, for example, to the leaders of his sect? Or, in another example, to refer a homosexual teacher who has been thrown out of his job 'under God's damnation' to his minister? Further, how many ministers or priests would be prepared to acknowledge their church's behaviour as sinful? Most probably the churches or sects of such 'outcasts' are sincerely convinced their action has been right. They can hardly be expected to ask for forgiveness.

What could psychotherapy have to offer to such 'outcasts'?

When you are excluded or expelled from your church for the wrong reasons, it is essentially the same confrontation faced by a young homosexual boy or a young pregnant girl who has been thrown out of the house by a self-confident but over-authoritative father forbidding him or her ever to return or to get in touch again. Could you ever again as a person be able psychologically to trust, to commit yourself, to summon up the courage to show your face at home? This theme is, clearly, appropriate for psychotherapy. Especially when, if you have not solved these things at a psychological level, you will feel that you cannot show your face to God either. Psychologically, people who are excluded from their religion have been thrown out of their family, cut off from their own roots. Psychotherapy can and should offer to help such people solve this problem and to help clarify their questions to God. Thereafter they may then be able to deal with the spiritual problem of how to restore what they experience as a broken relationship with God.

Therapy can also help such people as those in the examples with another aspect of their problem. It is important that such people face the fact that there are 'unhealthy' religious communities and bad religious leaders. Religious

movements and all established churches (like political movements and govern-
ments) can get hijacked by tyrannical factions, or can become collectively unbalanced by exaggerating one aspect of the religion over all the other aspects.
Obsession with waging religious wars, or with over-scrupulous demands for
conforming behaviour, are examples of such exaggerations. Such exaggerations build up from time to time, but we must not forget that religious institutions have as much trouble getting rid of such attitudes and behaviour as do
any individuals and secular institutions.

But people like the young student in our example do need some kind of
'healthy' spiritual life and 'sound' religious teaching. Otherwise life will, in the
end, become meaningless for them. For this an appropriate religious
community is indispensable. The persons involved have to appreciate that the
majority of religious communities are not so uncharitable, narrow-minded, or
fanatical as the ones they have left or been excluded from. But the question is,
how are they to judge? Could therapy offer some help in this?

While it is never warranted as a therapist to tell someone that you think their
church or sect is obsessional or bullying, nevertheless it is always appropriate to
ask questions about everything. This includes asking questions about religious
practices and attitudes, so that people can reflect and come to their own conclusions about what is right for them in their particular situation in life. Although
evaluating religions is outside the therapist's province, he is well qualified, and
even in a unique position, to recognise the signs of imbalance and to formulate
self-reflexive questions that can help the person make his own judgement and
his own decision whether or not to join another religious community.

CHAPTER 4

Vision or Hallucination?

Vignette 4

She was nervous when she came in. She was a down-to-earth woman, an industrious housewife. She had lost her husband, had acknowledged his loss and had been working through it, clearly acknowledging her feelings and what he had meant to her. She was open and honest. Her fear was in what her GP had asked her to share with me. Would I think her crazy? Would I refer her to a psychiatric hospital? 'You see,' she began, 'Every now and then I hear my name called, and I also have had a vision. I want to make sense of it. I want to know what you think.'

As a therapist, how would you respond to this woman?

Implicit in this example is the same discrepancy as we noted in vignette 2 (a religious patient who fears disrespect). But the difference here is that the conflict between the religious and the secular view is now *within the person*. Potentially, it was becoming a threatening situation for her.

The fear of being 'crazy' is quite common with visionary people, religious believers included. Many of them have internalised the popular view that people who experience voices and visions must be hallucinating. And many churches, having known more than their share of mental disorders and impostors, have quite understandably grown wary of these phenomena.

In reality, the art of distinguishing between visions and hallucinations is not complicated. Morton Kelsey says: 'If someone sees pink elephants, that is a vision. If someone sees pink elephants and hides under the bed for fear of being trampled by them, then that is a hallucination. The difference is really very simple.' Most people who came to him with visions knew perfectly well that these experiences did not originate in the physical world. Kelsey explains that, like a dream, a vision is a vivid image or series of images over which we have no control. If conjured up wilfully, it is not a vision. Unlike a dream, a vision does not happen during sleep but when the person is wide awake and knows he is awake.

Winnicott, too, sees hallucinations as dream phenomena that have come forward into the waking life. In his opinion, 'hallucinating is no more an illness in itself than the corresponding fact that the day's events and the memories of real happenings are drawn across the barrier and into dream-formation'. Although Winnicott does not differentiate between hallucinations and religious visions, he implies that he considers the criterion for pathology not to lie in the fact that people 'see' but rather in the way they deal with what they 'see'.[1]

Moreover, many quite 'normal' people at some time of their lives see visions and hear voices. Now that the taboo on talking about these experiences is diminishing, it appears that they happen to a much larger section of the population than was supposed. Current research in social psychiatry has compared three groups: schizophrenia patients, dissociative patients, and non-patients. These three groups all experience their voices in the same way. Professor M.A.J. Romme, head of the department performing this research, concludes that the big difference is that patients hear many more negative voices, whereas non-patients predominantly experience them as positive. Another difference he has observed is that psychiatric patients are mostly unable to cope with them, whereas healthy people stay in control and respond to them as persons who adopt a position towards them.[2] As an alternative to medication, which rarely helps in these cases, the research team now teaches people to accept the voice or vision as something that belongs to them personally. Rather than fighting the phenomenon, they begin with making these people realise that struggling with it only makes matters worse. Therefore they teach people how to stay in control and how to prevent the voices from weakening their concentration during work.

To return to the example of the woman in vignette 4, she could easily be reassured about hearing her name called and her vision. This is how the therapist, who was aware of the religious–secular conflict within her, responded:

Sequel to vignette 4

'People in the psychiatric ward definitely behave differently than you do,' I told her. 'Your hearing your name called reminds me of the story of young Samuel. He heard someone calling his name, but someone else had to explain to him it was God's call.' The woman, herself religious and familiar with the biblical story of Samuel, answered, 'Yes, I've had the same thought. Do you think it could be something like that?' I said, 'Maybe the Lord has something to say to you, but of course I cannot tell

you what that would be. So try to listen to him.' As the therapist involved, I advised her to cut down her household work and her prayers, and use that time to become rested and quiet so that she could listen better.

This therapist moves a step farther than just reassuring her! He suggests it might be a visionary phenomenon that conveys a direct message from God. This is of course not standard procedure, but here it makes sense because both the therapist and the woman share the same religious belief. This is probably why this woman's GP referred her to a Christian psychiatrist. They are both familiar with the biblical story of the prophet Samuel, who as a boy awoke at night hearing his name called. He then ran to his master, the old priest Eli, thinking he was the one who called. Eli denied that this was so and sent the boy back to his bed. However, the same incident happened again – and then for a third time. Then the old man told the boy it was probably God who was doing the calling and advised him to stay and listen to the voice next time.[3] Within this shared religious frame of reference, recall of this Samuel story is a valid model of how God may very well manifest himself, and how people may explore the spiritual meaning of the experience.

The question is, would the difference between religious visions in the strict sense of the term and other visionary experiences be relevant for therapy? In therapy you deal with patients, so would not their experiences be unequivocally pathological?

The answer is not so simple. First, these kinds of religious phenomena seem to happen to all kinds of people, to the healthy and to the sick, to the imaginative and to the unimaginative, to the educated and to the uneducated, to the religious and to the non-religious, to the good and the bad – criminals are no exception. Mental patients are no exception either, and that is why it makes sense that the validity of patients' experiences should be assessed.

Second, physical, psychological, and spiritual problems often tend to interact. Lingering marriage trouble, for example, may cause physical complaints. It may also cause spiritual complaints such as an 'empty' prayer life. But there are exceptions. Just as some artists may be very disturbed without their talent being much impaired, some patients may both be very disturbed and have a prayer life more healthy and authentic than that of most 'normal' people. In such a case, their religious life may be particularly relevant to therapy as a *positive* factor. And if in the context of their religious life they have religious visionary experiences (in the strict sense of this term), then these are of significant importance to the patient and should definitely be dealt with quite differently from pathological delusions.[4]

Let us illustrate this with another example:

Vignette 5

She is a housewife, in her mid-thirties, entering therapy because of bulimia nervosa. She is not given to vomiting or the use of laxatives, but whenever she over-eats she becomes high for several hours. When shopping she cannot resist ice cream, grilled chicken, and other snacks. She leads an isolated life. Although she is a member of the Pentecostal church she is keeping this at a distance from her too. She is married to a man who has become severely psychotic. Her little son is very withdrawn and himself a borderline case. Whenever she is high from eating, she is unable to keep a safe eye on him. Her little son is now in hospital for observation.

Her childhood has been sad and lonely. Her mother, her elder sister, and her grandmother were very close but always excluded her, the second and youngest child. Until she was 12 her father had supported her. He then became sexually attracted to her. At 17 she had attempted suicide and was hospitalised for some time. She still shudders when she thinks back to confinement in an isolation cell.

Her communication with God is very intense and in the course of it she sometimes experiences visions. In her visions she says she has seen Jesus crying when she could no longer resist over-eating. As a girl, she had experienced that the Holy Spirit showed her who she was, a 'mowed patch of grass'. More recently she has seen herself as a beautiful woman. She knew this woman was the woman that God would make her. She has also been given the knowledge that she would become a good and strong mother. To her these visions were very precious experiences, a real lifeline. But it was because of these visions that for some time she had hesitated to seek help. Was she hallucinating? Would she again be put in a psychiatric hospital – again be isolated?

She is recovering now, very slowly, very painfully. And all the while it seems as if God is guiding her healing process through visions.

It is not always therapeutically relevant to figure out whether or not a vision is a 'religious' one. But in cases like this bulimic patient it is. In these cases, one needs criteria for discovering the vision's source and spiritual meaning. Unfortunately, most psychological and medical theory does not consider as serious the possibility of a 'divine reality' manifesting itself. As a consequence of this, no such criteria have been developed to help assess whether this is so or not. Neither, unfortunately, is it possible to make a clear-cut distinction between religious and non-religious visions.

Such religious communities that recognise the possibility of receiving direct religious messages have developed tests and criteria for evaluating and interpreting such experiences.[5] Like a dream, a vision may have widely divergent sources and meanings. A well-known secular example is the discovery of the structure of the benzene ring by Kekulé von Stradonitz. One day he was travelling on a bus through southern France. He was half-asleep when he saw in front of him six snakes. Each held another by the tail end, forming a circle. From this vision came Kekulé's theory of the benzene ring.

Like a dream, a vision may also have a spiritual meaning. Therefore visions, like dreams, may validly be looked upon as being potentially a form of communication from God. As such they can be accepted and 'worked at' for an understanding of them, an understanding which may or may not be instantaneous. However, by no means does every voice or vision originate from a spiritual source. This is true even for those in which Jesus or Buddha or Krishna appears.

I would suggest that in such cases a therapist could profit from the information and expertise gained through 'spiritual direction'. Spiritual directors, also called spiritual guides or spiritual friends, are specialised in counselling people in their personal relationship to spiritual reality. They are not necessarily priests or ministers, and throughout history women have always figured prominently in this calling. Spiritual direction is directly concerned with a person's actual spiritual experiences.[6]

All through history spiritual directors have had to learn how to discriminate sensitively between deception, self-deception, psychopathology, and the 'real thing'. This art is called 'spiritual discernment'.[7] This idea of discernment is not to be confused with our concept of diagnosis. As Gerald May puts it: 'Discernment' (or the Greek 'diakrisis') refers to an act of separating apart. 'Diagnosis' refers to distinguishing through knowledge.'[8] Discernment is more subtle and intuitive than diagnosis: those who 'discern' are very much aware of the uniqueness and complexity of each human being. They seek to discriminate among inclinations so that a proper direction can be followed.

Within the practice of group analysis we can also observe that, while on the one hand it is necessary in group therapy to have a correct diagnosis of a problem, the nature of group analysis is such that it often also calls forth a collective sensitivity, which may function as some sort of 'collective discernment' capable of separating the authentic from the inauthentic. This is connected with the 'basic law of group dynamics', which Foulkes formulated so: 'The deepest reason why [these] patients...can reinforce each other's normal reactions, is that *collectively they constitute the very norm, from which, individually, they deviate.*[9] One effect of this 'law' is that the group can signal the overall direction in which a person is going as well as identify basic life choices. In other words, a therapy group as it progresses may also become increasingly competent in the art of spiritual discernment.

CHAPTER 5

Depression or Spiritual Darkness?

Vignette 6

To all appearances he was a successful man in his mid-forties. The confident expression on his face did not quite mask the look of sadness and desperation about the eyes. His recent 'accident' in the car was not really an accident. 'I really didn't mean to do it; it's not that I wanted to die, it is just that I cannot think of any reason to live. That is very important to me. Can you help me?'

As a therapist, how would you respond to this man's question?

'It's not that I wanted to die, it is just that I cannot think of any reason to live.' In his book *Psychotherapy and Existentialism* Frankl observed that as a psychiatrist he was more and more confronted with patients who suffered with a total loss of an ultimate meaning to their existence. Since then psychotherapy has known ever-increasing numbers of people with this kind of vague but nevertheless very urgent complaint.[1] Many of them are not patients in the traditional sense of the term because they are usually performing adequately. They are capable of intimate relationships and they do not suffer from depression. This phenomenon has given rise to an increasing interest in existential psychotherapy, based on the view that it is of critical importance to people to create a meaningful life in the face of a meaningless universe, and that in order to do this they have to face honestly and courageously the dilemmas of existence, and the confrontation with their own mortality.[2]

An experience very similar to that of such patients (feeling life to be meaningless without there being an obvious reason for this feeling) is quite commonly met in the practice of spiritual direction. To spiritual directors this is not in any way a new phenomenon, nor characteristic of our time. It is considered to be one of the signs that a person is on the verge of reaching spiritual awareness (it is then traditionally called 'spiritual darkness'), or, if the person is already engaged in a spiritual quest, that he is in a process of transition from one stage of spiritual development to another (such transitional depression-like

43

states are usually called 'dark nights'). The phenomenon reminds one of a rather similar phenomenon in the psychology of art. Many artists report knowing an 'incubation period', a period of despair and emptiness which precedes a new turn in their development as a creative artist. Vignette 7 is a clear example of 'spiritual darkness', taken from one of the numerous autobiographical reports of the phenomenon:

Vignette 7

...but five years ago something very strange began to happen with me: I was overcome by minutes at first of perplexity and then of an arrest of life, as though I did not know how to live or what to do, and I lost myself and was dejected... These arrests of life found their expression in ever the same questions: 'Why? Well, and then?'

At first I thought that those were simply aimless, inappropriate questions... that now I had no time to attend to them, but that if I wanted to I should find the proper answers. But the questions began to repeat themselves oftener and oftener, answers were demanded more and more persistently... I understood that it was not a passing indisposition, but something very important, and that, if the questions were going to repeat themselves, it would be necessary to find an answer for them. And I tried to answer them. The questions seemed to be so foolish, simple, and childish. But the moment I touched them and tried to solve them, I became convinced, in the first place, that they were not childish and foolish, but very important and profound questions in life, and, in the second, that, no matter how much I might try, I should not be able to answer them. Before attending to my Samara estate, to my son's education, or to the writing of a book, I ought to know why I should do that. So long as I did not know why, I could not do anything. I could not live... All that happened with me when I was on every side surrounded by what is considered to be complete happiness. I had a good, loving, and beloved wife, good children, and a large estate, which grew and increased without any labour on my part. I was respected by my neighbours and friends more than ever before, was praised by strangers, and, without any self-deception, could consider my name famous. With all that, I was not deranged or mentally unsound, – on the contrary, I was in full command of my mental and physical powers, such as I had rarely met with in people of my age...

The author of this autobiographical vignette is Leo Tolstoy. This period of despair about the meaninglessness of his life was followed by a conversion experience: '...I understood that faith was not merely an evidence of things not seen, and so forth... that faith was the knowledge of the meaning of human life, in consequence of which man did not destroy himself, but lived. Faith is the power of life...Without faith one cannot live.'[3]

Leo Tolstoy is by no means the only one in whose life such a period preceded a spiritual breakthrough or a new turn in their spiritual journey. It is not exceptional, too, that during such a period people do not realise that they are actually engaged in a process of spiritual progress. What is new and typical in modern Western culture is not so much that people suffer from it, as that many of them turn for help to a therapist and not to a spiritual counsellor such as a priest or a minister. This is why I suspect that among the increasing numbers of those who seek therapy with vague feelings of meaninglessness there may be quite a few who are unwittingly involved in a search for spirituality. We have coined a phrase for this phenomenon that will also be used in this book: 'spirituality in exile'.

It makes sense in the context of vignette 6 to ask whether this businessman is on the verge of a depression or of a spiritual awakening. His case may be a genuine case of 'spirituality in exile'. If so, his wrestling with the seeming meaninglessness of life would then be seen as a perfectly normal phase in his progress towards an authentic spiritual life.

Handbooks of spiritual direction mention a number of 'dark nights' normally occurring in the course of most contemplatives' lives. (A contemplative is a person who has chosen a radically and totally God-oriented life. Two forms of praying are particularly important for contemplative life: meditative and contemplative prayer. The latter is analogous to the practice of silence and openness known as 'meditation' in the Buddhist tradition. This terminology can be confusing because in the Western spiritual tradition the term 'meditation' is used for a different practice, one in which words and images play an important role. See also Chapter 17, section 2.) These 'dark nights' precede a new development towards another, more profound way of praying. They are periods of deep inner suffering and loneliness, in many aspects very similar to depression. Therefore it is very important for spiritual directors to be able to recognise whether the person is showing the first depressing signs of mental and physical ailment, or whether he is indeed entering a 'dark night' which has to be dealt with quite differently from depression.

One criterion for 'discernment' in such cases is that 'dark night' experiences, unlike primary depressions, are not usually associated with loss of effectiveness in life or work. Often the person is mystified at how well he is continuing to function. Furthermore, a sense of humour and compassion for others are both retained. While there may be a great superficial dissatisfaction and confusion, there is also a feeling that in spite of everything there is an underlying sense of 'rightness' about it all. This is in stark contrast to depression where one's deepest sense is of wrongness and (consciously at least) the desire for a radical change.[4]

This is but one example of an issue where it is necessary to differentiate carefully between psychological and spiritual phenomena because at first sight they look similar, but in fact they are different phenomena and need distinctly different approaches. There are more areas in which such subtle discernment is needed. I shall not elaborate on them here, because in this chapter the message is a general one: *as a result of the modern phenomenon of 'spirituality in exile', such people may enter psychotherapy* and therefore it is useful for a therapist to be knowledgeable about the dynamics of spiritual life. Part 3 and Part 4 will discuss some important aspects of these dynamics.

CHAPTER 6

Narcissism or Misdirected Worship?

Vignette 8

In his book Burnout: The High Cost of High Achievement, *Herbert Freudenberger describes the case of Clyde.*[1]

Clyde grew up in Texas, living with his mother, two older brothers and a younger sister. His father died suddenly when Clyde was a teenager. Because the family had little money Clyde, now at high school, spent his evenings working in a local restaurant. After graduation he took a full-time job as a waiter. He felt a responsibility to help support his family. His older brothers had gone off on their own leaving him to support his mother and sister.

He threw himself into his work. After a few years Clyde went into partnership with his employer to open a new restaurant. He worked even harder determined to make the new venture a success. He spent almost all of his time at the restaurant, building the business and worrying about the future. He had little time for recreation. The restaurant became a huge success and he worked even more hours.

When Clyde's mother remarried he was free to slow down a bit, to start a life on his own. Unfortunately, he had become trapped in a pattern of work addiction that was difficult to stop. He decided to go on to bigger and better things. He sold his share of the restaurant for a substantial profit and headed for New York. He was determined to open an elegant restaurant and make it the best in the city. He found the New York business world a lot more difficult than he had expected. He spent weeks trying to establish contacts. Neither his money nor his Texas reputation seemed to impress anybody.

He worked and planned even more diligently, more compulsively. He became more and more frustrated. One evening he met some people at a bar who introduced him to cocaine. The cocaine made him feel alive and supercharged. It gave him the same feeling of exhilaration that he experienced when working. Since his compulsion to work was not giving him the same satisfaction as it once did, he found cocaine to be an effective substitute.

He began spending more and more money on drugs. Although he still tried in vain to get his restaurant started, he met with failure at every turn. He became extremely dependent on cocaine, needing it every day. When he was not working compulsively he was using cocaine compulsively. He finally ended up with little money working as a waiter.

I shall use this story for a little imaginative excursion. First, I shall imagine how a therapist may evaluate Clyde's condition and consider an appropriate therapeutic approach. Then I shall take a second look at the same story, and imagine how Clyde's condition might be perceived from a spiritual perspective and what from that perspective could be a possible appropriate therapeutic strategy for dealing with his problem. The comparison is meant to illustrate how integrating the spiritual perspective into therapeutic thinking would enrich the latter by adding to the therapist's methodology a different approach and one that in some cases may be successful.

When looking at Clyde's *psychological* condition, a therapist could observe his lack of significant close relationships and his addiction to work and to cocaine. He could note that prematurely he had to take over his father's role to support his family – and did so quite successfully. He could also reflect on the possibility that Clyde's mother's remarriage may be a factor in his trouble – did not Clyde begin to come apart only after that? Yet another factor could be his inability to cope with failure. Probably narcissistic injury is playing havoc with his common sense.

When considering possible therapeutic approaches along these lines, the therapist could think of working primarily on the addictions, and on building self-esteem. Psychodrama could be helpful for helping him come to terms with his role in the family and how it has changed. Group psychotherapy could serve to help him sort out his problems and improve his ability to have significant close relationships.

The *spiritual* view would include more than the catalogue of his failures, his addiction, his lack of close relationships, and the probable cause of these. It would also say that what fails can lead one towards what is true. There is no doubt about Clyde's ability to work and to carry things through once he is on the right track. His years of working in a restaurant in Texas have shown that. It is also true that his original motivation was a good one, namely, to support his mother and sister. He is capable of following an ideal and of putting his heart and soul into it. When looking at Clyde's spiritual condition, it is obvious that he has also *lost* something: an overriding purpose in life to which he can devote himself.

These two views do not mutually exclude each other. The difference between them is, do we see Clyde primarily as a problematical case, or do we see him primarily as a person, capable of following his ideals, but a person who has lost his direction? In the spiritual perspective it is essential to discover whether there is some central concern in his life, something you might say he *devotes* himself to. In doing so, one may discover where his spiritual longing is possibly directed and what it is that he worships in his life. Looking at Clyde's case in this way, we observe that in the original situation with his mother, he was 'called' to do what he did through the twin demands of an outside situation and loyalty. Most importantly, on the level of selfless love, his had been a nurturing life. He nurtured his family and he nurtured people in the restaurants, some of whom may have appreciated what he did, some not. It was a loving action, at least to start with and before other concerns deflected it. Living a loving and nurturing life is an indispensable key to spirituality, be it Christian, Buddhist, Islamic, or whatever. So this observation suggests that spirituality may be important to Clyde and a clue to his healing, even though he is not yet conscious of this. If this indeed proves to be so and he indeed becomes conscious of it, then this could easily become the key to his recovery.

When considering possible therapeutic approaches to Clyde's recovery along these lines, the most obvious strategy would be to help Clyde discover what he might devote himself to at this particular time in his life. Focusing on that question may in and by itself already be enough to transcend his problem to a higher level. One possibility would be to take him back to the original good so he can reflect on where he lost it and where he wants to go from there. He could be encouraged to undertake his work at the restaurant with concentration and reverence, trying to discover and practise the essence of 'caring service' to others. Once he discovered this as a personal and genuine life experience, he could expand this same sense of caring to other relationships.

Another possible therapeutic approach would be to work on *idolatry*. Originally, the term 'idolatry' referred to the worshipping of idols. In modern language use it means that a self-defined 'good' takes on a life of its own and enslaves the person. Could this have happened in Clyde's case?

Psychoanalyst Erich Fromm writes in his *Psychoanalysis and Religion*:

> We picture ourselves as being far above such worship and as having solved the problem of idolatry because we do not see ourselves worshipping any of these traditional symbols of idolatry. We forget that the essence of idolatry is

not the worship of this or that particular idol but is a specifically human attitude. This attitude may be described as the deification of things, or partial aspects of the world and man's submission to such things, in contrast to an attitude in which his life is devoted to the realization of the highest principles of life, those of love and reason, to the aim of becoming what he potentially is, a being made in the likeness of God. It is not only pictures in stone and wood that are idols. Words can become idols, and machines can become idols; leaders, the state, power, and political groups may also serve. Science and the opinion of one's neighbours can become idols, and God has become an idol for many.[2]

Benner, in his *Psychotherapy and the Spiritual Quest*, shows how a lifelong illusory striving such as described above may express an underlying spiritual longing to be all that we can be, i.e. to be fulfilled.[3] This basic human desire, however, can be steered into a direction that ultimately proves unsatisfying. Benner shows how in our culture the same spiritual longing may hide behind the quest for identity or for happiness, for perfection or truth and justice, for beauty, emotional stimulation or mystery. Religious cultures offer models and accepted lifestyles for people who strongly feel this spiritual longing. In such cultures it is easier than in ours to recognise what is driving them, and to be aware of the pitfalls in life as a quest.

Quite often such idolatry can be heard in the way someone's life story is being told. When the absolute good is, for example, success, one's whole life story then becomes a story of successes and failures, everything that happens is defined in terms of how it contributed to his success, every failure as threatening the very meaning of his life. Then the only place for other people – the listeners to his life story included – is as possible 'worshippers and admirers' of his success. Others are viewed as an audience rather than as real persons. As a consequence, the person receives no real nourishment from relationships with others. As in our culture 'success' is mostly implemented by comparing our own accomplishments with those of people above us, this leads to a life in which one is forever striving at a goal that is forever elusive.

If considered from the viewpoint of idolatry, it makes sense to investigate whether Clyde's basic dilemma (in vignette 8) could be that he has lost the ability to discern when 'a good' becomes '*the* good', and therefore an end in itself. The loss of a purpose to which he can devote himself may have caused him to make an idol of success. As both spiritual longing and misdirected worship in our culture are often at an unconscious level, people like Clyde could be helped to focus on their sense of worship and reverence, and to probe into the power and the direction of their underlying motivation. The direction of their reverence could then change and deepen. As a result their actions might change towards something more in line with what they have come to feel is most central in their life.

The above is one profile of what might go on in the mind of a therapist who integrated a view of the spiritual nature of man into his therapeutic thinking. As regards methodology, this perspective would not necessitate the development of some 'spiritual therapy'. On the contrary, it could be integrated into the therapist's own methodology and suggest new lines of approach compatible with it. For example, if as a therapist your method includes exercises and rituals, you could easily design some of these for intensifying Clyde's sensitivity to his deeper subconscious longing for something to dedicate his life to.

This way of thinking is not too esoteric for use in groups. We have repeatedly found that groups come up with their *own* suggestions and approaches which are quite effective. For example, one group suggested that a workaholic, who always had many excuses as to why he was not able to spend more time with his family (whom he loved), should as a spiritual discipline commit himself to put his family first during the Lenten period (a period before Easter, during which the forty weekdays are devoted to fasting and penitence). The group checked frequently during this period as to how he was doing. Somehow it seemed easier for the person to change behaviour initially for such a time-limited period and as a spiritual rather than a psychological discipline.

The spiritual perspective, as can be seen with the help of our examples, is more inclusive than either the psychological or group dynamic perspective. It can be said to *transcend* the other two perspectives, more or less analogous to the way in which a system transcends its subsystems. This is to say, it embraces many more factors, data and dimensions. Introducing a more inclusive perspective is different from introducing a new perspective at the same level of inclusiveness. It is more encompassing and can clarify the factors involved in a more coherent way. The integration of the spiritual perspective into therapy at a more inclusive level would be analogous to Freud's adding the sexual and unconscious perspectives to psychiatry. Before Freud's time psychiatry was mainly trying to explain and handle psychiatric phenomena on the physical level. Freud did not make the physical approach superfluous or obsolete. On the contrary, his work gave rise to important and fruitful medical research questions. What he did was to add a new and more inclusive way of explaining psychological phenomena and therefore of dealing with them. Instead of just looking at symptoms as having physical causes, he looked at the body/mind together and at what the physical symptoms were saying. This was indeed a leap – a transcending of the strictly medical dimension.

The same point can be made about group analysis. When practitioners integrated the group level, via the introduction of concepts such as 'group matrix' and 'group resonance', they also exposed new and interesting psychological research questions. This, again, was a leap – a transcending of the strictly intrapersonal.

Yet again, the integration of the 'spiritual dimension' in therapy, which implies looking at the body/mind/soul together, is no less a significant leap in perspectives than the previous ones. It looks *beyond* the sickness/health dichotomy – it looks even beyond the life/death dichotomy to discover what gives purpose, meaning and direction in life.

Concluding Part 1

The preceding chapters have shown some of the many different ways in which religion and spirituality could influence, change and affect psychotherapy. Some of these examples were quite obviously related to religion or spiritual experience. In other cases the connection only became visible when they were viewed from the perspective of an underlying spiritual longing in the person(s) involved. There are obviously many more ways in which both areas may interconnect than those presented in the case histories discussed above. In fact, there is an enormous variety of ways. However, underlying that variety are some basic dynamics at work, and the emphasis in the coming chapters of this book will be on understanding the most relevant dynamics rather than on case histories and methods. So let these examples help us to take a first step towards bringing some order into this variety.

Vignette 1, the priest welcoming his imminent death, points to one of the many differences between a spiritual and the customary perspective on life and death. In our culture, you are supposed to be afraid of death and in most therapeutic situations, you are stimulated to be honest about such a fear. I shall return to the issue of attitudes toward death later on, but here the example is meant to serve as an illustration of how easily such differences may get overlooked in therapy, and how much therapy may gain in depth and scope by *not* overlooking them. Vignette 2 points to a problem that is caused by a similar difference between a religious and a non-religious perspective. In this case, it presents a problem *both* to the therapist *and* to the patient. The patient hesitated to begin therapy because he was afraid his faith would be disrespected or 'explained away', and the therapist did not know how to reassure him. Their problem is neither spiritual nor psychological. Essentially, it is a problem between two different subcultures, each espousing one of the two perspectives and being prejudiced and largely ignorant about the other one. The woman who heard her name called and the bulimic who experienced visions (vignettes 4 and 5) were both afraid that they were 'becoming crazy'. The cause of this fear is also neither psychological nor spiritual: it is again the difference between the two perspectives. In these cases, however, the persons involved experience it as an *inner* conflict because they have internalised *both* perspectives. Understanding such differences as originating from a break-up in our common cultural background may avoid such unnecessary problems both for patients and therapists. Part 2 will connect with the above examples or rather, with the type of interconnection between psychotherapy and religion or spirituality they exemplify. The chapters will outline that break-up in our cultural background that caused such incidents to become problematic in the first place. This information may help a therapist to recognise such differences and deal with them adequately.

Vignette 3, an ex-member of a religious sect, presents another type of problem. It is an example of how people's authentic spiritual longing and naïveté may be exploited and manipulated by dubious leaders. Unfortunately this type of problem occurs rather often, also with ex-members of the regular, non-sectarian churches. In this case it was a sect, but any religious community may at any time become prey to such leaders. People may suffer intensely and for a long period from problems of this type, which is now included in DSM-IV. In such cases it is clear what psychotherapy can contribute to their solution and that this psychotherapeutic contribution does not require any specific excursion by the therapist into the spiritual domain. If reliable spiritual direction or pastoral psychotherapy is available, it is preferable to refer such a patient to it. If not, or if the patient looks with distrust upon *all* spiritual or pastoral helpers as a result of his mistreatment, then the patient first needs to work through his feelings of being deceived and manipulated, of resentment, of being rejected, and so on. He probably also needs to acknowledge that he himself has also contributed to what has happened to him. These are the *psychological* aspects of his problem. A therapist does not require any specialised expertise on spirituality to deal with them. In doing so he can pave the way for the patient to deal with the *spiritual* aspects of his trauma thereafter and to find a better way to develop a mature spiritual life. That is however outside the scope of psychotherapy. For that, the patient will have to seek expert spiritual direction.

Vignettes 4 and 5, about visionary phenomena, and vignettes 6 and 7, about periods of spiritual 'darkness' or 'dark night' occurring before or in the course of spiritual life, are examples of rather well-known spiritual experiences. These and other phenomena have been reported over the centuries as often accompanying the processes of awakening to spiritual consciousness and spiritual growth. They can be easily mistaken for psychiatric symptoms, and depending on one's personality structure, they may indeed trigger off hallucinations or depressive states. But normally this is not so. Mostly they have positive effects or mark the coming of a new and deeper level of spiritual consciousness. If a therapist wants to avoid misinterpreting such spiritual phenomena and to allow therapy to profit from their positive effects, then he needs at least some elementary knowledge about the processes involved in spiritual awakening and spiritual life. The same is true for vignette 8 (the story of Clyde) which is an example of the intricate interconnectedness between misguided and unconscious spiritual striving and psychological problems. If a therapist is sufficiently familiar with the dynamics of spiritual progress and stagnation, he may find additional ways for assessing and approaching such complicated cases. These vignettes taken together are saying that what a therapist really needs is an in-depth understanding of the processes and challenges involved in spiritual awakening and spiritual development, in particular those that have to do with the initial phase because they are the most likely to surface in the context of a therapy. In that phase people are often confused and confusing to others because they are not yet really aware of their emerging spirituality. Such an in-depth understanding will then enable the therapist to recognise its manifestations, to empathise with those concerned, and to develop his own ways of dealing with them within his own methodology. Part 3 and Part 4 will connect with the problems exemplified by vignettes 4 to 8 by offering relevant information about the change processes involved in spiritual awakening and spiritual growth.

In the introduction to Part 1, I introduced the concepts 'religion' and 'spirituality'. Meanwhile I have also introduced two other key concepts, namely '*spiritual discernment*' and '*spirituality in exile*'. They will also be revisited in later chapters. Below is a reminder of their meaning:

'This or that?' (you may recall) asked the headings of each chapter. In doing so they signalled differences between psychological and spiritual assessment of each case cited. The answers, it was suggested, could easily be *both* 'this' *and* 'that' – and maybe even more. Nowadays, we are familiar with the idea that there is no one 'true' interpretation or cause of complex phenomena. Each one may be as true as the other, but the one rather than the others may suggest a more promising therapeutic approach. The thesis of this book is that the spiritual perspective (with its additional concern for the purpose, meaning and direction of life) is the one therapeutic approach that sometimes holds most promise. This is why the art of spiritual *discernment*, i.e. the sensitive discrimination of subtle signals of someone's underlying spiritual attitude, becomes relevant when a therapist considers integrating the spiritual dimension into his practice.

Interestingly, there seems to be something like a 'natural' spiritual longing in people all over the world, both within and outside established religions. They may not be aware of what it is they are seeking, or of why they feel so un-fulfilled. Such enduring but unfulfilled spiritual longing may give rise to psychological problems. And it takes discernment and insight in the basic dynamics of spiritual life to recognise such processes. The concept *'spirituality in exile'* refers to the current phenomenon that spirituality also exists *outside* the established religions, in a way that is relevant to psychotherapy. As explained above, it can be very confusing both for himself and for the therapist when someone is not yet fully aware of his spiritual longing. Or it may have serious psychological consequences if someone has awakened to spiritual conscious-ness and all on his own starts experimenting with mystical ecstasy, or tries to develop special spiritual powers such as performing miracles or exorcism.

In discussing the various vignettes in this part of the book, I have also raised some questions about *methodology*. What to do with authentic communication of feelings, views, etc., from religious people, feelings which may be contrary to what psychology and common sense lead you (as a therapist) to expect? What to do, for example, with a patient's fear that his faith will be disrespected or reduced to a psychological problem? How to deal with religious experi-ences? Or what to do with people whose religion seems to make them miserable? How do you recognise the 'spirituality in exile' referred to above? Some practical suggestions have been offered in these chapters, just to give some idea of how one could deal with such questions. But, of course, how a given therapist will actually choose to respond will depend on his own under-standing and methodology. Throughout the coming chapters further practical suggestions will be given. But I want to emphasise the fact that there are no quick answers to methodological issues such as these. The important thing in whatever methodology is being pursued is to become alerted to 'veiled signals' of spiritual concerns, and to integrate the spiritual perspective into therapeutic practice. With this in mind, the emphasis in the next chapters will be on insight rather than methodology.

An exercise in discomfort

If you have felt uncomfortable (intellectually, emotionally and professionally ill at ease) while reading these first six chapters, I now invite you to do some mapping of this uneasiness. As in working with countertransference, to analyse your own discomfort as a reader of this book is an important tool for gaining better insight into yourself. So I suggest analysing your discomfort by reviewing your answers to the questions that went with the vignettes. Could you specify where and how the vignettes and their commentaries feel odd, questionable, offensive, or difficult to empathise with? Reflecting on this could help clarify your own position in respect to what has been suggested or implied or claimed.

PART 2

A Grammar of
Western Consciousness

Introducing Part 2

The problems of the people figuring in vignettes 1, 2, 4 and 5 (welcoming death, fearing disrespect, visions and voices) are not confined to the individuals involved. The problems are more common than we would like: they signal an *underlying discrepancy between the spiritual and the modern secular modes of experiencing, conceptualising and communicating.* In certain respects the discrepancy has generated what can be seen, without exaggeration, as at least two subcultures within Western culture.

This discrepancy in our culture manifests itself in therapeutic interaction in all sorts of forms. It creates problems that secular therapists and patients involved in spirituality have *with each other* and which they have to solve *together* for therapeutic intervention to succeed. This is why the chapters which follow will outline some aspects of this discrepancy that are particularly relevant for therapists to know about. The chapters will also offer some suggestions to help find strategies for approaching and dealing with its manifestations.

CHAPTER 7

The Past Complicates the Present

1 Exploring the discrepancy between religious and secular subcultures

To approach problems connected with the differences between the religious and the non-religious perspectives in our culture adequately, a therapist needs adequate information about these differences. This chapter therefore presents a rough sketch of the most relevant points of divergence between the two: how they came into being in the course of history, and in what way this divergence influences the situation of the contemporary believer in general and in therapy in particular. The problem is partly ideological, partly linguistic. It is partly ideological, because the whole idea that there *is* indeed an invisible transcendent reality, and that it *does* somehow communicate with human beings, is at odds with the basic assumptions of current Western atheism. In other words, the ideas and ideals connected with the religious view have become *implausible* to many modern minds. It is partly linguistic, because religious and spiritual feelings, beliefs, practices and dilemmas are expressed in an infinite variety of religious languages and images, stories, symbols and metaphors. These are largely of ancient origin and therefore easily misunderstood and most often in need of explanation and interpretation.

2 Plausibility structures

Let us for a moment return to the first vignette: the priest who was excited at the prospect of death and the therapist who had to decide how to respond. Why do we so easily assume the patient's excitement must be interpreted as a manic flight from facing the reality of his impending death?

When people are asked, 'How do you want to die?', most of us want to die without knowing what is happening to us and without great pain to ourselves and others. However, at other times and places this understanding of death would have been considered irrational if not immoral. For example, medieval people most feared a sudden death that would not allow them to make proper spiritual preparation. Preparation for death was important. The emphasis was upon dying well, and there were several guides that described the 'art of dying'. The medieval world preferred those illnesses that gave one a lingering death, or at least time to prepare for one's death. Our understanding of violent death shows the same difference: the medieval person could look forward to dying in war, since prior to battle there was time to prepare for his possible death. This is in sharp contrast with most of us today. Indeed if we had the choice, we might very well prefer to die in unanticipated automobile accidents.[1]

We have no communal sense of a 'good death'. Most of us would agree that death is a very unfortunate aspect of the human condition, something that should be avoided at all costs and ever feared. In *Momma and the Meaning of Life*, Yalom describes a conflict between two patients about this view on death and how his group of terminal patients made him question his own therapeutic scepticism.[2] His article implicitly shows how the cultural agreement about death has crept as an unspoken assumption into therapeutic practice, too. That is why the priest's excitement looks implausible, why we tend to look upon it as untruthful. Ideas such as looking forward to afterlife or hearing your name called by God are implausible in the secular frame of reference, but plausible in a spiritual one.

This is but one manifestation of many modern people's difficulty in believing in the existence of a spiritual reality – even in understanding what it would mean for someone else to have a real and meaningful relationship with such a reality. Much more plausible to the modern mind would be to see such a relationship as a purely subjective project, somewhat like a child creating a fantasy bosom-friend.

Sociologist Peter Berger in his influential book *The Heretical Imperative* has introduced the term 'plausibility structure'.[3] He uses it to explain how in the history of Western collective consciousness a fundamental shift has taken place in the overall structure of what people can accept as believable and what not. When people, for example, say 'I cannot believe in God', this is not one isolated statement. It is part of a whole structure of interrelated beliefs with which the consciousness makes sense of itself and the world. Berger shows how modern technology, economy, mobility, and many other factors construe the daily life of ordinary people – and in its wake their consciousness – in such a way that the whole source of intelligibility has changed.

3 Losing our sense of unity

Louis Dupré in a more detailed study in the history of this shift in consciousness shows how since the time of the Renaissance many key ideas in the make-up of a worldview and of self-identity have disintegrated, changed, sometimes even gone into reverse. As an overall result, the originally prevailing sense (of society and self) of unity with the world has been fragmented. One such fragmentation is the idea of a fundamental separatedness and difference between, on the one hand, the physical and human world and on the other the transcendent Being. But there is more: as a second fragmentation, Western cultural consciousness also came to see a fundamental separatedness and difference between, on the one hand, the human person and, on the other hand, the whole of organic and inorganic nature.[4]

This double break-up has resulted in a radical transformation in how we experience our world and ourselves. For example, we have great difficulty in believing in the existence of a transcendent realm, whereas in Antiquity and in the Middle Ages you just had to look around you – or to look into yourself – to find it. The 'book of Nature' (natural phenomena decoded with the help of Scripture) told you so. Your own self, being a microcosm of the macrocosm, told you so. But now we experience the physical world as an independent, often antagonistic, reality without any inherent meaning and value of its own. We are convinced that as human beings we are the only ones that allocate meaning and value to it, because our human subjectivity has become the sole source of meaning and value.

Unfortunately, this human subjectivity has suffered from a similar break-up, one which has fragmented the very way we experience ourselves. As the self became distanced from nature and made into an observer of the world, it became also a spectator to its own experiences and even to itself. Ideas such as self-actualisation, or searching for your identity, all suggest that our 'real' selves are not where you would suppose them to be: emphatically and continuously present on the front stage of our consciousness. People experiencing themselves as partaking in a meaningful cosmos would probably have difficulty in understanding our search for our elusive selves. Similarly our ideas of individual freedom, the autonomous person, equal rights for everybody, and other items high on our collective priority list, would be quite puzzling to our ancestors as they still are today in certain parts of the world.

These break-ups are part and parcel of the modern Self, and give modern plausibility structure its character. The point here is not that our plausibility structure is right and the earlier one is wrong, or vice versa. It is even less true that we are worse off than our predecessors and should return to the old self-consciousness and old society. Quite rightly, we cherish ideas such as the intrinsic value of each individual person, equal rights, freedom, and so on. Moreover, such historical changes are irreversible and in any case any structure of ideas which shapes experience and consciousness has its own particular benefits and liabilities. The point to be made is, our plausibility structure is at the background of the discomfort about spiritual and religious expression in therapy. It is also at the background of much longing for a sense of unity, harmony and belonging that surfaces in therapy. Unity is high on the agenda of spirituality and religion; disintegration of unity is one characteristic of our collective consciousness – and therefore of our culture. But there is no way back. Our culture has to find new ways to integrate the broken relationship between the cosmos, its human partaker/interpreter, and their common transcendent source – and part of psychotherapy is about individuals embodying this cultural quest.

4 The break-up between spirituality and theology

Yet another development in Western culture has resulted in making the situation of religious people difficult: the practice and theory of spiritual life became alienated from theological thinking. Tragically, the discipline of systematic theology, which is the theoretical reflection on religion, has been one of the stimuli for the double break-up of the original sense of unity in Western consciousness. How did this come to pass? In the Bible the world is seen as created by God. Originally, this was explained as implying some likeness between the world and God. Somewhat in the same way that you can learn something about Picasso from studying a painting of Picasso, you could supposedly learn something about God from studying nature and the human heart. The world was thought to be the place where God's 'footprints' (vestiges) could be found, for example in the predictability of what we now call 'laws of nature', or in 'moral law', or in 'human reason'. At the beginning of the 'modern' period in Western thinking (which lasted roughly from the early Renaissance until the rise of Postmodernism in the late twentieth century), however, theology took a new turn and started to theorise an ever more increasing difference and distance between Creator and creation.[5]

But with such a sharp separation between Creator and creature, the question arose how then to conceive the *tie* between them? Spirituality is all about the tie between the person and his God – how was spirituality supposed to fit into this modern trend in theological thinking? The answer to the latter question is: it did not and still does not – although new developments are in the air now. Spirituality and theology each went their own way, to the detriment of both. Theology contributed to the emergence of modern culture and its plausibility structure – and became ever more incompatible with the spiritual mode of experiencing and thinking. So spirituality was forced to become a separate tradition within its own religion, developing its own terminology, techniques and ideas. The price it had to pay was isolation. In the course of time it became largely confined to the subcultures of contemplative monasteries and minor Protestant congregations, suffering there from the sociological inbreeding effects of all isolated communities.

In doing so, spiritual practice and thinking kept a surprising continuity with the past. Several historians observe that in times of great cultural change, spiritual attitudes do not change in the same way and at the same pace as other areas of the culture. Interestingly, this is happening again in our time. Our culture is again involved in an all-embracing change process. One aspect is a renewed interest in spiritual life. Spiritual books are selling like never before. Again there is this surprising continuity with the past: many of these bestsellers date from the late Middle Ages. Many others are not just ancient, but also stem from faraway cultures like Buddhism or Native American religion. This suggests that spirituality may be more like an anthropological category *sui generis*. Like art and music, it cannot be fully explained by psychological or sociological factors.

In short, there has been yet another break-up, the one between mainstream religious teaching and practice on the one hand, and on the other the spiritual life of seeking a personal relationship with God. For an individual in search of this spiritual dimension of personal life, this means that he may have difficulty in recognising his inner longing for what it is, even within his own religion. This is one major cause of the phenomenon of 'spirituality in exile'. Unfortunately such an 'exile' may not be restricted to people outside any religion. People may feel lonely within their own church, which has forgotten the language, the symbols, and the dynamics of spiritual life.

5 The impoverishment of religious language

In the preceding sections, I have discussed implausibility, a diminished sense of unity, and a split between theology and spirituality as cultural factors behind difficulties and incomprehension between religious and non-religious patients and therapists. Yet another 'collective' problem is a linguistic one.

The 'objectifying' of nature has opened the way to the development of the natural sciences and the prominence of their way of thinking. Now science demands a very peculiar kind of language. To do its proper job, research has to limit itself to a particular set of categories, terms and methods. Each key term has to be as precise as possible, adapted to the subject under study. And each subject has to be reduced to those elements of it that lend themselves to scientific method.

Of course any professional scientist knows his language is artificial, that it covers only a small section of reality, and that it is insufficient for the many varied tasks language is needed for in human interaction. However, with the rising prestige of the sciences its language use, too, has deeply influenced 'ordinary' language use. As a result, there is a strong tendency in our culture to cleanse 'serious' language from ambiguous meanings as much as we can. We prefer clearly defined concepts, unequivocal words, and literal meanings. There is much to be said for that, particularly in science and legislation. But the other side of this coin is that we tend to underestimate 'unserious' imaginative language, and largely neglect to educate young people to understand its richness and its adequacy for communicating intricate subjects like religion, art and music.

As a contrast to scientific and science-influenced language, religious language has to be highly symbolic and metaphorical to do its job properly. All thinking, knowing and communicating about God is characterised by awareness that it is dealing with a mystery whose *full reality is inexpressible* in literal language. This is also why, next to symbols and metaphors, parables and riddles are so much used in the teachings of various religions. These are meant to startle people into an awareness of an alternative reality, one which transcends our everyday ideas and wisdom.

Another factor in this linguistic difficulty is that up to a hundred years ago the mode- and tone-setting classes in society enjoyed symbolic and poetic expression and used it profusely in all kinds of areas. As a result, many religious writings from former times are even more symbolic and metaphorical than they need to be, simply because people admired the richness of such language and wanted to use it.

If one supposes that religious language has but one precise meaning, one is in for misunderstandings. Reading the biblical creation stories in the book of Genesis *only* in this way, to use a well-known example, does both oneself and religion a poor service. Not only has this resulted in the conflict between 'creationism' and 'evolutionism', but, worse still, it has also caused people to forget the richness and depth of its earlier meanings, such as its allegorical meaning of the six days as six periods in the history of man's redemption, or its spiritual meaning of six illuminating insights helping people towards spiritual growth.

This is not to say there is no objective content in religious language. It is not just a chain of symbols and metaphors, nor a series of lyric expressions of feeling. The alternatives in religious language use are not *either* factually true *or* metaphorical. A fundamental biblical statement such as 'God is love' is meant to say, directly and objectively, something important about the nature of transcendent reality. A religious expression such as 'When I pray, I stand before God' is also meant as a statement of an important truth. As Cavell points out, 'speaking religiously' is not accomplished by using a given form, metaphorical, factual or whatever; it is to speak from a particular perspective.[6] To understand a metaphor you must be able to interpret it; to understand an utterance religiously you have to be able to share or empathise with its perspective. But as soon as you want to explain a fundamental religious statement such as 'God is love', or want to reflect on its implications, or to understand how it applies to your own life, or to express your happiness about it, the need arises to use exemplary stories, lyrics, metaphors and symbols.

6 Symbolic miscommunication

Even if you are aware of the symbolic and metaphorical character of religious language, there is a further problem. We are all aware of the fact that *words* can change their meanings with time. The meaning of the word 'person', for example, has since the arrival of Latin civilisation on the world stage changed into its exact opposite. Its original meaning was 'mask' (for example the masks actors used when acting a part in a play), while in its modern meaning a 'person' refers to who somebody really is when he is *not* hiding behind a 'mask'.[7] The same is true of *symbols and metaphors*, albeit that their meanings change more gradually and unnoticeably than do the meanings of words. The effects of such changes in the case of characteristically spiritual metaphors will be discussed in Chapters 10 and 11. Here I shall limit myself to just one example of what happened to one symbolic picture. The example illustrates how deeply confusing such a change of meaning can be, to both the religious and the non-religious.

In most Orthodox Church icons of Mary, the mother of Christ, there are three stars on her cloak. Quite often these icons also show all kinds of other symbols connected with her. One of these other symbols is a burning bush. This is taken from the Old Testament story of Moses, to whom God made himself known by speaking from a burning bush that never burned up.[8] The symbolism of these connected images is lost to most of us. The three stars mean that Mary conceived her divine child as a virgin, and that she remained a virgin during childbirth and from then on. Quite apart from the biological aspect of this virginity, what is the point of being and remaining a virgin, and what has this to do with a burning bush?

The original meaning is that Mary symbolises that part in the depth of the human soul that is receptive to God. The idea is that if you listen to yourself very sensitively, you will find somewhere behind all complexity a yearning for harmony with God. Now a deep yearning means there is already something like a hidden 'entrance' or 'image' for whatever the yearning is directed to. This 'receptacle' for God is supposed as being very quiet and pure, and to be most of the time stifled by the turmoil of psychological drives, emotions, conflicts, and so on. It is supposed to be that place in your soul where 'God can be born in you' – we are more likely to say something like 'your spiritual core' or 'your spiritual Self'. It is traditionally called the 'pars virginalis', i.e. the 'virgin part', or the 'apex animae', i.e. the 'summit of the soul', as if your soul had a kind of aerial or sensor for the Divine at its top. In this context, Mary and her virginity are not primarily feminine symbols. Men and women, every human being is supposed to have such a pars virginalis and everybody can become conscious of it.

This symbolism of the three stars is directed to people having a religious experience that is reportedly not exceptional and is occurring all over the world. It is brilliantly analysed by Otto in his classic book *The Idea of the Holy*. However different their cultures, most people are at first terrified when actually experiencing contact with the Holy. The experience is so overwhelming that they are deeply afraid to lose themselves in the confrontation. That is why Otto calls it a 'mysterium fascinans et tremendum', a fascinating and terrifying mystery.[9] The three stars of 'virginity' are directed to this spiritual fear. Mary represents the ideal human attitude (both for women and men!) of unhesitating and unpretentious willingness to let God have his way with us, body and soul. The three stars of virginity are meant to reassure us that we need not be afraid to surrender freely and willingly to the Biblical God because he will not 'rape' our souls. He respects human personhood and will leave it intact. This is also the connection between the virgin Mary and the burning bush that is never consumed by the fire. The bush too reassures the human person that the contact with God will inspire but never destroy the personality. The message of both pictures is that the God of the Bible asks for a free and conscious assent. He will speak and act through human beings, but not by undue pressure and not by 'taking possession' of their bodies and minds as in ecstatic religions. The issue is still pertinent in our time. Whenever you elicit autobiographical stories of people who have been through an overwhelming spritual experience, they quite often tell you that their first response was a fear of 'losing themselves'.

The very fact that so many words are needed to explain the traditional spiritual meaning of only one rather common icon shows how difficult such symbolic language is for us to understand and appreciate today. It also shows how such centuries-old symbols may convey a spiritual message that applies to every one of us today as much as it did to earlier generations.

As an aside I would mention this is not to imply that this particular spiritual meaning of the eternal virginity of Mary and the burning bush is the *only* and the *only valid* meaning. It does not *per se* make the belief in the reality of these events unfounded or superfluous. Millions of Christians believe that the statements about these events are *also* literal truths. They ground their belief in doctrine and Scripture. Others contest these beliefs, using arguments taken from modern methods of historical criticism. These discussions inevitably remain unresolved so long as both parties start their arguments from different presumptions. Nevertheless two important comclusions may be drawn from them. First, these discussions show how important it is *to keep symbolic and literal communication apart.* They take place at two different levels of interpretation. Questions about the impossibility of remaining virgin at conception, childbirth and thereafter, and of being on fire but not burning down, belong to the literal level of interpretation. But they simply do not apply to the symbolic level. At that level, the pertinent questions are about the truth of the *spiritual* message. Second, such discussions are part and parcel of the problematic situation your religious patient, as a contemporary believer, finds himself in. I shall return to the issue of 'levels of interpretation' in Chapter 10, section 5, while making the problematic situation of the contemporary believer the subject of the following section of this chapter.

Let us now, after this excursus, return to the main subject of this section which is to point out that there is also a *communication problem* for religious and spiritual people. As illustrated above, they are more or less caught between the devil and the deep blue sea. On the one hand our dominant linguistic system offers them objective language which is as inadequate for conveying religious and spiritual meaning as it is adequate for scientific studies and procedures. On the other hand the religious traditions, which in themselves are so important to the believer, invite understanding in a language of symbols and metaphors which, while once adequate for the task, are no longer so. Many have lost or changed their original meaning and coherence. This exacerbates the communication problem between believer and non-believer, and can easily put a halt to any useful dialogue between the two.

7 The problematic situation of the contemporary religious believer

Let us now return to psychotherapy. The question we are exploring in this book is, how can a therapist empathise with, and approach adequately, patients who are involved in spirituality (i.e. the personal, relational aspect of religion), despite the fact that he himself has no religious background and no detailed knowledge of the many different churches and other religious communities?

A first answer to this question is that a relatively sketchy knowledge and awareness of the existence of today's religious and secular subcultures and its implications will ensure that he does not miss or ignore the significance of sub-culture differences in a therapeutic situation. Second, that the long and conflict-ridden history of ideas about religion and spirituality will manifest itself explicitly or implicitly in both individual and group therapy. Third, that the cultural break-up referred to will colour and possibly account for the way in which spiritual concerns are expressed – or concealed. And fourth, that these same break-ups will inevitably influence, for better or worse, the therapist's and the other patients' response to the believer and his expressed or unex-pressed spiritual concerns.

All of this is to say that awareness of and some knowledge of religious versus non-religious subcultures allows a therapist to anticipate the sort of situation that the believer, non-believer and therapist himself (who may be either) is likely to find himself in where spiritual concerns are playing an implicit or explicit role. Situations of such a heterogeneous (religious–secular) profile will be recognised as potentially problematic for some or all of the indi-viduals involved.

Let us now look at how this historical information and awareness allows us to be more specific about the characteristics of the problematic situation of the contemporary religious believer.[10] First, for the first time in human history, belief in God has become implausible in Western civilisation, and to the very same extent it had been plausible for earlier generations. As a result, the religious believer is *in a defensive position*. He knows his belief will be challenged and that if this happens, he will have to explain himself either in religious terms that more often than not irritate the other rather than enlighten him, or in secular terms that are not adequate for expressing transcendence. Therefore you may expect people to draw back from talking about their religion and their spirituality, and to be afraid of encountering incomprehension if not downright rejection. In a therapeutic context, an example of this was the reaction of the orthodox Protestant of vignette 2.

A second characteristic of the problematic situation of the modern religious believer is caused by the fact that no one can ever put himself completely outside his culture. Contemporaries cannot avoid being contemporaries. Religious believers of today are themselves, of course, also products of a culture that has lost the transcendent dimension. This means they are faced with the difficult task of acknowledging the atheism *within themselves* and of dealing with it. If they don't do that, they will inevitably have a kind of schizoid life. Inevitably, because they will then hang on to beliefs that they (at least tacitly) assume or feel to be incompatible with other beliefs that they continually encounter and respond to in their daily 'modern' lives. Berger has convincingly shown that even such ordinary activities as for example using a telephone are not 'neutral' in this regard. He writes:

> The telephone, in the most obvious way, is an external fact in the individual's life; indeed it is a material fact, embodied in innumerable physical objects, one or more of which may clutter up the individual's house. Equally obviously, this external fact shapes many aspects of the individual's everyday life. Thus he can utilize his telephone, and the enormously complicated and powerful machinery to which it is linked…to carry on a trivial conversation with a friend vacationing in Indonesia. But that is not the whole story. An individual who uses the telephone must know how to handle this particular piece of machinery. This is a skill, which after a while becomes a habit – an external habit, a bit of learned behavior. But the use of the telephone also means learning certain ways of thinking – internal habits, as it were. It means to think in numbers, to absorb a considerably complex framework of cognitive abstractions…to have some notion of what could go wrong with

the machinery (even if one must call on an expert for repairs)… But there is more yet. To use the telephone habitually also means to learn a specific style of dealing with others – a style marked by impersonality, precision, and (at least in this country) a certain superficial civility. The key question is this: Do these internal habits *carry over* into other areas of life, such as nontelephonic relations with other persons? The answer is almost certainly yes.

The issue raised by Berger's key question is: do these internal habits also carry over into the area of religion and spirituality? I have no hesitation in answering 'yes, they almost certainly do.' Berger published his book in 1980, so he could not at that time anticipate the influence of the mobile telephone and internet. In his essay *Heidegger, Habermas and the Mobile Phone*, published in 2001, Myerson has reflected on the ever increasing use of the mobile telephone and its implications for the future. He thinks that in the course of the twenty first century it will considerably change both human identity and society. I think that at this point of time the influence of internet is already apparent and this, too, does and will undoubtedly continue to create its own external and internal habits, which in their turn will carry over to the area of religion and spiritual-ity.[11]

Life in our modern society seems therefore inevitably to result in an *inner in-consistency* with traditional religion and spirituality. This may easily lead to anxiety and over-defensiveness. This problem is probably at the background of the women of vignettes 4 and 5, who simultaneously take their visionary expe-riences seriously and at the same time are afraid they are 'becoming crazy'. It could also be one of the sources of the orthodox Protestant's fear of entering psychotherapy (vignette 2): he may have sensed that at some point he will have to confront his *own* internalised cultural atheism as well as the atheism of the therapy group.

A third characteristic of the problematic situation a modern religious person finds himself in is that individual spiritual experience has become *private* and thus essentially removed from any possible meaning for an outsider. As thinking and science became separate activities alongside but separated from religion, the experience of Transcendence as sacral reality lost its cultural context. As a culture, we do not know how to cope with it. There is no consensus about what constitutes the experience of the sacral; people connect it with highly divergent content. Even within the churches there is little talk about it. The only *space* our culture has left for Transcendence is private life. As a result, an individual's 'transcendental experience' is at best assumed to have some value for this one individual, for example as satisfaction of emotional needs and therefore private. It is not thought of as a real issue, and one addressed to all of us. This attitude is not only generated by our surrounding culture in general. It is also generated by an individual's and community's cherishing of his or its *own* religiosity.

As a fourth characteristic, religious people are at a loss as to how to *communicate* with other people about their own spiritual and private experiences, particularly with non-believers. Even more problematic is the fact that they have to a large extent also lost the 'linguistic and symbolic means', as mentioned earlier, to connect their *own* experiences with the sources and symbols of their own spiritual tradition – sources and symbols which are meant to help them in their spiritual quest. This should be kept in mind whenever religiously minded patients in a therapy session struggle to make themselves understood or are seen to fall back on traditional dogmatic formulations, formulations that are not easily comprehended by others and often irritate them. Such 'strugglers' may seem to fellow patients and possibly to the therapist to be inauthentic, whereas the underlying experience may in fact be quite profound and relevant to their therapeutic process. A therapist who is sensitive to their situation can help them to communicate in simple words and in words that are *as close as possible to their actual experience*. When this is so, communication is more likely to be on a person-to-person basis instead of reproducing the break-ups and misunderstandings inherent in our culture.

In closing this chapter, I should like to reiterate that even a general knowledge of the break-up of our culture provides a helpful tool in facilitating communication in a 'religiously heterogeneous' therapeutic group or dyad. But it must also be kept in mind that the *degree* to which such knowledge can help depends upon (among other things): the particular prejudices existing in the particular religious subculture, in its particular surrounding secular culture and in the particular therapeutic environment in which communication is being sought. Detailed knowledge of forms of religious belief (Christian, Jewish, Buddhist, New Age, and so on) and their concomitant spiritualities is of course extremely useful. But it is not a *necessary* starting point for therapists to be helpful.

The next chapters will illustrate how a general and minimal knowledge of religious/non-religious cultures allows us to understand what can be accounting for communication difficulties and the ensuing lack of genuine dialogue, in both group and dyadic therapy sessions.

CHAPTER 8

Bringing the Background to the Fore

1 The foundation matrix

The opinion in Chapter 7 is derived in part from a concept in group analytic theory known as the *'foundation matrix'*. Group analysis uses this concept to describe and analyse where and how the 'outside' and the 'inside' impinge on each other in therapy groups. Formulated in group analytic terms, the cultural tensions described in Chapter 7 are part of the foundation matrix and therefore likely to be reproduced in therapeutic interaction. As seen in this book, this concept and knowledge of it is also relevant for other therapeutic methodologies in addition to group analytic practice. One need not be a group analyst to use it as a helpful instrument for observing and analysing the effects of background issues in all or any psychotherapeutic methodology.

Since, however, this concept from group analytic theory is not widely known outside the circle of practising group analysts, I should like to elaborate on it with the help of an example taken from group analytic practice. The example will also be used to point out why reproductions of the foundation matrix can be problematic for the therapeutic process and to suggest how any negative effect this may have, can be counteracted. In later sections I shall use this same concept to explore more deeply in what ways a therapist can understand and help patients who are involved in spirituality despite the fact that he himself has no religious background and no detailed knowledge of the various religious communities and their beliefs.

The 'foundation matrix' and the 'group matrix' or 'dynamic matrix', as the latter is also called, are two core concepts of Foulkes, the Founding Father of group analysis. About the foundation matrix he writes:

I believe that a good deal of what is usually called external or social is at the same time deeply internal and of very powerful dynamic influence for the total being as he develops. This comprises our social, cultural, vertical inheritances transmitted over generations, even for the building up of one's own image of one's body, as Paul Schilder in particular has shown. There are some basic things shared by our groups even before the individual members have met, such as language, the particular culture, even class and education. This is called the *Foundation Matrix*. They bring this common ground with them into the group. What we traditionally look upon as the innermost self, the intrapsychic as against the external world, is thus not only shareable, but is in fact already shared.[1]

Elsewhere he compares this matrix with a pyramid from the less to the more and more individual: collective, species culture, class, family, individual.[2] The concept 'foundation matrix' refers to the bottom layers of this pyramid. It includes all that is common to us as members of our culture, as well as all that is common to us as members of the human species.

This foundation matrix is a precondition for the gradual emergence of *a particular group's own matrix*, i.e. its own specific and ever-changing 'concert of interactions which is our primary basis for orientation, for interpretation, confrontation, and other contributions'.[3] Foulkes writes about this particular matrix:

> Apart from this fundamentally shared life we can see this matrix growing and developing more and more, embracing more and more complex issues which are very important for the therapeutic process altogether. This, which develops under our own eyes, is called the *Dynamic Matrix*. All mental processes, including of course all therapeutic ones, take place in this hypothetical web of communication or communion, in this matrix.[4]

In short, he views the group (or dynamic) matrix as the web of communication and relationship in a given group, the common shared ground which ultimately determines the meaning and significance of all events, communications and interpretations, verbal and non-verbal.[5] This concept of Foulkes may be difficult to grasp, but its use is essential for the practice of group analysis, because a group analyst 'focuses on the total interactional field, on the matrix in which these unconscious reactions meet.'[6]

Let me illustrate this with the help of an example.

2 A group acting out themes of the foundation matrix

In the German journal *Gruppenanalyse*, Haubl describes what happened in the seventh session of one of his therapy groups:

Vignette 9

Mrs P. tells how during puberty she has been sexually abused by her father. She tells this clearly and in detail, but it shows how difficult it is for her to tell this. She addresses herself mainly to the male co-therapist. This co-therapist notices that he starts fantasising about putting Mrs P.'s father to trial.

Mrs P. says she doesn't feel any hate, only grief and mourning. She cannot maintain any contact with her father, he has become a non-person to her.

Then three other female group members take over and verbalise the hate. An empathising older man tries to verbalise what he feels, but the women cut him off.

The two therapists involved intervene. They make clear that now at last Mrs P. shows she is willing to communicate about her traumatic experiences. It is not therapeutic to prohibit her effort.

After that the three women also tell about their experiences of sexual abuse. In contrast to Mrs P., their stories are in general terms, sketchy and not in detail. They tell about a father entering the bathroom and teasingly caressing his daughter's thigh. They tell about men making obscene jokes, ending up in the 'telling' look of an uncle. They then make disapproving remarks on the non-responsiveness of group member Mrs Q., who has kept silent all the time. Mrs P. has also been reduced to silence.

Now the therapist tries to stimulate a more concrete exploration and invites the women to tell more about their life experiences. The theme becomes still more general. 'Women have always been abused by men, for centuries.' – 'Women are always victims.' – and so on and so forth.

Both therapists confront the group with the silence of Mrs P. They also point to the female group members' pressure on Mrs Q. One woman argues aggressively and pedantically that this is necessary 'because only merciless openness can liberate; survivors of the Holocaust have known this for a long time.' Spontaneously and just as aggressively, the therapist says he is outraged by this analogy. The group falls silent; every now and then someone makes a hostile remark. They are all shocked and after a while cautiously say so.

During the last minutes Mrs Q. starts talking. She has read a lot about sexual abuse and has attended some lectures on the subject. But it did not help her. She feels mentally and physically exhausted. This resembles the symptoms of sexually abused women, but she cannot remember any abuse. This session has made her even more confused; she doesn't know what to believe.[7]

Haubl analyses how the *foundation matrix* influences the group matrix here. Our collective consciousness is shocked by the theme of incest and other sexual abuse. As in virtually all cultures, ours too has put a strong taboo on incest. Until recently the cultural myth has been that it hardly ever happens, and the cultural coping strategy has been to keep silent about it. Now in the days of victims coming forward, the myth is obviously contradicted. Incest and other sexual child abuse appear to happen all over the place. This is of course a welcome change, opening the way to help the people involved. The other side of the picture is, however, that the theme has become a sensational subject in the media, always good for television programmes with very high ratings. According to Haubl, this has led to a change in our consciousness, resulting in a collective fantasy about universal sexual child abuse.[8] In this cultural context any authentic testimony of an individual woman automatically becomes stereotyped. Women have recently gained an interest in the status of a victim, because the media teach them this is a sure way to get attention. It is quite obvious that the three women in this group are acting out this collective scandalisation fantasy. Mrs Q.'s confusion can be seen as one other expression of the same, but now at the individual level. She tries to connect her own vague feelings with what she has picked up from the media about incest. The group matrix now becomes infused with another emotionally highly charged collective theme from the foundation matrix: the demanded solidarity between the women group members against the men. I shall stop the analysis here, however. The above seems to me to suffice as an illustration of what is meant by 'foundation matrix'.

To sum up, Haubl's group (vignette 9) is a beautiful example of Foulkes' observation that a therapy group is a miniature representation of the world at large, with which it is coterminous. Many other group analysts have expanded on this idea and shown how political conflicts, economic problems and social classes are reproduced in therapy sessions. To this day there is still an ongoing discussion in group analytic literature which keeps therapists alert to the contextual nature of many group phenomena.[9] As the influence of the foundation matrix is *contextual*, i.e. determined by the specific circumstances within which an action or event takes place and therefore the determinant of its *meaning*, its themes are quite often not expressed explicitly but rather acted out. This makes it often difficult to recognise what is happening and therefore to deal with it adequately.

3 Foundation matrix and spiritual concerns

So much for the explanation and illustration of how the concept 'foundation matrix' enables a therapist to gain insight into how cultural themes and ideologies sometimes direct the interaction in a therapy session. Now let us return to the foundation matrix's effects on *religious and spiritual* concerns.

A first point is that the effects of the culturally predetermined problematic situation of the contemporary believer (already noted in Chapter 7, section 7) may manifest themselves at any moment in psychotherapy, either explicitly and verbally or implicitly and acted out. These effects may easily surface in connection with situations that at first sight may have little or nothing to do with religion or spirituality.

A further point to be made is that the analysis of Haubl's group alerts us to the fact that some themes associated with religion and spirituality, such as suicidal cults, deprogramming of sect members, anti-abortionism and radical 'fundamentalism', are also hot items in the media. Therapists should therefore be prepared for foundation matrix's themes, conflicts and prejudices concerning such issues to influence the group matrix in a similar way to incest in Haubl's group. And they should, moreover, be aware that these are quite often acted out implicitly rather than expressed verbally. Once a therapist is aware of this, it is not really difficult to recognise and counteract the dialogue-disturbing character of this phenomenon.

A third point worth noting is that the analysis of Haubl's group illustrates how themes *within* a religious subculture may come to dominate and possibly befuddle therapeutic communication. This is particularly worth noting because what I have for the sake of convenience called 'the religious subculture' is itself also far from homogeneous. This in itself can complicate the therapeutic process in group and dyadic sessions. Here is an example of how a theme from *within* a specific religious subculture may be acted out implicitly in the group matrix rather than expressed verbally:

Vignette 10

In a group of Roman Catholic religious sisters one member, a charming old lady in her seventies, said she was afraid of death. The other group members responded by giving her all kinds of, to their minds, good advice. They tried to reassure her that she need not be afraid. They tried to help her by suggesting she should meditate on Jesus' fear in the night before his execution. They told edifying stories about devout people dying in dignity and peace. It went on and on and on. The old nun kept silent and seemed to shrink a bit. At last she said, 'I know all this, it's what I keep telling myself.'

I know it and I believe it, but still it remains words, words, words to me.' In fact the others were not helping her at all. They refused to take her fear seriously. After I had pointed this out and asked them why she was not allowed to be afraid, it gradually became clear that this group was acting out a myth in the foundation matrix of their subculture, namely that nuns have an exemplary faith and lead exemplary Christian lives, and therefore have no reason to fear death. A much more fruitful discussion then developed. It appeared that the old nun had indeed reason in her own mind to fear the confrontation with Jesus after death. This in turn prompted another group member, a professional nurse, to tell how she also was very angry with herself. She explained that she was nursing a much respected but terminally ill Sister, but that she was angry at herself because she personally had great difficulty in performing this task patiently and lovingly. It appeared that in fact she was very angry with her patient, because this Sister was experiencing an agonisingly painful and debilitating terminal phase, instead of dying an edifying 'beautiful death' as saintly nuns are supposed to do. In the same way as the group had refused the old nun's right to be afraid, this nurse denied her patient the right to die in her own way. Why? She was imposing on her the subcultural (foundation matrix) norm for dying.

4 Metacommunication

Awareness of the significance of the foundation and group matrices leads us to another equally relevant and significant concept. This is that a particular type of *metatransference* and *metacountertransference* is likely to occur between the religious and non-religious parties in a group or dyadic therapy session. These two types of transference were first highlighted in transcultural psychotherapy, in which therapists and patients come from different cultures. In such situations there are by definition large cultural differences that complicate therapeutic communication. So let us first look at transcultural psychotherapy theory and see what relevance this may have for communication in 'religious–secular' therapy.

In a seminal article on transcultural psychotherapy, Michel characterises the communication between patients and therapists from different cultures as 'a game with four partners'.[10] These 'four partners' in the transference–countertransference game of a therapeutic dyad are: the personality of the patient, the personality of the therapist, the cultural identity of the patient, and the cultural identity of the therapist. Michel uses a helpful diagram to visualise this. This diagram indicates that dialogue in a therapeutic dyad is determined by (1) the relationship between the two individuals, (2) the relationship of each partner to his own cultural group, (3) the relationship of each partner to the other partner's cultural group, (4) the wider relationship between both cultural reference groups, and (5) the cultural context in which the session is held, for example, therapist and patient in a specialised institute of professional psychotherapy.

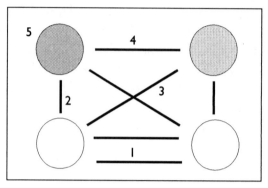

1. intersubjective relationship: transference/countertransference;
2. relationship between the individual and his cultural group;
3. relationship between the individual and the other's cultural group;
4. relationship between the cultural reference groups: metatansference;
5. cultural context in which the session is held.

From LucMichel 'The significance of the patient's and the therapist's cultural groups' in Group Analysis 29 (1996), 3, p.398.

Michel calls the fourth determinant, the relationships towards and between both cultural reference groups, '*metatransference*'. As a result of it, the transferential communication involves not only the individual and personal identities of the therapist and of the patient, but also a group transference between their respective cultural groups. Analysis of the meta*counter*transference then may, for example, show the therapist either eliminating systematically the cultural aspect by overdetermining the psychodynamic or intrapsychic factors, or alternatively exaggerating cultural explanations of any possible pathology. On the patient's side, metatransference may result in vague feelings of guilt or shame, to which the therapist in turn may react inappropriately in a hyperprotective way. Michel writes about the phenomenon of metacommunication in individual psychotherapy. Obviously the transference-countertransference situation in the transcultural *group* is more complex than in the dyad, but in essence not different.

As indicated in Chapter 7, some problems in the interaction with religious patients arise from conflicts and misunderstandings concerning religion and spirituality which still run so deep that they produce a situation that is rather similar to the intercultural (transferential) one. Consequently, metacommunication of the type Michel describes is likely to occur in religiously heterogeneous therapy sessions too. In other words, when patients communicate their personal spiritual concerns, they are likely to become involved in the metatransferential 'four-partners game'. The difference with the transcultural situation is, however, that in heterogeneous *religious/non-religious* therapy sessions this gap between different plausibility structures and symbolic systems cuts straight through the very heart of our *own* culture. As a result, its metatransferential phenomena tend to be much more veiled, unrecognised and more prone to being overlooked. Sometimes it is quite obvious that this is happening. At other times it is not so evident, because it is intricately intermingled with the other factors operative in the complexity of the therapeutic interaction. It is therefore useful for a therapist to be alert to signals of metatransference and metacountertransference in his own and others' interaction with patients who are involved with religion and spirituality.

To trace such often veiled and confusing signals of religious metatransference and metacountertransference, one could usefully try to observe and analyse how Michel's five determinants of the intercultural interaction also determine the actual therapy session. To do this, the therapist would need to try to answer the following questions:

About determinant 1, the relationships between the individuals:

> To what extent do therapist(s), non-religious patients and religious ones communicate with each other as *individual persons*?

About determinant 2, the relationship of each one to his own cultural group:

> How do therapist(s) and patient(s) relate to their *own* (non)religious subcultures? Enthusiastically? In conflict? Defensively? And how does the therapist himself relate to therapeutic theory and practice – in general and in particular?

About determinant 3, the relationship to the cultural group(s) of the other participant(s):

How do therapist(s) and patient(s) relate to the (non)religious subcultures of *each other*? And how does the therapist himself relate to religion and spirituality?

About determinant 4, the wider relationships between different cultural reference groups:

What is the relationship between the participants' *religious and non-religious reference groups*? The general information offered in Chapter 7 becomes relevant here, but more specific information is needed. In the encounter with the real person, one can ask for more information or infer it from the person's expressions. The resulting more detailed insight will then enable the therapist to observe the influence of this relationship more accurately. A therapist would usually also need to have some idea of how the particular religious subculture of his patient regards professional psychotherapy. It is, for example, quite possible that the man who feared disrespect for his religion in psychotherapy (vignette 2) belonged to a religious community that is suspicious of psychotherapy. Such a community may, for example, think that all psychological problems are caused by sin and should be cured by prayer. Or they may have stereotyped psychotherapy as antagonistic to all religion because of a popularised version of Freud's views on this matter. Such a stereotyped judgment is often behind the suspicion that religion is 'explained away' in psychotherapy. A therapist can discover such influences by asking questions about the patient's view of psychotherapy. In this way he can bring this issue into the open so that it can be addressed directly.

About determinant 5, the influence of the 'cultural context':

What is the influence of the *professionalisation of psychotherapy* on the interaction? For example, what is the effect of the fact that therapist and patient(s) meet each other in a specialised institute of professional psychotherapy? Or, what is the influence of the implicit assumptions about disease, abnormality, irrationality and unhappiness on which much methodology is based? This is very difficult to find out, but nevertheless very important. Here is an example of this type of influence, in another area than that of religion and spirituality: research on intake procedures in psychotherapy shows that patients are rarely treated for the problems they present in their first interview. The intake procedure appears to be a kind of negotiation of meanings, as a result of which the intaker repeatedly reformulates the original complaints and verifies whether the patient can accept each new reformulation. Characteristically, these reformulations are sequenced so that the problem is described more and more as a therapeutically manageable one. Concerning a number of such presentations of patients with *identical* problems (interpersonal problems and problems at their jobs) this transformation process was analysed and compared. It appeared that the intakers *reformulated these identical problems differently for women and for men.* Women's problems were reformulated as caused by weak ego-boundaries and dependency, and their treatment was directed towards strengthening their weak egos. In contrast, men's interpersonal and job problems were usually accepted as formulated by the patient himself. But to make these acceptable for therapy, the intakers added something. They added, for example, the men's emotions about these problems, or their lack of emotions. In this way, men's problems, too, became located *within* the person.[11] This example shows how quite ordinary standard procedures of the institution may unconsciously be allowed to influence the present and future communication much more significantly than anybody would want. Such processes may also unwittingly happen to patients formulating their problems as related to their religion or their spiritual life, either at intake or in the course of their therapy.

Some of the above questions require self-reflection on the part of the therapist. Others depend on sensitive observation of what is happening in the interaction, and still others can be answered only by asking the patient(s) for further information. The latter links up with Michel's suggestion on how to *counteract* metacommunication. In his opinion, the best strategy is to bring any metatransference and metacountertransference into the open. For religiously heterogeneous therapy, this strategy would mean bringing the therapists' and the patients' religious-cultural backgrounds and stereotypes explicitly into the therapeutic communication. This would create enough of a common background to facilitate a two-way recognition of the phenomena. Against such a background, personal identities and intersubjective relationships can then become clearly recognisable as the arena or foreground where the interpersonal things that really matter will and must happen.

5 Why concern ourselves with the foundation matrix?

So what if the foundation matrix *does* determine therapeutic interaction? Is this important? The answer is 'yes'. The influence of the foundation matrix, including the influence of (sub)cultural misunderstandings and metatransference phenomena, is often counterproductive for the therapeutic process. The examples of Haubl's group and of the nuns' group both show a group process directed at *un*differentiating and even at impeding differentiation and discovery of a personal stand. This process of undifferentiating can be observed in Haubl's group (vignette 9) in the enforcing of solidarity, in the ways in which the women win the status of victim, in the silence of Mrs P. who is not permitted to be non-vengeful nor permitted to communicate with a man about her grief. It can also be observed in the pressure put on Mrs Q. to comply with the popularised idea of 'necessarily' repressed traumas. A similar process of undifferentiating shows up in the example of the old nun (vignette 10) expressing her fear of death. The group offered standardised pseudo-religious help, and in this way refused her the opportunity to differ from the collective ideal of a 'beautiful death'. Both examples illustrate how in reproducing the foundation matrix, the group matrix may impede a reorganisation of the members' attitudes rather than stimulate it. As a result the therapeutic process can stagnate and can continue only if the therapist first intervenes at the foundation matrix level of the interaction. Such an intervention can also clear the way for the person to seek needed *spiritual* help by, for example, a spiritual director or a pastoral psychotherapist.

CHAPTER 9

Psychotherapy and Cultural Root Metaphors

1 Foundation matrix and metaphors

In this chapter I shall look at yet another way in which elements of the foundation matrix may be used as an entrée for acquiring insight in religious and spiritual problems even if one has not much detailed knowledge of the religion or spiritual tradition concerned. Using again Haubl's group (vignette 9) as an example, I shall show how some *metaphors* are deeply engrained in Western consciousness and function as structuring principles of therapeutic interaction – and can also be the source of many people's problems, spiritual ones included.

What is a metaphor? Aristotle defines it so: 'Metaphor consists in giving the thing a name that belongs to something else.' One of the examples he gives is: 'As old age is to life, so is evening to day. One will accordingly describe evening as the "old age of the day" – and old age as the "evening" or "sunset of life".'[1] As you see, the study of metaphor (a figure of speech based on perceived similarities, in which a name, descriptive term or phrase is used for an object or action to which it is not literally applicable) is very old. All through the centuries the subject has been written about. Since the 1970s there has been a veritable explosion of studies in this terrain, particularly of philosophical and psychological theories. Small wonder, because we are doing it all the time: linking objects, processes, functions or concepts from one area with ones taken from another area, on the basis of perceived similarities. We do it for example when we talk about a 'computer *virus*' or the 'millennium *bug*'. A random look at a psychology text on my bookshelf revealed via its index the following metaphors: introspection, displacement, projection, attitude, empirical law, transference, narcissism, shut-in personality, slip of the tongue, stress, defence mechanism, and many more.

Metaphors and their underlying processes of looking for similarities between quite different things are basic for our comprehension of complex matters. In science, the finding of a good metaphor may be a real breakthrough. I have already mentioned in Chapter 4, for example, Kekulé's discovery of the structure of the benzene ring. He saw six snakes forming a circle by holding each other by the tail end. How could this vision become an extremely fruitful theory of the benzene ring? Because Kekulé used it as a metaphor: six groups of atoms can be visualised as connected with each other in a similar way that six snakes biting each others' tails connect with each other. Note that this is not just an ordinary figure of speech, it is a highly unconventional and novel metaphor. It is precisely because it is both unconventional *and* suggestive of new and satisfactory insights and experiments that this metaphor could cause a whole new turn in organic chemistry. Outside science, too, apt unconventional metaphors function as eye-openers because they disclose new ways of perceiving reality and structuring thought. There are many more functions of metaphors, like the suggestive ones used in advertising, the manipulative ones used in propaganda, the humorous ones in jokes, and the entertaining ones in games like Monopoly and Stratego. It becomes increasingly clear that human experiencing, understanding, acting and interacting are thoroughly metaphorical in character.

2 Root metaphor theory

In the next sections I shall look specifically at *root metaphor theory*. The term 'root metaphor' refers to the most common principles that in our culture organise people's thought, perception and experience as a kind of underlying 'grammar of consciousness'. Such root metaphors have been shown to be very relevant for counselling and psychotherapy. They function at the level of the foundation matrix as well as at the level of the group matrix and at the individual level, so they can be seen as communication links between these three levels. Because there is only a limited number of root metaphors, awareness of these enables us to gain a rather comprehensive and structured view of the field in such a way that its complexity becomes more manageable without requiring too much detailed knowledge of, for example, religious philosophies and dogmas. I shall use Haubl's group (vignette 9) once again, to show how underlying 'cultural' root metaphors organise the ways in which the foundation matrix influences the group interaction. Then I shall show how the same root metaphors are also operative in religion and spirituality, and how this may offer opportunities for therapists to be helpful to religious patients.

Many novels, plays, films and stories are implementations of popular themes such as the Cinderella theme. Virtuous but destitute girl, undeservedly held in contempt and ill-treated by family, superiors, or life in general, meets prince and catches him despite competition and other obstacles. The setting in a novel, play, film or story may differ from prehistoric cave to medieval castle to modern California. The depth and sophistication may vary from so-called soap to world literature. But the basic storyline is the same. In narratology (the study of the structures and functions of narratives), such a recurrent storyline is called a *'primary narrative structure'*.[2]

People tend to make sense of their lives in primary narrative structures. These establish what for them is to count as pertinent data in determining the structure of their autobiography. These 'ordinary' narrative structures are usually much simpler than the ones used in literature and drama, and moreover, most are used unconsciously. However, more often than not people use not so much a narrative story *line* for structuring and giving meaning to the chaos of their actual life events, but something more simple, more like a *metaphor*. A recurring metaphor, for example, is that of the prison. Even though the word 'prison' is not always used in such autobiographies, it is quite evident that people using it make sense of their lives by regarding themselves as prisoners. Their marriage is a prison, their job is a prison, and so on.[3] Wives and bosses are allocated guardian jobs, God is of course the superguardian, the least easy to fool if you dare want to escape. The individual stories vary widely in their setting and detail, but the structure is the same, because they are all implementations of the same prison metaphor. Of course the prison metaphor *may* be adequate to characterise a life situation. Some jobs, some marriages, some religions are indeed prison-like. But if somebody always and everywhere sees himself as a prisoner, then his prison is likely to be largely of his own making. Both in pastoral care and in psychotherapy it is important to discover such primary narrative structures and metaphors, because some of them are more restrictive than helpful for coping with life. The person involved must first move to another metaphor or another structuring principle before change and growth can get on their way.

The same phenomenon can be found at the more general level of a culture. In our culture quite a few metaphors are in use, but some of them are particular favourites. In the same way that at the personal level a metaphor may structure and give meaning to a whole life, a culture's favourite metaphor may generate the worldview of a whole culture. Stephen C. Pepper showed how in our Western culture some of them are particularly widespread and influential, mostly without people being aware of the fact that they are using them. He introduced the term '*root metaphor*' to refer to such widely used metaphors. The term 'root metaphor' distinguishes this function from other uses of metaphors, like the heuristic ones in scientific theory, the eye-opening ones in poetry, or the cliché-type ones in everyday language.[4] In this book I shall use the term '*cultural root metaphors*' for the ones identified by Pepper, because in the next chapter I want to distinguish these from '*spiritual root metaphors*' – metaphors that are specifically designed to function in spiritual life.

One such cultural root metaphor is the one of *similarity*, leading to the organisation of facts, experiences and ideas into categories. As an example, a therapist does this when comparing the symptoms of his patient with DSM-IV, eliminating one or another until arriving at a diagnosis that includes most of the available information. Another one is the cultural root metaphor of the *machine*, leading to organisation into linear cause-and-effect processes and mechanisms. This metaphor is functioning when for example a therapist looks for the cause of mental disturbance in order subsequently to find a cure. A third one is the cultural root metaphor of *context*, including personal biography, time and place. In therapy this is practised by taking into account the personal context of the patient, as in looking rather at the neurotic family system than at the individual's symptoms.

Another one is the cultural root metaphor of an *organism*. It characteristically emphasises growth, maturity, development and interaction. Five properties of plants have been of particular importance for structuring thought in fields as widely divergent as economy and poetry: the idea of the supremacy of the whole without which the parts are nothing; the idea of growth (both in the sense of development through time and of extension); the idea of assimilation (the plant converting diverse materials into its own substance); the idea of internality (the plant being a spontaneous source of its own energy and transformation from seed to full-grown plant); and the idea of interdependence between part and part, and parts and the whole: pull off a leaf and it will die.[5] Many modern therapies, including group analysis, use this metaphor of an organism for understanding complex change processes.

In our culture, these few cultural root metaphors identified by Pepper function as comprehensive key models which *provide coherence for a conceptual scheme for understanding life and the world*. Because of this function, some authors suggest using the term 'key model' rather than 'root metaphor', because once you have discovered which one is being used in a particular case, it provides you with a key to the way in which people – individually or collectively – make sense of their lives and their world.[6]

As for psychotherapy, the individual level is obviously the most interesting. The above mentioned cultural root metaphors are at the root of how many people – therapists not excepted – unwittingly structure their lives in addition to making sense of what is happening to them. The research of Lyddon and Adamson, for example, has shown a correlation between, on the one hand, success or failure of a therapy, and on the other hand, correspondence or difference between the cultural root metaphors therapist and patient are (unconsciously) using.[7] In other words, this research shows how important it can be for a therapist to discover such 'keys' (both his own and his patient's), because without either realising it, the cultural root metaphors they use influence their interaction and therefore the outcome of the therapy, significantly.

3 How cultural root metaphors may become problematic

Any one of these cultural root metaphors is no better than any other. Their applications in many different disciplines, therapy among them, show how each of them contributed to our understanding in a way one single metaphor could not do on its own. Trouble starts when one of them is assigned the status of a universal theory that pretends to cover *all* facts exclusively with one organising principle. It has then been *made absolute* and structures people's minds into *an ideology*, a closed system (in Pepper's terminology: a *'world hypothesis'*). An ideology with the similarity metaphor at its centre is called *'formism'*. In formism, categorising is no longer used as a handy instrument to approach a particular set of phenomena. It expands into *enforcing* a particular category system onto people and their experienced reality. Anthropologist Mary Douglas has shown how whole cultures may be characterised by the rigidity with which they enforce their category systems on reality.[8]

In the same way the machine metaphor is at the centre of the world hypothesis called *'mechanism'*; the context metaphor of the one called *'contextualism'*; the organism metaphor of the one called *'organicism'*. Each of these cultural root metaphors may be made absolute into an all-encompassing ideology. Once one of these has become such an ideological '-ism', it is fully adequate in the sense that it cannot exclude anything whatsoever because it structures *all* thought, perception and experience. Whatever does not fit in is overlooked or seen as irrelevant. For the very same reason it is dangerously *in*adequate, because its absolutism excludes other approaches to people and their reality.

In individual lives these cultural root metaphors function, too, but then in a personalised way, often in combination with other metaphors such as that of the prison or with primary narrative structures such as that of Cinderella. There is a difference, however, whenever they function as the personal cognitive and perceptual structure of an individual – even though that individual is of course part of the culture generating these metaphors. The difference is, first, that at the personal level they function largely unconsciously. A person telling his biography as a linear cause-and-effect story is rarely if ever aware that he is using the mechanistic root metaphor to structure his life experiences, that is, in such a way that all responsibility falls upon whatever he thinks to be the 'First Cause'. Second, there is much less correction. Whenever a professional uses, for example, the mechanistic metaphor inadequately, by looking for linear cause-and-effect processes when a systems approach would be much more sensible, other professionals will quickly correct him. As a contrast, if the personalised version of such a metaphor is being used inadequately or made absolute, this may easily go uncorrected. In therapy, disrupting such personalised metaphors may sometimes be an essential precondition for effecting any real change. If not, the only change that may occur is likely to be superficial and temporary, because it will stay within the same restrictive frame.

4 Cultural root metaphors in psychotherapy

As an illustration of this discussion on cultural root metaphors and how these may help us recognise the links between foundation matrix and group matrix, let us now try to analyse what happened at the level of cultural root metaphors in Haubl's therapy group (vignette 9). Apart from the media-influenced incest theme, another decisive factor in the group's poor differentiation is how they get stuck in a pseudo-antagonism between men and women. Haubl described which group analytic strategies the therapists have used to counteract this antagonism and to make space for careful exploration of authentic experiences of subgroups and individuals. However by restricting his analysis to this antagonism and its solution in this particular group, a much more fundamental change has been hidden from view.[9] Now that we have explored cultural root metaphors and how they may be applied inadequately and made absolute into an ideology, we can see how at a deeper level, his group had also unwittingly *implemented the cultural root metaphor of similarity*. It had organised itself into male-oppressor/female-victim categories. The group members had made this similarity metaphor *absolute* and had given birth to formism when the group started to forbid individual members from crossing these category boundaries: for example, as the victimised woman tried to cross them by communicating with the male co-therapist, and a male group member tried to cross them by expressing sympathy with the female experience. In such a formist matrix with its strictly rigid character, some specific behavioural and psychological characteristics are expected to be normative and unchangeable. Every individual deviation from this is now felt as a threat. Any differentiation is effectively blocked.

Through their interventions, the therapists in Haubl's group have not only made the group aware of how they acted out the foundation matrix's 'scandalisation' themes. At a deeper level of the group matrix, they unwittingly changed its root metaphor from the formist into the contextual one. In this new matrix, categories can and should be criticised, changed, individualised, even abolished if they are dysfunctional. It goes without saying that a group matrix implementing the contextual metaphor is much more conducive to group differentiation and therapeutic change. The same is true for the organic growth metaphor. It should be kept in mind, however, that *each* root metaphor can become counterproductive for therapy.

To sum up, the content of the discussion in the previous pages is meant to alert therapists to the way in which *cultural root metaphors of the foundation matrix,* functioning as deep-rooted cognitive instruments for organising experience, influence people's thought and feeling in their actual life situation. They are also *operative in both individual and group psychotherapy.* I have also pointed out how such cultural root metaphors may become an unchallengeable *ideology* when they are made absolute. In a (sub)culture (i.e. at the foundation matrix level), in the group as a whole (i.e. at the group matrix level), and in an individual (i.e. at the person level), *badly chosen or misapplied cultural root metaphors or root metaphors that have been made absolute may obstruct therapeutic change.* Then there may be need first of what Watzlawick calls a 'second-order change' before the group process can become truly therapeutic.[10] For a therapist, it makes sense to be aware of this, because *analysing the metaphorical structure of problems may help determine the level at which therapeutic interventions may be used most effectively.*

5 Spirituality and cultural root metaphors

Let us now apply this insight to the function of these cultural root metaphors in religion and spirituality.

Spiritual life is living within a transcendent perspective. This perspective is characteristically and significantly *relational*. Everything revolves around the all-important relationship with the God or the gods of that particular religion. A simple example can illustrate how 'relational' and 'non-relational' perspectives differ: everybody can be happy because the sun shines on a holiday trip, but not everybody can be grateful simply because of that. Being grateful is relational, because it makes sense only when there really *is* somebody who *intentionally* did something to *make* you happy. It makes no sense to be grateful when nobody is responsible, i.e. when it is just a happy coincidence that the sun shines at this particular moment and no personal relationship is involved. Within the religious perspective, on the other hand, expressing your gratitude for the sunshine is just as straightforward as saying thank you to anybody else who did you a favour. The difference is, in the religious perspective there *is* actually somebody to thank for making you happy and you *can* communicate with him, in the non-religious perspective not. It is precisely because of the 'relational' and 'perspective' character of things religious, that the goals of therapy and religion, despite their obvious differences, also parallel each other to a large extent. Ideally, both try to help people toward authentic relationships and a wider perspective. This is why *spirituality*, which is about the personal aspect of the relationship with God, can have so much relevance for therapeutic change. It has been shown that any change toward a more authentic and loving *spiritual* relationship transfers to other relationships as well, and vice versa.[11]

Any perspective and any relationship is compatible with many different metaphoric ways of organising perception, cognition and action. Religious communities and individuals, like everybody else, use a great variety of these, among which are cultural root metaphors. The *similarity* metaphor, for example, is much in use whenever new situations demand new policies. To answer modern questions on for example how to deal with environmental problems or with *in vitro* insemination, religions characteristically search for similarities between these new situations and the ancient ones described in their Scriptures. The *organic* one, to give another example, is in use for evaluating the quality of religious experience. One of the criteria most religious communities then use to justify its existence and character is that you have to look at its 'fruits', i.e. the quality of the long-term personal and community effect.

Like everywhere else, both the specifically religious and the 'ordinary' non-religious metaphors may be used inappropriately, idiosyncratically and in a totalitarian way. This is so particularly in their personalised versions where fewer corrective processes can come into play or be brought into play. As for the dominant culture's root metaphors, you may expect these to be given a religious character when used by religious persons. That is to say, God will be allocated a role in them. In doing so, each cultural root metaphor *may* be made absolute or otherwise applied wrongly in a religious context just as it may happen in a non-religious one. If, for example, 'absolute formism' turns religious, God will be seen to demand strict, clear and eternal categories, somewhat like the idea of apartheid. All deviations and mixed or intermediate forms will be considered sinful, because they are in conflict with the divine order. 'Absolute mechanism' will turn God into the ultimate cause of every-thing, 'absolute contextualism' will allocate him one role amidst many other elements featuring in personal history, while 'absolute organicism' will see him enhancing growth and development but ignore reality's dark sides of death and evil.

The point here is *not* that God should have no role at all in a person's life structuring. The point is that a cultural root metaphor, that has been made absolute in a religious perspective, has been expanded into an ideology, and therefore into a closed system. And allocating God a role in a closed system, be it idiosyncratic or not, is not what religion is about. It comes down to denying God any freedom, which prohibits spiritual growth to the very same extent that it prohibits therapeutic growth. Spiritual life is more like an *open* commitment, the kind of mutual commitment underlying marriage, parenthood and friend-ship. In open commitments you do not pin the other down to one single role or task. You do not know beforehand how the relationship or your view of it will develop, what kind of persons both of you will become by engaging in this re-lationship, and so on. It is rather an attitude of mutual love and support you promise to maintain than a set of prearranged absolute obligations. (I shall return to this in Chapter 22.)

Although the foundational Scriptures of the major religions do not know these modern insights into cultural root metaphors, study shows they are obviously sensitive to the need to use such metaphors appropriately and flexibly. Sutherland points out, for example, that when the apostle Paul in his letter to the Galatian community writes that there is neither Jew nor Greek, neither slave nor free, neither male nor female, he is in fact urging his audience to change from the similarity root metaphor to the mechanistic one.[12] Essentially, his line of reasoning is thus: God created us all, therefore we are all the end-results of one and the same linear cause-and-effect process, and therefore we all belong in the same category in spite of obvious differences. This is a second-order change, allowing people to see each other in a radically new way.[13] In the Old Testament, the book Job in its turn fights the tendency to make the mechanistic metaphor absolute. It does so by denying emphatically any direct cause-and-effect relationship between human guilt and human suffering. Misfortune is not necessarily caused by misbehaviour.

6 How cultural root metaphors can shape spiritual concerns

When dealing with religious patients and with groups within which religious and spiritual issues surface, therapists may have to deal with basically the same phenomena in the use and misuse of metaphors as do these biblical examples. An example of this would be:

Vignette 11

One of my patients, a woman of about 40 years old, has lost a child in a car accident. She is a member of a small Protestant church. She is convinced that the death of her child is a punishment of God, because she has been unfaithful to her husband. How am I to approach this?

The interconnection of psychological and spiritual aspects is very clear here. Like so many parents mourning a child's death, this woman probably suffers from irrational guilt feelings. Her theology allows her to rationalise these feelings falsely by connecting the accident with her real guilt of adultery. It is quite clear, first, that this theology is a serious obstacle for any psychological healing. It is also quite clear that it is a serious obstacle for any spiritual healing too. Who could ever love and trust a God who is prepared to kill a child to punish the parent? It is bad theology too. In the Bible, there are indeed texts about the wrath of God and punishment. But these texts are abundantly nuanced and counterbalanced by a great variety of texts emphasising his compassion and forgiveness for whomever sincerely repents. Why didn't this woman apply these to herself? And she is no exception as a 'religious person' in not doing so.

If she were to communicate her feelings to the group, then this might be an opportunity to separate the pernicious bond between her loss and her guilt. But how are therapists to use this opportunity? Aren't we supposed to respect the individual or group religions? Who are we (as therapists) to pass judgement on any theology whatsoever?

As a therapist, you are not in a position to judge religious truths. Nor would you be likely to have them discussed in your groups, as this would too easily divert the group's attention from their real work. However, whenever religious or spiritual issues emerge in therapy you have to deal with *significant individual- and group-generated versions*, and you will feel the need to assess *their* therapeutic significance. With this in mind I think it is useful to distinguish in your own mind (albeit somewhat artificially) between the person's relationship with God on the one hand and cognitive structuring on the other. The latter is where cultural root metaphors enter the picture. Religious cognitive systems may or may not be based on inflexible and absolute root metaphors. But if they are, this may be a serious obstacle both for therapeutic and spiritual growth. But do not lose sight of the fact that an individual's or group's authentic search for a harmonious relationship with God may still be present, which in its turn is favourable for therapeutic and spiritual growth.

Looking at such cases from the viewpoint of cultural root metaphors may well provide a handle on how to deal with such religious obstacles to therapy. It enables us to see for example that this woman in vignette 11 has been making the mechanistic root metaphor absolute and thereby into an ideology, that is, a closed cognitive system. Within that closed system, there can be no other role for God than the leading role in linking causes to their appropriate linear effects. Unfortunately, in most cases such insights cannot be used directly in a therapeutic intervention. Too many people would be prone to think that you are attacking their faith. But there is another way. You could try to explore, first, whether the patient is indeed organising the rest of her life in the same linear way, and second, whether perhaps the whole group is or is not organising itself by this mechanistic metaphor which they too have made absolute. Are the group members always looking backwards for external, earlier causes of their trouble, or always trying to find a scapegoat whenever their interaction gets out of hand? Could it be the group matrix that triggered and is reinforcing this woman's interpretation of her loss? In the event that your observation would confirm one or other or both of these hypotheses, you can undoubtedly find a way to work at changing or making more flexible this underlying organising principle, at the individual and/or at the collective level. To do so would bring about a second-order change, which in its turn would probably trigger off a gradual change in both theological thinking and feeling.

I shall return to this problem of how to deal with theologies in Part 4. I have illustrated here how some insight into the functioning of cultural root metaphors can already provide a first step in understanding and dealing with such a problem.

CHAPTER 10

Psychotherapy and Spiritual Root Metaphors

similarity
mechanistic
organic

1 Spiritual root metaphors

To appreciate the significance of the religious element in psychotherapy, I have in this book made a distinction between 'cultural' root metaphors (the ones from Pepper's theory explained in Chapter 9) and 'spiritual' root metaphors (root metaphors that function specifically as key models for structuring spiritual life and thought). I shall now turn to the latter and show in what ways spiritual root metaphors – and insight into them – are pre-eminently relevant for psychotherapy with patients who are involved with spirituality.

Religions and their spiritual traditions use a great variety of metaphors, symbols, parables and other linguistic devices in their prayers, liturgies, teachings, etc. Some of these are quite widespread. Versions of these are found in quite different traditions all over the world. Although I shall continue to use Christian spirituality as my model, it is precisely at the level of spiritual root metaphors that keys can be found for understanding people of other religions and religious movements as well.

Spiritual root metaphors are characteristically meant to guide people in growing towards a mature spiritual life, to help them in structuring their lives accordingly and to provide a language for communicating about it. Such spiritual root metaphors have had a deep and enduring influence on individuals and societies. They still have a deep influence, although largely unconsciously.

Being aware of this is important for therapeutic interpretation and helpful guidance. First, because these spiritual root metaphors organise religious people's lives to a much greater extent than we tend to realise. Second, because, unexpectedly, non-religious individuals and society are also still deeply influenced by them. Since a therapy group, as stated earlier, reproduces society, it is necessary to be alerted to these 'implicit metaphoric influences', particularly when spiritual concerns are allowed to be expressed and admitted into the arena of group discussion in therapy.

2 What is the function of spiritual root metaphors?

We have already noted how spirituality, for those consciously engaged in it, is living within an all-inclusive perspective. We have touched on how this affects literally everything from major life decisions up to trivial experiences like saying 'thank you' for the sun shining on a holiday. It is about individual and community life being led as a meaningful whole, striving for unity with the transcendent foundation of the universe as a whole. This meaning and unity is found in living life as a continuous search for a harmonious relationship with God – whatever the circumstances may be. Now we all know how life is wildly discontinuous and complex, and frighteningly insecure and unpredictable. And this is where the spiritual root metaphors come in, to help you find this meaning and unity in the most varied circumstances, to help you listen to how they may lead you to an ever-deepening relationship with God. A spiritual root metaphor is a basic means of perceiving order, meaning and unity in the seeming chaos, meaninglessness and discontinuity of life. It helps people to organise thoughts and feelings, focusing on how such situations and experiences affect the relationship with God. It provides a language and images to communicate the spiritual way of seeing reality. It helps in making choices, regardless of whatever other pressures may be brought to bear by outside forces. By helping people to make such choices, a spiritual root metaphor also helps them to find and create their personal and collective identity.

In short, the function of spiritual root metaphors is to help people find spiritual meaning and wholeness in the most divergent both positive and negative real life situations and experiences.

3 Criteria for adequate spiritual root metaphors

To accomplish such a diversity of tasks, spiritual root metaphors have to possess at least three properties.

To begin with, they need to *share a basic structure with a large number of common experiences.* A volcanic eruption, an avalanche and a shipwreck, for example, share a basic experiential structure. They occur quite suddenly, they confront people with overpowering external forces, they are highly perilous, they create feelings of extreme terror and helplessness, they overshadow all other interests and occupations by the all-important struggle for survival, and so on. Because of this shared structure, any one of these three calamitous situations can be used to characterise the experiential qualities of any one of the others – and also to communicate the felt experiences of people involved in all kinds of *other* crisis situations which may be widely divergent but *share the same basic structure.* Use of the metaphor of the shipwreck to communicate the experience of a personal crisis is a familiar example of this. As an attempt to explain the effect upon the self of the unexpected and the irrational in psychological terms, the shipwreck metaphor can also be used to characterise the situation in psychological terms as 'the conscious being surrounded and impinged upon by uncontrollable irrational forces'.[1]

(2) Second, spiritual root metaphors need to be such that they can *generate a variation of narratives that can be broken up into a sequence of situations that can be seen as 'stages'*. This permits widely different situations to be related to each other as well as to a larger whole, while preserving the individuality and uniqueness of each particular situation. So the shipwreck could be one stage in a larger narrative of a sea voyage, whereas the shipwreck itself could be divided into stages, each of them focusing attention on a particular kind of experience: the stage of foreboding, then the stage of the first perceiving of the threat, then the stages of the sudden onslaught of the hurricane, the wild waters, the loss of control, the breaking of the ship that was supposed to provide safety, the drifting around helplessly, the absence of any outside help, the drowning of friends, the being cast ashore, the total isolation of an uninhabited island or the finding of hostile powers there, the need to start a new life and find a new identity which are completely discontinuous with the earlier ones, and so on. *Each one of these experiences may be analogous to the outer and inner situation of a particular person or group in a particular crisis that in itself has nothing to do with a shipwreck.* But the analogous basic structure helps him to give it a place in the larger whole of his existence and in doing so to see it as transient. He can then focus on its potential meaning in the context of his relationship with God. In this way it helps him organise and unify his perception in accordance with such a phased structure.

(3) Third, in order to function satisfactorily as a spiritual root metaphor, the real life situation from which such a metaphor is taken would have to be *familiar to most people*, at least from hearsay. It should not be difficult for them to imagine what it would do to them were they indeed involved in such a situation.

The metaphor of life as a spiritual journey, for example, meets these requirements beautifully. As Landow puts it, it is one of those few metaphors whose variations should command the attention of the student of Western culture. The notion that life is a journey has provided one of the most pervasive commonplaces of Western thought for two and a half millennia, and it is easy to see why. The figures of voyage, progress, or pilgrimage all enable us to spatialise – and hence visualise – our existence.[2]

It enables people to ask themselves meaningful questions about their lives as a whole: when and where it started, what progress they made during their life, what has guided or misguided them, what obstacles and stagnations they met, and so on. We don't need to look far to discover that a lot of our thinking is still being done in terms of progress and stages demarcated by battles, trials and crises. Any description of a journey (an exploratory expedition, a sea voyage, a pilgrimage, a mountain climb, an odyssey, a treasure hunt, a quest for the Holy Grail) which contains enough structural likeness to everyday real situations may become a cultural root metaphor or a spiritual root metaphor, provided it is well-known enough in that culture or that spiritual tradition.

Other examples of widespread spiritual root metaphors are life as a *love story* (falling in love, engagement, wedding), as an *education*, as a *trial*, as *warfare*.

4 When spiritual root metaphors are disconnected from their context

Unfortunately, even the most adequate spiritual root metaphors fail when they are used in an invalid way. Then they generate misery instead of direction, hope and fulfilment. Spiritual root metaphors are quite as prone to being made absolute, misapplied and distorted as are the cultural root metaphors discussed in Chapter 9. This is particularly so in their 'personalised' or 'group-generated' versions. For a therapist, it is useful to keep this in mind and to know something about the proper functioning of spiritual root metaphors. I will now use the example of vignette 11, the woman who lost her child, to illustrate two major ways in which *spiritual* metaphors may fail: when they are made absolute and when they are disconnected from their context.

In Chapter 9 I used vignette 11 to show how the cultural root metaphor of the machine, with its preference for cause-and-effect connections, may be operative in a 'religionised' version. This 'religionising' is done by using 'punishment' as the connecting factor in the woman's linear cause-and-effect thinking. That is, she combined the mechanistic cultural metaphor with a powerful spiritual one, the 'trial metaphor', taken from the sphere of criminal law and punishment in court.

What went wrong in this case with the trial metaphor, and what would the valid (spiritual) application of the metaphor taken from court procedure be?

In the first place, *she made this spiritual root metaphor absolute*, just as she did the mechanistic one. As with the cultural ones, it is important that people (and communities) do not make spiritual root metaphors absolute but keep an open mind for other spiritual views, in this case views on the death of a child. As the research of J. Cook and Wimberley (described in Chapter 17) for example shows, there are actually other authentic perspectives on the death of a child operating within this woman's own Protestant tradition.

Second, in applying this metaphor of crime and punishment, it has been *disconnected from its proper context*. Spiritual root metaphors are in Christianity mainly taken from the Bible and in other religions from their sacred traditions. These traditions provide the natural context for these spiritual root metaphors, and it is important that the metaphors are kept within that context.

The case of the woman in vignette 11 is thus both an example of a metaphor made absolute *and* of what can happen when a spiritual metaphor is disconnected from its original context, and in this disconnected form determines the person's spiritual response to life incidents.

As the woman in vignette 11 was a practising Christian, a member of a Protestant church, she most probably took the juridical metaphor from the Bible in which there are indeed large parts about prescriptions and laws for how to live as a just and holy people. So thinking in terms of 'breaking laws' in events relating to moral issues is certainly encouraged in all religions which consider the Bible as their foundational text. The woman's example even relates to a case of breaking a major law, as the ban on adultery is one of the Ten Commandments that are the most authoritative laws of the Old Testament. She obviously feels guilty about that, and in the Christian ethic she will have to be sincerely repentant and ask forgiveness before she will feel her relationship with God is restored. What interests us here, however, is how she *constructs* the spiritual situation she finds herself in. What has happened here is that the spiritual metaphor of trial and courtroom has become *isolated from its biblical context of the spiritual journey*. The effect of this double isolation has been destructive, both religiously and psychologically. The woman expects to be punished, justifies the punishment but invalidly makes this punishment the death of her child.

In the next section the case of this woman will be used to analyse in detail the biblical context of the trial metaphor she uses, in order to show what may happen if it becomes disconnected from that context. This analysis will help the reader to understand the many other ways in which such misapplied or absolute versions of spiritual root metaphors will continue to haunt people's religious lives – and have negative effects on their therapy too. To consider in detail the implications of this relationship between text and context, I shall use material from the illuminating study of Borg about the connection between the biblical travel stories and the texts about laws and punishment and about the relevance of this connection for contemporary spirituality.[3] This excursus is necessary to give the therapist reader simultaneously an example of the *kind of thinking* that is involved when people try to relate their own lives to biblical narratives. It is relevant for a therapist to have at least some understanding of how this kind of thinking functions, if he is to understand such patients as the woman in vignette 11.

5 Excursus: journeys and laws

What then is this biblical context and why is it disastrous (spiritually and psychologically) if the trial metaphor becomes disconnected from it and in that form assumes an out-of-context life of its own?

Three major journeys are reported in the historical parts of the Hebrew Bible. They are of primary importance and have many meanings and functions in Bible-based religion, shaping the ways in which people understand themselves and their relationship to God. They also shaped the way in which the authors of the New Testament understood Jesus and themselves. Now in the history of Christian Bible interpretation, texts were always supposed to have at least four meanings: (1) a meaning at the literal level; (2) a meaning at the allegorical (or typological) level (as redemptive history of humanity); (3) a meaning at the moral (or tropological) level; and (4) a meaning at the spiritual (or anagogical or mystical) level.[4] The latter meaning is important here, because here we have the journey quite explicitly taught to relate to each individual's life as a God-given guiding principle in his spiritual search during his earthly life. For countless centuries these journeys have been used as metaphors to understand and direct the religious communities' and an individual's spiritual life. They are the story of Abraham, the story of the Exodus, and the story of the people's return from Babylonian captivity.

In the first one Abraham is called by God to take his family and leave his home and his country. He is promised a country of his own and as many descendants as there are stars in the sky. His trust in this promise is severely and repeatedly tested, however, and at the end of his life he and his wife Sarah still have only one descendant, and the only space he owns in their promised land is a grave. The second story of a journey is about the history of the people of Israel being liberated from slavery in Egypt, wandering for forty years through the desert guided by God himself and arriving at last in their promised land which they then still have to conquer. The third story tells how the people are brought home after a long period of estrangement. When used as spiritual root metaphors and applied to individuals or communities, they point out three types of situations that may serve as a point of departure for people's journeys through life under the guidance of God: in search of their spiritual identity they may have to depart from the safety of their ordinary lives, from oppression by internal or external forces, or from estrangement from their true spiritual 'home'.

These biblical histories are still much in use. People who never have been outside their country, for example, communicate quite intelligently about their spiritual experience of being in 'the desert'. And in spiritual group work people have no trouble at all in responding whenever they are asked to choose one of these journeys and to make a drawing of its course, indicating from where they started, where they have been during their life, and where they are now. And the insights following from discussing these exercises are usually quite realistic and helpful for growth and healing. What must be emphasised is that *apart from their other religious functions, these stories clearly function as spiritual root metaphors. In that context they are not only stories about the past, they are structuring the present and the future.*

Returning now to the structuring in terms of crime-and-punishment in the context of Christian religion, it should be noted that within two of these biblical journeys there are many texts about laws, trials and punishment. The journey metaphors provide the larger context for these juridical texts. It is critical to realise *where and how* the juridical texts are related to the larger context of the 'master' narrative. The ban on adultery, which the woman in vignette 11 applied to herself, is part of a quite large part of legislation given to the people during the forty-year period of their wanderings through the desert. To understand the connection between legislation and desert, it should be realised that both in everyday life and in spirituality, being liberated from slavery is not in and by itself enough for a life of freedom in any meaningful sense. If a whole ethnic group has been subjected to slavery for generations and then set free, it has to learn from the bottom up how to live as autonomous and responsible people. Hall would probably even say their soul has been murdered, that is to say, their capacity for love or joy, their response-ability, as well as their identity has been obliterated.[5] They would also have to learn how to sacrifice which part of their freedom for the sake of the others. They would have to curb their own innate desire for violence. And so on. They will get nowhere if each of them individually understands freedom as being free to do anything he likes without regard to the well-being of the community. They would be a flock of escapees, soon to be breaking up, instead of uniting as one people. This is what the story about the wandering through the desert teaches. The chosen people has to go through a process of unlearning old dependencies, of learning to trust God's guidance unreservedly, and of training to become a responsible and righteous people.

When viewed from the first level of meaning mentioned above, i.e. the literal one, this is the way the legislation texts fit into the Exodus narrative. When viewed from the fourth (spiritual or mystical) level of meaning, it is clear that there, too, the juridical metaphor belongs in the larger context of the spiritual journey of individuals and communities. Spiritual teachings of all major religions, not only the Bible-based ones, know an extended period of spiritual disciplining. To put it simply: it is not true that you are suddenly converted and there you are! The promise is indeed that God will set you free, and in the course of your spiritual life you will find this to be true. But freedom will only restore wholeness if its destructive aspects are restrained. Group analyst Van der Kleij, comparing group therapy with Roman Catholicism, observes in both this same paradoxical feature of strict discipline and restraint in the context of being set free and being made whole again.[6]

There is also much talk about 'punishment' in the narrative about the Babylonian exile. Here the contextual 'master narrative' is mainly about the kings and the priests of the Temple in Jerusalem. They are the spiritual and moral leaders of the people, but they have corrupted their own and the people's relationship with God. Prophets bring messages from God that warn them they will be punished if they continue in this way. (Differently from how we understand the word 'prophecies' in the Old Testament meaning these are simply messages from God, which may concern either the past or the present or the future. Prophets are thus messengers who are accredited with conveying God's will or promise or judgement.) The Jerusalem elite refuse to listen and we are told the Temple was therefore destroyed and the upper classes exiled. From that moment on, the prophets' messages change direction: they now proclaim God's love and forgiveness and promise he will rescue his people. After seventy years the exiles are indeed allowed to leave Babylon and rebuild the Temple which is the residence of God on earth. So the homeward journey is located right within a context of both punishment and forgiveness. The Temple as an institution is quite central in this master narrative. It is the site where rites are performed to cleanse the impure and where sacrifices are offered to expiate the guilty. Because of this context the 'journey' is not just a story about returning exiles, it is also a story about a journey with God and towards God, in which God's enduring love and forgiveness is revealed. It proclaims that his punishment does not last forever, and that his punishment does not mean abandonment but rather recovery from self-inflicted estrangement. When the above story is applied as *spiritual* root metaphor, it may for example help people who are disturbed, sometimes deeply, because of an intense religious experience in which they simultaneously felt how far they have estranged themselves from God and how passionately they desire to be reconciled with him.

In the New Testament the meaning of Jesus' life, death and resurrection is seen in the contexts of the Exodus and Exile journeys and the institution of the Temple. They have decisively influenced later thinking about Jesus through the centuries till the present day. The Exodus journey can be recognised in the view of Jesus as overcoming 'powers' that keep us emprisoned, such as sin, death and demons. When Jesus is pictured as revealing God's love and compassion he is as it were the embodiment of the homeward journey. And the context of the Temple functions is clearly present in the view of Jesus' death as a sacrifice to expiate sin, as a sign of God's great love for us. Psychologically, the latter is very important for people with a negative self-image, because it emphasises that we are accepted just as we are. Our own awareness of sin and guilt will never truly separate us from that love. We need never remain the slaves of our past; again and again we are allowed to start anew.

Other influential texts about the theme of trial and punishment are the prophecies about the Last Judgement, in particular such as those in the New Testament book called 'Revelation' or 'Apocalypse', prophesying the end of this world. This expectation of the world's end has given birth to many 'apocalyptic' movements. We are inclined to associate the influence of apocalypticism with its more bizarre manifestations. But we must not lose sight of the fact that this 'sense of an ending' has had – and has to this day – quite an impact on popular culture, literature, science, politics, art and modern thought, as for example reflected in the works of Marx, Hegel, Milton and Blake. The term

'Last Judgement' means that at the end of time everybody will be resurrected, after which the real and persisting enemies of love and justice will yet be brought to justice and get the punishment they deserve but which they had all too often and all too obviously escaped in this life. Connected with the Last Judgement is the expectation of a coming period of a thousand years, a millennium in which justice, mutual love and happiness will reign on earth.[7] In the book of Revelations this period is stated as coming before the final judgement and the beginning of a completely new world. In the course of history up to this day this millenarian expectation has also led to many religious and non-religious movements which are convinced of the imminence of a Reign of Peace.[8] When used as a *spiritual* root metaphor, i.e. interpreted at the fourth (spiritual meaning) level, the notions connected with the Last Judgement may for example help people in desperate and corrupting circumstances to persist in acting compassionately and justly, and help them keep their belief in the ultimate victory of love and justice.

To sum up, the biblical thinking in terms of guilt, trial, punishment, sacrifice, atonement and being forgiven is firmly located within the context of the 'master' narratives of liberation (by a loving and compassionate God) from estrangement caused by external oppression or by people's own injustice and egotism. Applying this juridical theme spiritually to individual lives should give people courage and hope rather than the kind of despair the woman from our example shows. And let us keep in mind that she is by no means the exception. What has happened in her case at the spiritual-psychological level? Some points Borg has made clear can be helpful in finding an answer to this question.

6 The consequences of disconnecting the trial metaphor

In his study of the connection between the biblical journeys and laws, Borg explains what happens if *in spiritual application* the texts taken from judicial court and sacrificial Temple service become detached from their context and become dominant metaphors of their own, determining the way in which people think about Jesus and the Christian life. When this happens this metaphor leads to a *static* spiritual life, an ever-repeating circle of sin, guilt and forgiveness followed by more sin, guilt and forgiveness. Historically, this indeed happened in the Middle Ages. At that time the metaphor from the juridical court became ever more the dominant one. When systematically taught over a long period, such a juridical metaphor detached from its context may lead whole (sub)cultures to a static religiosity. In the meantime there have been strong counter-movements, emphasising the Christian teaching about forgiveness and social commitment. Nevertheless there are still people who tend to structure their thinking and feeling in this juridical way, among whom will probably be the woman in vignette 11. It leads to a type of religion in which God is predominantly known as legislator and judge, with the result that people concentrate all the time on their shortcomings and guilt.

Another effect of detaching the juridical and sacrificial Temple texts from their context and using them as an absolute spiritual root metaphor is *passivity*. People then tend to forget to ask themselves, 'Now that I am forgiven, where am I on my journey with God and towards God, and what will the next step be?' Religious life is no longer seen as *an ongoing process of spiritual change*. This is so because people think that in repenting sin and receiving forgiveness they have already done everything that needs to be done. Such detachment from the context may also lead mistakenly (at the spiritual-psychological level) to a passivity towards one's culture. Such a development is quite contrary to the spirit of these punishment texts when they are connected with their respective master narratives. The journey stories stimulate people not to be passive but to look critically at their present culture. The story of Abraham leaving his home country, for example, may invite them to ask themselves whether their spiritual 'home country' is perhaps so self-righteous that it suffocates any true spiritual life. In the Exodus story a cruel foreign government is the main object of divine punishment. When applied to the present, it may invite people to oppose oppressive political systems. In the Exile story the people's own political and religious establishment is targeted for divine punishment. It may encourage people to investigate and openly criticise their own leaders. The story of Jesus' own life journey ending up in trial and execution has even more radical potential. The subsequent resurrection turns the whole juridical situation upside down. The political and religious establishment, as well as the foreign occupying forces, appear to be the ones who were really on trial in this trial.

7 Therapy and spiritual root metaphors

We may conclude that the thinking structured by the trial metaphor can be very important for spiritual life. Yet neither this spiritual root metaphor nor any other should be made absolute, distorted or detached from its context. For a therapist, there is no need to step respectfully aside for a religious expression of a person who obviously misconstructs his spiritual life by making absolute, distorting or detaching biblical metaphors. And to return to the woman of vignette 11 who was convinced the death of her child was a punishment for her adultery: the Bible itself offers counterbalances to this way of thinking and believing. She herself should be able to discover that; other religious group members could tell her that; the leadership of her own church may even have told her that. Were the essence of the biblical view on these matters known and understood by her, this would very likely bring significant relief to her as mother *and patient*. It would probably not take away her guilt feelings, but once the inappropriate and dysfunctional *spiritual* overtones are disposed of, she will quite possibly be more responsive to the *psychological* approach in a therapeutic process.[9]

As a therapist, you may not want to contradict her directly and explicitly, but it is sensible to *be aware* of what she is doing. That enables you to think about how to counteract her invalid use of a spiritual root metaphor via her cognitive structuring, and to help her find a way out of the vicious bond between guilt and mourning. The *sincerity* with which the woman of vignette 11 repents and mourns and the *passion* with which she craves to restore her broken relationship with God, *that* is what we should respect – and that is where the therapeutic process can begin.

I have suggested that it is useful for therapists to be alerted to the way in which metaphors drawn from biblical stories may generate and structure people's problems, and to the *kind* of interpretation and reflection people use when they seek to relate their lives to their Scriptures. I have chosen this approach because in my opinion it provides a non-religious therapist with a key to access the inner world of spiritually oriented patients. After all it is not realistic to expect such a therapist to gain real in-depth knowledge of Bible, theology and spiritual traditions with their specific and often quite peculiar language use. Both the cultural root metaphors Pepper has identified and the specifically spiritual root metaphors can therefore serve as a key because (1) they are rather common and widespread, (2) they are relatively limited in number, (3) they are traditional and therefore it is rather predictable which ones will be chosen, and especially (4) they determine the *structure* of people's thinking, feeling and acting.

That key may be used at two levels. At the level of *empathising*, an understanding of the function of spiritual root metaphors gives access to how someone construes meaning and cohesion in his life – and therefore experiences these. This makes it easier for a therapist to empathise with that person without needing first a detailed knowledge of his religious belief. It also makes it easier for a therapist to make it clear to the person *that* he is able to empathise.

At the *analytical* level he can not only investigate *which* root metaphor is operative in someone's problems and whether it is an adequate one, but also look at *how* it functions – or dysfunctions. It also enables him to observe whether that person is doing the very same thing in other areas of his life, or to look into the metaphorical structure of the group matrix and the foundation matrix. If it appears that the same phenomenon, for example the making of one such metaphor absolute, is also happening in another area or in the matrix, then it makes sense to ask reflexive questions at that underlying level.

Understanding such processes may also help him differentiate validly in a given case between 'spiritual guilt' and 'neurotic guilt feelings'. Within a spiritual context adultery not only creates guilt toward the partner, but the guilt is also toward God, that is to say, it is also *spiritual guilt*. This of course intensifies the guilt feelings beyond what secular society at large would consider to be proportionate. In the spiritual context this intensification is *not necessarily neurotic*. For someone whose life centres around a spiritual relationship it is not out of proportion.

8 Psychotherapy and the Bible

The foregoing excursus on Bible texts and their interpretation is meant to help therapists understand the *kind of thinking* that traditionally went into mainstream Christianity's interpretation and application of messages of the Bible. If a therapist wants to go more deeply into the inner world of spiritual people, he needs to familiarise himself with the characteristic way of thinking that goes into theology. Lack of awareness of this is where the communication between 'religious' patients and non-religious therapists most often breaks down. Most patients will of course not be able to present such an informed professional account as the one about the 'punishment' texts and their contexts presented above, *but they will use this type of thinking*. It is easily mistaken as being irrational, capricious, or purely subjective, yet it has its own logic and objectivity. This thinking can be erroneous and/or a distortion of the biblical message. Should this be so, such thinking may need to be corrected and when necessary should be. Such correcting is of course not the task of the therapist. However it is important that the therapist is alert to the possibility of a religious patient making either valid or invalid biblical connections; that he takes the patient's religious thinking seriously where it is indeed serious and sincere, and to see through it where it is being misused – for example as resistance to therapy.

As a second objective, the excursus is meant to show something of the *richness of biblical language and images.* Around the year AD 400 Augustine expressed his enthusiasm about the richness in meanings of the Bible, 'How amazing is the profundity of your words! We are confronted with a superficial meaning that offers easy access to the unlettered; yet how amazing their profundity, O my God, how amazingly deep they are!'[10] Although nowadays we read with quite different eyes from Augustine's, many people still have this same experience. In the biblical religions, spiritual growth goes hand in hand with this process: to the extent that someone grows spiritually, he discovers ever deeper meanings. If he integrates these into his life that again leads to further spiritual growth.

Since the rise of rationalism the literal interpretation has become much more influential than it had been in earlier times, but there is now once more a tendency to pay attention to the many levels of meaning that can be found in all great literature and therefore in the Bible too. This attention to levels of meaning constitutes a different way of thinking and formulating from the one used in the sciences. It is also different from the way of interpreting used in psychotherapy, *but nevertheless is concerned with issues that are as real now as they were in earlier times*: about human dignity, about responsibility, about solidarity, about justice, about resistance or passivity. The same is true of most of those strange-seeming doctrinal formulations such as those about the Trinity and about the two 'natures' of Christ. And the same is also true about many of the discussions on heresies in the first centuries of the current era. These discussions are about God and Jesus, but they are simultaneously about people: about human happiness, about what it means to really love your neighbour, about the value of the body and the physical world, about the despair of people who simply *cannot* succeed in living decently, about the arrogance of some who succeed in doing so and assume the right to a special place in heaven, and so on. If you decide to integrate spiritual concerns into psychotherapy, it will be helpful if you have some idea of *how* people connect their own life events with the textual and doctrinal information they have been taught, and how this in turn can result in guilt feelings, fear and so on to a point where psychotherapeutic intervention is called for.

Incidentally, dealing with a richness of meanings is not that strange. All great literature and great art has it, which is precisely why they kept fascinating people all through the ages. For example, one may read *Romeo and Juliet* as a story of a boy and a girl's sexual awakening, or as a story about how the young always want exactly the opposite of what their parents want, or as a story about the kind of pressure medieval social and political structures exercised on people, or as a cautionary tale, 'See what happens when you have sexual intercourse without your parents' agreement or try to make up your own rules', or as a story with a spiritual message: their dying and the subsequent reconciliation of their families as one manifestation of something that happens all the time on a cosmic scale and therefore also in human souls. A battle of love against destructive forces, in which love conquers beyond death. Through Romeo and Juliet's deaths, something positive emerges which echoes also in the lives of subsequent generations who read the story, because we ourselves are involved in manifestations of this same battle. Our own tenderness, our own innocence are also in danger of getting crushed, perhaps by our own destructive powers. Yet these interpretative possibilities are neither capricious nor unlimited: you may interpret Romeo and Juliet in many new and surprising ways, but you cannot make them into an Othello and Desdemona. And that is of course also true of the Bible. That explains this ongoing process of dialogue, i.e. again and again alternating between opening oneself up to deeper meanings and going back to the actual text to validate one's insights.

To sum up, this chapter as a whole is meant to make you familiar with the idea that it may make sense to analyse religion-related problems in terms of 'personalised' or 'group-generated' versions of spiritual root metaphors, and to be aware of what effects they may produce. Such metaphors, when used validly, are important pointers and guides towards a meaningful and harmonious spiritual life. They are intended for everybody as pointers and guides in all kinds of real life situations. But, precisely because they have this function, their misapplication can damage or even ruin both spiritual and psychological health. Understanding these metaphor-driven processes will help you as a therapist to come closer to the essentials. It will help you draw out hidden or vague background influences of a religious character and bring them to the fore.

CHAPTER 11

Spiritual Root Metaphors and Modern Western Consciousness

1 Spiritual metaphors as hidden navigators

'God is dead – and we have killed him!' cries the madman in Nietzsche's *Fröhliche Wissenschaft.*[1] Unfortunately for them, the parricides neglected to kill God's metaphors as well.

For generations upon generations the biblical and doctrinal texts from which spiritual root metaphors originate have had the ultimate authority of revealed divine truth. Applied as spiritual metaphors, they have helped countless people to shape their relationship with the divine reality and their own lives into a meaningful whole. This accounts for the enormous ideological power of spiritual root metaphors. God may be killed, but his metaphors survive and have gone, so to speak, 'underground'. *And from there they continue to structure our lives.*

As a result, the most important spiritual metaphors are not just detached from their appropriate context, as discussed in the section about the metaphor from criminal court disconnected from the contextual travel narratives (see section 5 in Chapter 10). In dominant modern culture, there is no longer a context for them, *their context has largely disappeared.* They are no longer universally taught, so that the individual can choose for or against adopting them, rejecting them, or questioning the appropriateness of their application in specific situations. Nevertheless after such a long period of explicit teaching, they have become the normal, standard way of organising thought, feeling, action and society. But by continuing the practice without explicit teaching, they have become more an 'unconscious habit' than a deliberate choice.

Thus the main spiritual metaphors *continue to function as organising principles.* However, their original meaning is now changed and their application remains unquestioned and uncorrected. As with a grammar, you don't need to be cognisant of such a structure to be able to use it. They have become a sort of 'unaware grammar of life experience and action', much in the same way that one may speak one's mother tongue correctly without being cognisant of its grammar. In this way they shape our culture up to today. In that form they, too, are part of the foundation matrix determining the group matrix. Just as one cannot deny that economic and political structures are reproduced in group formation, the same is true for spiritual metaphors that have for centuries determined our culture. In their new secular context, however, *their meaning has changed, often even to the point of complete reversal*. When 'God is killed', the source of hope and orientation is taken away from these metaphors, and without this source they can become a cause of despair and disorientation.

Once again, here is something curiously reminiscent of what Michel writes about the intercultural relationship. According to him, even if one of the partners in such a relationship rejects his own culture, *it still remains present as a void*, a sort of negativity. This void appears when psychiatric disorders manifest themselves. Vignette 3 (the case of the student who had been a member of a religious sect) shows such a process at work. He had renounced his 'faith', and yet it was still present, albeit as a sort of negative element. His was an extreme case because he had clearly been involved in a tyrannical religion. But even in less extreme cases, such an underlying void or negativity seems to be latent in the unconscious.

It would seem we have an analogous phenomenon in the collective unconscious too. To give an idea of what to look for, I shall take a second look at the metaphors of the journey, the trial and warfare, and now focus on the consequences of them going, so to speak, 'underground'.

2 When the journey metaphor goes underground

In section 3 in Chapter 10, I explained that the metaphor of the journey is pre-eminently adequate to function as a spiritual root metaphor. That is why it is used as such in many Christian and non-Christian traditions. Its impact has been so forceful and enduring, that the journey metaphor now functions in a variety of other goal-oriented activities that have nothing to do with spirituality. As a result, it has almost the same status as the four cultural root metaphors identified by Pepper (see Chapter 9, section 2). In psychotherapy, for example, it is used whenever we talk about setting *goals*, designing treatment *strategies*, taking *steps*, about *progressing*, *regressing*, and overcoming *obstacles*. It is also employed in economic and political language use, where strategic thinking on how to attain set goals is particularly relevant. When the journey metaphor is made absolute, it takes the form of *progressivism*, a closed system in which every popular new idea or technological development is labelled and hailed as a 'progression'.

When functioning as a spiritual metaphor, the life journey is a journey with God and towards God. It is easy to imagine what happens if you take out the divine partner in such a view on life: it means loss of destination, of the compass, of the anchor, of protection, of the meaning of disaster as a transition to the next stage of the journey, of the certainty that in the end everything will be set right. It also means that the stronger partner has fallen away, so that the weaker one, the human being, is the one who all by himself has to determine the direction and stay in control. In fact, he had better drop the 'life journey' as a structuring principle and not use such a frightening one!

In the course of the nineteenth century, when scepticism about biblical religion spread among the educated classes in Western societies, two responses can be observed, responses which I think show how the metaphor continued and still continues to structure Western thought and feeling. One of these is the increasing faith in 'progress' as if guaranteed by 'Inborn Reason' (enabling man to conquer destructive natural forces by science and technology), or by the 'Laws of History' (providing for a succession of ever more 'civilised' societies), or by the 'Laws of Nature' (unerringly pushing the evolution process to its highest product, i.e. Western man). It is commonplace to note that Marxism and liberalism assume a secular 'promised land' based on the eventual triumph of a proletariat or, respectively, of freedom and reason in a capitalist society. In other words, science, evolution and/or civilisation took over the function of God, in the sense that they provided for a destination, an inborn compass, a trustworthy guarantee that in the end all shall be well. Belief in progress became the dominant ideology.

Simultaneously, as a second response to the journey metaphor getting disconnected from its spiritual context, disbelief in the inherent goodness of nature, reason and civilisation began to manifest itself. Art and literature of that period show an explosive increase of the theme of sudden natural disaster. Paintings, poems and novels about volcanic eruptions, avalanches, shipwrecks and deluges become widely popular. However, the disasters are clearly no longer meaningful parts of a life with God. They are pictured from the viewpoint of helpless victims surrounded by irrational destructive forces.[2] The popularity of these paintings and literature means they express something that is widely felt by many people. What they actually express is a deep existential anxiety and insecurity.

Taken together, these two reactions seem to signal how culture kept seeing life as being 'on the way' but now has to invent its own hopeful end. Now they have to find the guarantees of success either in themselves or in the world, and discover these to be precarious. A spiritual metaphor of hope and meaning (the spiritual journey) has in essence become a metaphor of despair and meaninglessness.

Writings on the meaninglessness of existence prior to the nineteenth century are rare, but then, rather suddenly, the world seemed to be deprived of its intrinsic purposefulness and meaning. In the twentieth century, when modern secular thinking spread over ever larger parts of the population, and two world wars and the great depression had effectively undermined faith in progress, this growing feeling of meaninglessness culminated in the existentialist movement that openly declared life and death to be meaningless.[3]

In the early 1970s, when an even larger part of the population had become non-religious, the effects of this tension began to become manifest in psychotherapy. Psychotherapists repeatedly reported that patients now had other complaints than before. In the first half of the twentieth century their complaints largely corresponded with the clear symptoms and their underlying dynamisms as described and analysed by Freud. But now an increasing number came with much vaguer complaints such as a daily experienced feeling of meaninglessness and emptiness. Often they even lacked any hope that treatment could help them to have a meaningful life, because the world itself was experienced as empty and meaningless. Yalom is one of the important theorists responding to this development. He points to the basic existential conflict flowing from the individual's confrontation with four ultimate concerns: death, freedom, isolation and meaninglessness. Psychopathology he conceives as the result of defensive and ineffective modes of dealing with these central givens of existence.[4] But in his view the world is meaningless, so each individual has to create meaning in his life as a creative response to this meaningless universe. In his view, meaning does not exist outside the individual who creates it for himself. Consequently, since most individuals are at least dimly aware of the self-created nature of their personal meanings, fear for meaninglessness is always hovering at the threshold. This fear is often intensified by an awareness of the inevitability of disaster and death.

Yet in Yalom's view a sense of meaningfulness of life is regarded to be essential to mental health. Acknowledging the precariousness of self-created meaning, he stresses that *commitment* is the therapeutic answer to meaninglessness. It makes sense indeed to distinguish between 'meaning in life' and 'meaning of life'. 'Meaning in life' is the meaning people subjectively find in their own lives, for example the meaning their work, their family, their hobbies may have for them. 'Meaning of life' would then be an objective concept, referring to whether life as such indeed has meaning, irrespective of one's subjective experience. Yalom is of course quite right that commitment to significant activities or relationships would help people to find meaning in life. But the question inevitably arises, would not such commitment contain the danger that in their commitment to 'meaningful activities or relationships' they could *again* be confronted with disaster and death and *again* suffer from the ensuing existential anxiety and meaninglessness? That seems to be the weak point of any meaning *in* life that is not embedded in meaning *of* life.

Research can never determine once and for all whether life in fact has meaning. That is a matter of philosophy and religion. However, one can do research on whether people subjectively experience meaning in their lives, and how this relates with therapy results. Such research confirms that indeed meaning in life, whether embedded in an overall religious meaning of life or not, is related to improvement during psychotherapy and predicts the outcome of therapy, independently of patients' pre-treatment levels of well-being. In Debats' research, young adult patients who have a low sense of meaning in life, as measured with the Life Regard Index, were found to have significantly worse outcomes in regular treatment than patients with a high sense of meaning in life.[5] There has been an increasing number of studies on the impact of meaning in life on addictive disorders, on physical diseases such as AIDS and cancer, and on coping with traumatic life events. The conclusion from these studies must be that the concept of meaning in life has significant relevance for current clinical practice.[6]

3 When the trial metaphor goes underground

'At the heart of many cultures (perhaps of all) are metaphors of a major test or trial... In Western culture, the theme of the trial is coded in terms of a Last Judgement that lends significance to earthly trials in everyday life or in courts of law', writes Fenn in his study of the secularisation of religious language.[7] As a central religious theme, it is nowadays largely located in peripheral groups and movements such as religious sects heralding the rapid approach of the end of the world. But this marginalisation of the explicit version should not obscure the fact that the trial theme is very much alive, organising our lives, thoughts and feelings in many subtle ways. It gives implicit meaning to many activities that are remote from courtrooms. Some examples from Fenn's book are: science, politics and education. In science, the most basic assumptions behind the search for the 'truth' in scientific inquiry are very similar to those used in trial proceedings. In politics, periodic elections ensure that policies and politicians are on probationary terms, subject to a review by the electorate that resembles the deliberations and verdicts of a jury. In education, the schools, colleges, and universities of Western societies put the majority of youth through a process of continuous testing and evaluation. Another example is psychotherapy: therapists scrutinise a patient's account of feelings and experiences for significant distortions and omissions on the assumption that, beneath the surface and despite the profusion of irrelevant detail, there is an underlying complex of related motives and wishes, of fears and evasions at work in the patient's life. The discovery of the unconscious has opened up a source of accusations or of offensive motives that turns a lifetime into a perpetual trial with fresh evidence continually arising from buried sources.

Fenn concludes from these and similar observations that the cultural theme of a trial has lent to everyday life the awareness that the individual is on trial, and that to social institutions the cultural theme lends the right and obligation to be certified as creditable or authoritative witnesses to truth embedded in molecules, legal texts, medical records, or other significant repositories of information. In short, the going underground of the spiritual root metaphor of the trial has made everyday life and social relations deadly serious, because these entail the justification of individuals, of social institutions, and of society itself.[8]

Here, too, the taking away of God as the final Judge turns the metaphor into a trap. As a contrast to divine judgements, secular judgements are never once and for all. New knowledge changes the very 'laws' of nature and society and alters the composition of those whose testimony is to be taken especially seriously. New elites emerge as authoritative witnesses and the new laws of nature or society give enhanced credibility to those whose testimony has previously been found irrelevant or lacking in proper weight or validity. The secularisation of the religious demand for justification, then, has led to a dynamic process in which elites emerge and decline as laws change and new knowledge becomes authoritative.

As a result, many individuals in Western societies are caught in an inner conflict. On the one hand, they take seriously the role of the credible witness and seek, on the grounds of their own testimony, to be taken seriously. On the other hand, because of the professionalisation of procedures for reliable and authoritative testimony, most individuals face the likely prospect of being tried and found wanting in the classroom, in the doctor's surgery, in the employer's office, as well as in the courtroom itself. The same process has transformed virtually every context into a place of potential judgement, where personal or corporate credibility and authority are perpetually problematic. 'A lifetime on probation' can fairly characterise life in Western society. From a guarantee that, contrary to appearances, in the end justice and compassion will triumph over injustice and oppression, the trial has become a main source of continuous insecurity and subjection to professionalised elitism.

4 When the warfare metaphor goes underground

The idea of spiritual life as warfare is not restricted to the Christian tradition in which hymns like 'Onward, Christian soldiers' find a home. This metaphor, too, is fairly universal in widely divergent religions, as a battle between two cosmic armies, or between the gods, or with devils, demons, dragons, witches and other enemies. It is also found in the Scriptures of Islam and Hinduism, and is the many sagas and myths in which heroes set out to fight monsters and witches. Its occurrence as spiritual root metaphor does not mean the religion is a bloodthirsty one. In the most important Hindu Scripture the war of Ardjuna is even the 'master narrative', though Hindu religious culture is in principle peaceful. In the Bible it is God himself who decides when, why, and against whom to declare a war and (as a spiritual metaphor), always to restore justice, compassion and holiness.

This warfare metaphor has such a universal appeal as a spiritual metaphor because it offers people a way to understand the difficulties and struggles of spiritual life. Such war stories refer to the fact that there is much effort and risk involved in the choice for a spiritual life, that one has to fight one's own egotistic and destructive tendencies and quite probably external pressures, too. This is because the most important teacher of spiritual growth is reality itself, which admittedly is conflict-ridden. Of course people may use spirituality to escape the dark aspects of reality, as they may use anything else that comes to their mind for that purpose. But that escapist tendency is precisely what the major spiritual teachers and traditions continually warn against. Reality's seemingly senseless suffering and cruelty are emphatically not to be escaped. Neither should our own inner reality be escaped. Again and again strong destructive unconscious forces have to be confronted. Religious language expresses this in picturesque terms of a continuing battle against sin, demons, devils and temptations, but this process coincides for a considerable part with the fears and struggles we know to exist in the therapy process as well. The objectives are different, of course. In therapy you work with patients and try to help them towards 'normal' social and psychological functioning, whereas the spiritual person strives for a life with God which does not necessarily coincide with 'normal' functioning as understood in our society. Spiritual life may even start from an experience in which the person discovers how much the 'normal' performance in society in fact alienates him from a true relationship with God. The inner spiritual struggle often makes this realisation its point of departure and develops from there in a process of spiritual growth.

Obviously this metaphor can easily be misused by calling whomever you happen to dislike the enemy of God or by using it to justify dubious military operations.

This metaphor, too, keeps influencing secular thinking and behaviour much more than we realise. Davies' careful analysis of twentieth-century European and American militarism, for example, shows how deeply our very identity has been formed by this way of thinking and how the secularised version of this metaphor can be shown to have been uncomfortably influential in, for example, the 'smart weapons' justification of the Gulf War.[9] A fascinating example at the individual level is to be found in the content of ex-President Richard Nixon's autobiographical book *Six Crises*. Cochran's thorough analysis of this book shows Nixon to be dominated by the repetitive elaboration of one single metaphor. Political life is warfare to him, a series of battles in which Nixon consistently sees himself as a selfless hero. No crisis is ever initiated by himself. He is thrown into it, which right from the start defines his activities as selfless. Then each crisis is magnified into a battle in which 'Causes' such as world peace, the survival of freedom, or national security are at stake. Through this magnification he feels purged of petty personal concerns, and in his personal assessment his actions become those of a selfless champion totally dedicated to the well-being and safety of millions.[10]

5 Psychotherapy and disconnected spiritual root metaphors

I have tried to show how spiritual root metaphors have as it were 'gone underground' and in that form are still influencing many people's philosophy of life, often held unconsciously but apparent in the ways in which they conceive and experience life. For psychotherapy, this means this chapter can be relevant for understanding some common basic attitudes of non-religious patients and also for understanding what I have called 'spirituality in exile'.

In my experience, the effects of such underground metaphors at the individual and group level manifest themselves most often in *anger and resentment*. For example, it has been known to happen not infrequently that, when a theology student explains what it is he is studying, this awakens a latent anger in his listener. Not at the student personally, but at anything that has to do with religion. The older students are used to it, but the first-years are sometimes quite upset. This is but one way in which a deep-seated resentment against an absent or non-existing God surfaces. In the later chapters, I shall discuss the fact that it is quite common for even spiritual people to feel resistant to God and to their own spiritual yearning, but that is not the issue here. Here I am describing the *anger* of quite a few *non*-religious people – either at the God they have rejected, or at life itself. This scorn, resentment or actual anger can also be observed in modern art and literature, and in the media.

When a therapist allows spiritual issues to be brought up in therapy sessions, he can also expect this anger to emerge in his non-religious patients every now and then. Vignette 2 (the religious patient who feared disrespect) showed how religious patients themselves may expect that other people will respond to them in this way. If the situation is such that you (as a therapist) can just let the storm blow itself out, then, surprisingly, a quite moving genuine dialogue may follow. From behind the anger a personal distress and disappointment can emerge. Some then tell that they have been religious in the past but have rejected religion for some reason; others have never been religious but are nevertheless quite emotional about it.

Tuning in attentively to such anger often reveals an underlying spiritual conflict or need. Because a conflict or need at the spiritual level can easily be a source of other psychological problems, it may be relevant to pay attention to *why* they are angry and *at whom or at what* they are angry. The latter is an indication of what spiritual root metaphor is unconsciously still operative in their lives and with what they have filled the gap left when God is left out of it. You may hear them angrily rejecting God because he is the ultimate cause of all their bad luck, illnesses, losses, or whatever is the *immediate* cause of their anger. They then in fact reject the mechanistic metaphor of God. Or they deny his existence but the anger is still there, only now it is directed to another address, at coincidence or at blind natural forces, for example. The same root metaphor has been kept alive, but is now related to life itself as if, for example, it were an omnipotent power which *should* concern itself about the well-being of its helpless underlings but fails to do so. Or, as another example, one may hear in other people's anger their disappointment about the general injustice of life, indicating that even though they do not believe in God, they deep down still relate to life itself as if it were a supreme judge who *should* administer justice but neglects to do so.

The great Christian message is and has been that God loves humankind with a deep, unconditional and infinite love. Whatever root metaphor is used or taught, his power is always portrayed as beneficial, his justice as compassionate, his guidance as leading towards true happiness, his allotting of fortune and/or misfortune as ultimately a liberation towards spiritual fulfilment, and so on. In short, whatever kind of role he is supposed to fulfil in whatever kind of dealings with man and the world, that role is primarily a sort of channel for reaching out to man in a continuous outpouring of his infinite love, and a sort of permanent invitation for man to return that love.

It is easy to observe what happens when this divine love becomes disconnected from its spiritual context and people try to fill the gap that is left by other means. We see many people in whose lives an unfulfilled yearning for unconditional and infinite love is a persisting life theme. Putting their hope for infinite love in one lover, friend, parent, or leader after another, they heap disappointment upon disappointment and end up in bitterness because the love they are actually receiving never meets the standard of being 100 per cent unconditional and infinite. This is inevitable because however loving human beings may be and however impressively they give all they can give, human beings are finite and not divine. An alternate way to fill this gap in the spiritual metaphor is to assume the role of the absent divine partner oneself and act accordingly, all the time pushing oneself to the limit in order to offer divine-like love instead of giving wholeheartedly and generously of the *human* love which one can indeed give.

To sum up, when spiritual concerns emerge in therapy, it may be illuminative for the therapist also to pay attention to those who are responding negatively. *Which* God do they reject? From *which* spiritual metaphor has the absence of God left a gap, and *with what* do they try to fill that gap? Becoming aware of it is in and by itself already an important insight. Moreover, such insight opens up options and opportunities for change at two levels. At the first level, the one involved may decide to continue relating to life according to the same root metaphor, but now consciously. He may then either fill the gap left by the absence of God with something else, or he may decide not to fill it at all. At the second level, one may abandon one's current metaphor. This amounts to a second-order change, a fundamentally different way of relating to life itself. He is then in a position to try out a different model with its different implications - and through it possibly still find God after all.

There is much more of course that could be written about the spiritual root metaphor theme. But my goal is no more and no less than to alert you as a therapist to inherited and unsolved tensions of this kind and to help you to recognise how these spiritual root metaphors are still there and can determine numerous lives (group lives included), but no longer helpfully.

Concluding Part 2

The chapters of Part 1 gave an impression of the great variety of spiritual concerns that may surface in psychotherapy – or remain submerged and unsolved and as such possibly obstructing therapeutic progress. Where do we find instruments for understanding and approaching such problems adequately while staying within the task and competence of professional psychotherapy and operating from a limited knowledge of the many religions and their concomitant spiritualities of individual patients? And in addition, we have the complex sentiments of the 'spiritual exiles' too. That is our main question. The chapters of Part 2 have offered a first approach to finding answers to this question. In this approach the concept of 'foundation matrix' plays a crucial role.

Although the problems under consideration are real and pressing problems for the individual patients involved, many of them are *also* shaped by the foundation matrix. 'Foundation matrix' refers to all that connects us as members of our culture, which functions as the background and context upon which the interaction pattern of the individual members of the group (the group matrix or dynamic matrix) is built. It is both external and at the same time deeply internal to individuals and groups. The use of this concept leaves the group analyst free to move between background and foreground, between the levels of the transpersonal, the interpersonal and the intrapsychic. Although 'foundation matrix' is a group analytic concept, the phenomena connected with it can be observed both in group and in dyadic therapeutic interaction. Using the insights resulting from such observation is therefore not the exclusive terrain of group analytic practice. It can be a powerful tool in any and all approaches to psychotherapy.

As a first approach to the above question, the chapters of Part 2 have looked at how this concept may be used to develop such an instrument. This has led to the following insights.

First, because of historical developments in Western culture, many religious beliefs and practices are *no longer plausible* to many people. As a result, in any encounter between religious and non-religious people (the therapeutic encounter included) the religious are likely to find themselves in a *defensive* position, knowing that their religion and spirituality will probably be challenged explicitly or implicitly. They also know that they will have *difficulties in communicating* adequately what is most central in their lives. This may of course manifest itself in various ways, for example by keeping silent about the spiritual aspect of their problems, or by being shy or just the opposite, by over-compensating. Furthermore, their religious experience is likely to be seen, both by themselves and by the others, as *private* and therefore subject to being 'explained away', that is, reduced to its psychological aspects only. Obviously, the secular thinkers will find themselves in a *complementary* position, secular thinking therapists included.

Second, people involved in religion and spirituality in Western secular culture need to deal with their own *internalised atheism*. If they refuse to do that, this inner inconsistency may be at the background of psychological or relational problems they express or manifest in therapy.

Third, metatransference and metacountertransference, themes of the foundation matrix, including themes generated by religion and spirituality and themes having their roots in specific spiritual traditions, may be *acted out* rather than expressed explicitly in therapeutic communication and in that form are likely to obstruct therapeutic progress.

Fourth, a therapist does not need to know many details of a given religion to see how a particular person *construes* his spirituality. A limited number of *cultural* root metaphors are universally used as structural principles organising people's perception, thought and action. In addition, spiritual traditions use a limited number of *spiritual* root metaphors that are specifically designed to guide people's development towards a mature spiritual life. It is therefore therapeutically profitable to approach religious and spiritual concerns by analysing *which* metaphors (or combination of them) are structuring the problem or conflict under consideration, as well as *how* they are structuring them. It can also be worthwhile to do this with people who respond negatively to spiritual concerns.

In the preceding chapters I have also put forward some tentative *methodological* suggestions. They can be summarised as, first, a suggestion to bring such underlying influences from the foundation matrix on the therapeutic interaction into the open. Then they can be dealt with separately and no longer hamper person-to-person communication. A second suggestion is to encourage patients to express their spiritual concerns in terms that are as close as possible to their own experience and to have them give examples from their own experience. That is critical to avoid mutual irritation and makes it easier for the other(s) to understand them.

PART 3

Existential and Cognitive Aspects of Spirituality

Introducing Part 3

In Part 1 I have looked at how spirituality may occur as an element in a variety of therapy situations. At the end of the concluding section I have sorted the vignettes out into (1) problems that had to do with the tension between religious and secular subcultures, (2) problems that had essentially to do with religious persons whose own communities were misleading or mistreating them and (3) problems that have to do with people's own spiritual life. In Part 2 I have discussed the problems behind the first category vignettes. In doing so, I have moved to the cultural context, which to a large extent is the underlying cause of the way in which religion and spirituality can be a problematic factor in therapeutic interaction.

In Part 3 I shall turn to the background of vignettes 4 (a housewife hears a voice), 5 (a patient has therapeutic visions), 6 (a near-accident), 7 (Tolstoy's confession) and 8 (Clyde's addiction). The problems these vignettes illustrate have to do with an individual's spiritual change process. In order to understand what may be happening at this level, I shall look at spirituality from the viewpoint of *the individual person involved in a process of spiritual awakening and, on the basis of that, committing himself to spiritual life.* Such coming to spiritual awareness and choosing a spiritual life *involve complex change processes with great inherent potential both for personal growth and for regression or disorientation.* Understanding the dynamics of these change processes is relevant because they may influence therapy either positively or negatively. Spiritual change involves not only a person's inner life: it involves his whole life. No aspects are untouched, not even the most common daily activities such as eating or gardening. So there is in principle an infinite number of aspects, everyday and special, that are affected. The content of this part is therefore necessarily selective. I concentrate on what I think is most relevant for therapists if they are to recognise what is happening and to figure out what help can best be given in an individual case.

CHAPTER 12

Spirituality as a Change Process

1 An ancient theory of spiritual development

To structure my account of how modern people may be involved in spirituality, I have adopted and adapted elements from a very ancient theoretical systematisation of spiritual development which is still in use in contemporary Christian practice. Therefore I shall first give an outline of it and then tell how it is adapted for this book.

The notion of '*spiritual development*', or '*spiritual growth*' is rather widespread in the mystical traditions of various religions. '*Mystical*' refers to a particular type of religious experience described in numerous reports of a personal and immediate encounter with God or whatever Ultimate Being/ Reality is perceived in the person's spiritual tradition. The person directly experiences the Divine in an innermost realm of self where mind, senses, and feelings seem to come together. This inner 'spiritual sense organ' is referred to as one's Self, Atman, Christ within, or spirit, depending on how the nature of human beings is conceptualised in the various mystical theologies. *Mystics* are people who in their life combine two dimensions of spirituality. On the one hand, they put their whole life into the service of God, training themselves to become ever more receptive to his will and ever more obedient in doing his will as they perceive it. On the other hand, they are exceptionally receptive to mystical experience, which they consider to be a free gift from God, not a product of their own efforts. The tension between their own efforts and self-training on the one hand, and on the other hand their recognition of the free gift nature of their experience is sometimes compared with dancing: initially for a relatively long period in dancing (as in mysticism) you exercise to get your body under control, and then it may happen that *you* are no longer in control. In the case of dancing the music is in control. You surrender to the music that makes your body dance. And it not only *feels* like that. The onlookers can *observe* this is happening.

In the long run the lifestyle of the mystics results in a personality change so fundamental that it is often called a *'spiritual transformation'*. A mystical or *spiritual tradition* is a corpus of educational theories and training practices (we would say a methodology) assisting people and their counsellors in this striving. The latter are traditionally called *'spiritual directors'*, even though it is one of the few functions that has also been held by women from way back. Nowadays there is a tendency to choose less 'directing' terms like 'spiritual guide' or 'spiritual friend'.

In Europe, the dynamics of this development process are known to have been studied from the time of the ancient Greeks and thereafter. Possibly from even earlier times than Greek culture stems the systematisation of spiritual development under the guidance of a spiritual director in three stages or phases: *purification* (or *purgation*), *illumination* and *unification*, alternated by intermittent *'dark nights'*. (I have already discussed how a period of spiritual 'darkness' is often precursor of someone's spiritual awakening, and how 'dark nights' may occur in the course of one's further spiritual development. This was in the commentaries on vignettes 6 and 7, the businessman who had a near-accident and the text from Tolstoy's autobiography.) For each of these three stages of spiritual development different practices, exercises and prayers are called for on the path of spiritual growth. There is a case for hypothesising that the *structure* of this old Christian methodology is not specifically Christian but reflects the basic dynamics of any training that is aimed at devoting oneself to transcendent reality. Despite the obvious differences between religions, there are many and striking similarities between their spiritual traditions, their reports of spiritual experiences, and their practices. This suggests that we are dealing with a universal human capacity as, for example, the artistic capacity. Such capacities never function in the abstract. They develop only when they are implemented and exercised. In Western culture they are mainly implemented by the Christian religion. If this is true, it may rather be the implementation of the systematisation than its structure that identifies it with Christianity.[1]

The *purgative* stage consists of a variety of disciplined self-denying practices. A person learns to surrender his ego and to 'die' to the egocentric and defensive self. In the *illuminative* stage the person tries to become ever more receptive for transcendent reality. This is done by reading and reflecting on spiritual literature, by training the capacity to concentrate, and by 'untraining' the preconditioned categories of the mind that ordinarily filter perception of and reflection on experience. In the *unitive* stage the person feels himself to be in the presence of, sometimes even to participate in, the pure altruistic and creative love of God.

At some precious times he is so absorbed in this experience of being in communion with God, that he becomes less conscious of himself as a separate entity. Underhill, whose writings from the early twentieth century are still widely read, compares this with the appreciation of great music or art, for which, too, the eyesight or hearing needs to be supplemented by trained powers of perception and reception:

> The condition of all valid seeing and hearing, upon every plane of consciousness, lies not in the sharpening of the senses, but in a peculiar attitude of the whole personality: in a self-forgetting attentiveness, a profound concentration, a self-merging, which operates a real communion between the seer and the seen – in a word, in *Contemplation*.[2]

There are more of such theoretical systematisations, some of them very recent, but this one is still very influential in Western spiritual tradition. Some writers try to integrate it into modern psychological theory, for example into Erikson's famous theory of epigenetic development stages.[3]

In psychotherapy we will generally not deal with mystics, but in my practice I have often found that the old concepts of purgative, illuminative and unitive experience are very useful for making sense of 'ordinary' spiritual life and its pathways. Such evidence suggests that there is a *continuum*, i.e. a significant convergence, *between mystical and 'ordinary' spiritual experience*, particularly with regard to the *dynamics* of spiritual development. These processes are not so far apart from each other as we might at first suppose. Let me explain this with an example.

2 Adapting the ancient systematisation to modern experience

Vignette 12

In my first years at university, I was much impressed by the explanatory models of psychology. They seemed to be so comprehensive, so universal, so consistent. They had all the answers.

I

But in that same period I felt myself being called by God. I resisted that feeling. I tried to find a rational explanation for it. I thought it to be the voice of my superego, the result of my education having nestled itself in my conscience, which was dictating how I should live and obstructing me from making my own free choice. Often enough it seemed indeed to be the voice of my superego. Many times I had to expose a so-called 'voice of my conscience' as dependence. Many times I found I should say no to it. This is a process that is still going on. But still – not all of it could be explained in this way. Somehow this longing for God would not really leave. It would always return, chafing me like an abrasion. For a long time I kept thinking this was a morbid inclination. It seemed to me I lacked the courage to throw the thing out forever.

II

But then, in my postgraduate studies, I read the writings of Viktor Frankl and Abraham Heschel. What a relief! They put into words my dormant and unformulated idea that my inner conflict was not morbid. It had to do with what is most human in man, which is the question whether he is alone in the infinity confronting him. Since then I got to see more and more how in Jesus Christ the thirst of man for depth and eternity is assuaged.

III

Now my longing for God has evolved into an intimate personal relationship.

At this point we are interested in the *structure* of this student's experience and the path it followed according to his own account. To show how strikingly it parallels the ancient three stage schema, it is divided up into three main paragraphs:

In *paragraph I*, the student tells how he has *purged* or *purified* his feeling of being called by God through critical self-examination and saying 'no' to anything he felt to be inauthentic. These activities roughly correspond with what people are supposed to do in the 'purification' phase. I prefer to use the term '*existential aspect*' of a process of spiritual development rather than 'purification phase', because the type of activity involved can essentially be characterised as a process of self-discovery at the existential level.

In *paragraph II* the psychology student describes how *illuminative* the writings of Frankl and Heschel were to his self-understanding, and how he discovered a deeper, experiential meaning behind the formulations of 'that old time religion'. I take what is happening here to correspond roughly with what in the ancient system of process mapping is called 'illumination'. I prefer the term '*cognitive aspect*' of a process of spiritual awakening to refer to this activity rather than 'illumination', because the person is trying to acquire valid spiritual knowledge here.

In *paragraph III* the student tells about what happened to him after he affirmed the call and opened up to God. He describes this as an ongoing 'intimate personal relationship' with God. Though the story gives no details, this is probably not the immediate encounter of a mystical experience. But nevertheless I consider this personal relationship to be *unitive* in the sense that people feel such ongoing communication to be an essential part of their spirituality, and consider their striving to maintain it as the very purpose of their life. I prefer to use the term 'relational aspect' of a person's spirituality rather than unitive phase, because the activities the person engages in essentially come down to establishing, maintaining and deepening a personal relationship with God.

3 Why 'aspects' rather than 'phases'?

Many writers have pointed out that this ancient systematisation should *not* be understood as a strictly hierarchical and temporal one, as if earlier phases are once and for all left behind, and as if each stage is 'higher' than the earlier ones. To understand it as so is to contradict reality. For example, not only at the end of the spiritual journey, but also right from the beginning, there has to be some elementary 'unitive' experience, i.e. some awareness of the third and 'highest' phase of spiritual development. Otherwise people would simply not be motivated enough to keep striving for it. And the other way round, too, people who are considered to be advanced mystics report that they still struggle with egocentric tendencies. As for the 'illuminative' phase, in the first and final stages 'illuminative' spiritual intuition is also needed. This is so in order to integrate the 'gained experiences' at ever deeper levels of the personality. Therefore many spiritual directors nowadays consider purgative, illuminative, and unitive experience to be aspects rather than stages of spiritual growth – somewhat as there is now a general consensus that the phases in the grieving process that Elisabeth Kübler-Ross distinguishes in her famous book *On Death and Dying* are not so much stages that one follows – and should follow – in strict time sequence, but rather fluid steps that one can cycle through as many times as is needed as one grieves a loss.[4] Despite the reality of this there is obviously some kind of logical sequence in the process, because a person's process of awakening necessarily precedes his conscious decision about whether or not to commit himself to spiritual life and its concomitant process of spiritual change. The example of the psychology student (vignette 12) testifies somewhat to such a 'logical' sequence.

I shall use the terms of the classical schema therefore in the same loose associative way as I did in structuring the student's autobiography, i.e. describing *the spiritual change process as a dynamic interplay of aspects presupposing and influencing each other all the time.*

To sum up, my adaptation of this ancient systematisation of purification preceding illumination and followed by unification is threefold. First, I assume a *continuum* between the mystical transformation and the change process of 'ordinary' people. This implies that I use its *structure* and *characteristic experiences* also for describing 'ordinary' spiritual experience. Second, I consider the three phases of this schema to be *aspects* of individual spiritual development. Third, I have chosen modern terms for them. I prefer to use the term *'spiritual change process'* instead of 'spiritual transformation', and I shall analyse that change process by considering the *existential*, the *cognitive*, and the *relational* aspects, each roughly corresponding with the central theme people are working at in each of the three phases of the ancient schema.

These three aspects constitute the basic structure of Part 3 and Part 4. Chapters 13 and 14, entitled 'The existential aspect of spirituality' and 'Psychotherapy and the struggle for authentic spirituality', correspond roughly with the first main paragraph of the student's biography (vignette 12), describing how the process of spiritual awakening often entails a 'purgative' struggle for authenticity. Chapters 15 and 16, entitled 'The cognitive aspect of spirituality' and 'Psychotherapy and illuminative experience', correspond with the second paragraph of vignette 12 (the student reads Frankl and Heschel and in doing so gains in-depth spiritual insight), discussing the cognitive problem inherent in spiritual awakening and spiritual growth, and the nature of 'illuminative' understanding. The chapters of Part 4, 'Relational aspects of spirituality', correspond with the third paragraph of vignette 12 (the student develops an intimate relationship with God) discussing how people who strive for an intimate 'unitive' relationship with God need to learn some particular relational capacities. Depending on what *kind* of relationship they conceive the spiritual relationship to be, these relational capacities may converge, diverge or conflict with what most therapies want their clients to achieve.

4 Psychotherapy and the spiritual change process

Engaging in spiritual change is basically engaging in a healing process. If all goes well, it results in a way of life that is experienced as deeply fulfilling. Spiritual awakening and the craving for a relationship with God are in and by themselves normal phenomena, occurring largely in healthy persons. Moreover, falling prey to the inner conflicts and doubts inherent in the spiritual change process is in itself quite normal too. There is not necessarily a causal connection between struggling with these and mental illness or dysfunctioning. People may struggle spiritually or suffer for years without their other capacities being seriously harmed. And the other way round, people may be patients for years, even hospitalised, while at the same time being spiritually much more advanced than the people taking care of them. An example of this is the bulimic whose therapeutic progress was guided by visions (vignette 5). Her psychiatrist told me that he was much impressed by the sincerity and depth of her prayer life. In that respect, he felt she was undamaged despite her obvious mental illness. He spoke of his awareness of how much he had spiritually profited from his contact with her.

However, it can still be said in general that progress and stagnation in the spiritual terrain or in the psychological terrain are likely to affect each other at least indirectly. And it is the therapist's responsibility to be aware of what may go wrong in both areas and how this may affect people's mental health. From this point of view, the dangers are obvious, particularly if people set off on a solo self-prescribed journey or fall victim to inadequate or inappropriate spiritual leaders. Self-denying practices appeal to masochistic tendencies and encourage dependency; training consciousness to open up indiscriminately may lead to severe disorientation; paranormal phenomena may be seen as divine messages; regressive oceanic experience and its concomitant euphoria is easily mistaken for a genuine experience of being united or in communion with God. History is full of individuals, even whole communities falling prey to such pitfalls. Instead of healing, a blocked or distorted spiritual development aggravates pathological self-aggrandisement, self-destruction and dissociation. This is more or less analogous to Erikson's description of how serious disorders may result from the stagnation in psychosocial development that happens when people do not succeed in solving the dominant conflict of each of the 'eight ages of man'.[5] To circumvent this, nearly all spiritual traditions of the various world religions urge that people get supervision from an experienced spiritual director.

The first stirrings of spiritual awakening are the most difficult for a therapist to recognise. The psychology student of vignette 12 is now (fifteen years later at time of writing) a renowned psychotherapist. He has made his 'coming out' as a Christian and specialises in treating patients who want their religion to be an integral part of their therapy. But in the period of inner conflict he went through, it could easily have happened that he had decided to undergo psychotherapy. During such a period people are often not yet quite aware of what is happening to them and therefore cannot express themselves clearly. They may be overwhelmed by religious experiences they cannot yet integrate, they may think they are going crazy, or indeed become psychotic – for example, when they prematurely start experimenting with spiritual techniques aimed at altered states of consciousness. In short, this is a category of people who are most likely to be confused and, equally significant, themselves confuse others, their therapist included. Once people are *consciously* on their spiritual journey and know what they are doing, they are more likely to communicate this better. It is to be hoped that they will also have discovered where to turn to for reliable spiritual guidance.

5 Spirituality and customary religious behaviour

The psychology student's autobiography (vignette 12) also indicates how experiencing a personal calling may sit uneasily with churchgoing or other customary religious behaviour. Like many other people, this student had before or during his studies rejected religion and church. He later on rejoined his church, but many others stay outside. This is also a well-known phenomenon in mysticism, and one that again points to the earlier mentioned continuum between mysticism and 'ordinary' spirituality. Wakefield writes, for example, 'The relation of spiritual pioneers…to the institutional church is ambivalent. There is a sense that the institution quenches the spirit; there is an element of protest in all religious insight and a desire to break free of the tyranny of ecclesiastical systems…'[6] This is something to keep in mind when reading research on psychology of religion. In some of these studies, in particular the earlier ones, religiousness is defined in terms of overt behaviour such as church membership and traditionally expressed beliefs. As a result the population whose characteristics they investigate are usually participators in church activities. And these people are investigated about the behaviour and opinions that are supposed to be religious by the researchers' definition. However, the spiritual experience described above does not necessarily coincide with church membership, nor with conventional religious behaviour. According to these criteria, Dag Hammarskjøld and Simone Weil would qualify as 'non-religious' – whereas they are two of the most influential spiritual writers of our time.

Church life and theology nevertheless *do* have a relevant function for spiritual life. As Wakefield observes: 'The institution may confine if not crush, but without it there might be no spiritual life at all, and it is necessary to those forces which may overthrow it.' Note that the student from vignette 12 forgot to report that he was thoroughly educated in the Dutch Reformed religion. Having rejected that in adolescence, it seemed to him that psychology had 'all the answers'. But he did not realise that long before he had already been taught to *ask* 'all the questions'. Nothing is more conducive to 'illuminative' experi- ence than asking the right questions. That is what led him to interpret his un-easiness as a call from God. And when he found Frankl and Heschel illuminative, he did not realise that he was able to intuit their meaning because his religious education had already prepared him for grasping it.

CHAPTER 13

The Existential Aspect of Spirituality

1 Psychotherapy and the existential dimension

In the existential approach each person is viewed as a unique individual facing the responsibility for, and the finiteness of, his own life in the concrete historical situation of this world. This is different from the usual approach of psychology as an empirical science concerning itself with data and theories that can be generalised.

Mainstream British and American psychotherapy has discovered the importance of the existential approach somewhat accidentally. Victor Frankl hit upon it when observing inmates of Nazi concentration camps. It struck him that people who entertained a firm conviction of purpose and meaning in life were more likely to survive than those who did not. Had he not been a prisoner himself in such extreme circumstances (where life and death were genuinely and continuously at stake), he might in his ordinary psychiatric practice never have met this issue in its extreme consequences and therefore never have realised its importance. He developed an existential psychotherapy called 'logotherapy'. His ideas and those of others working along these lines met with little response, being too far removed from mainstream therapeutic thinking at that time.[1]

This situation changed when Yalom in his famous research on group psychotherapy made the same kind of discovery. He writes that in designing the interview questionnaire asking ex-patients what had been the major curative factors in their therapy, the category 'existential factors' was added by the researchers involved at the very last moment, 'almost as afterthought'. Factors like ultimate responsibility for one's life, recognition of our mortality and the ensuing consequences for the conduct of our life, the thrownness or capriciousness of existence, did not fit easily into the, at that time, dominant theories about what could possibly be curative. Therefore it had hardly occurred to the researchers to ask their patients about such matters (see also Chapter 11, section 2). Quite unexpectedly, the research outcome showed precisely these factors to be among the most curative ones accounting for positive results in psychotherapy.[2] So it turned out that this experienced research team nearly overlooked what was apparently vital to their own patients, and had been happening all the time under their own therapeutic noses! This realisation changed Yalom's view dramatically and inspired him to write his *Existential Psychotherapy*.[3]

Existential factors, Yalom recognised, figure in therapy much more than therapeutic theory would suggest:

Existential factors play an important but generally unrecognised role in psychotherapy. It is only when therapists look deeply at their techniques and at their basic view of man that they discover, usually to their surprise, that they are existentially oriented. Most dynamically oriented therapists who use analytically oriented technique inwardly eschew or at best inattend to much of the fundamental, mechanistic analytic theory.[4]

2 Existential consciousness

Let me now introduce another vignette, as a model of the characteristic structure of existential experience.

Vignette 13

A successful scientist says: 'I have given birth to a mentally retarded and physically handicapped baby. The paediatrician, my family doctor and my husband all insist on having me put the child into an institution. They reason that it will be cared for in a professional way I cannot compete with if I were to care for the child personally. They also point out that I would jeopardise my marriage and my development as a person and as a scientist if I undertake the all-consuming task of taking care of my child, which among other things would demand many hours daily of patiently exercising its muscles and its limited mental capacities. Certainly society in general would profit far more from my continuing to contribute to my academic discipline.

Nevertheless I have a strong feeling that I have to look after my child personally. The paediatrician attributes this to false and unnecessary guilt feelings for having 'failed' to produce a healthy child and warns me of the danger of becoming trapped in a vicious circle of ego-centred self-denial. I have considered this advice seriously but I still feel a strong inner conviction that my life lies with this child even though this means giving up my career and putting my marriage at risk'.

This mother is caught in a difficult dilemma. Should she decide for common sense and competent advice, or should she acknowledge her 'strong feeling' as sufficient reason for sacrificing her career and family life? What is the nature of this strong feeling? Is it indeed the false guilt mothers so easily become prey to? Or could it be something else? The dilemma faced by this mother is not unique. Many people have known comparable dilemmas. A couple that 'just know' that in their heart of hearts they are life and soul partner to each other, still have to decide whether this is really the ultimate truth about their relationship and if so, whether they should act upon it against severe odds. A youngster who wants to be an artist, but who, everybody says, will most probably become a mediocre and poor one, has to find out how much of his desire is fed by true artistic vocation.

What to do when you are totally and personally involved in such a situation, when some decision has to be taken, and has to be taken by *you*? You are free to choose what is best in your own interests or to follow some expert's advice. Or to toss for it. Indeed you can do these things, but you may be one of those people for whom this just doesn't work. You may feel strongly inclined to choose what is not in your best interests or not wise in some expert's view. This inclination refuses to go away and invites you to self-examination. Are you inflating your maternal instinct, your sexual desire, your artistic ambition? Are you self-denying? Spiteful? Stubborn? A self-appointed hero? Or is there something else, something you just find yourself to be utterly committed to, apparently for no other reason than this is what you are, what you have to be, what you want to be, what you ultimately stand for? At this point your self-examination has brought you to *existential consciousness*, that is to say, to self-awareness at the existential level. To some people some issues have this existential quality, some of them discover this when challenged by a dramatic situation, some of them 'just know', some of them discover it happily or unhappily only in the hour of their death.

An existential dilemma always involves being true to one's ultimate identity when being confronted with decisions regarding one's own life in this world. Sometimes circumstances force people to think about the meaning and direction of their own life as a whole, for example in major life decisions, in ethical dilemmas, or while facing death. Characteristically, they may then become aware of an inner core of their personality that they just find themselves to be. The decisive factor then is: 'this is a matter of who I truly am'. For want of a better term I shall call this inner core '*True Self*', a term coined by Kierkegaard and taken up by Jung and others. Rollo May calls it the 'I-am' experience. The term '*existential consciousness*' will be used to indicate that people are aware of such an inner core. The term '*existential awakening*' will be used for the process of self-discovery that leads to existential consciousness. This terminology, like others of its kind, needs two caveats in order to prevent misunderstanding. First, people can be aware of their True Self without having the concepts of True Self or of existential consciousness. The scientist-mother talks about her having 'a strong feeling'. Other people may express themselves in terms such as 'I just know I have to do this' or 'I don't know why, but I simply have to do this'. Second, the use of 'True Self' should emphatically not be understood in any reified and proprietary sense. 'Selves', be they true or not, are not entities, and neither are they possessions of the 'I's' that 'have' them.[5]

Existentialist philosophers hold that *everyone* has such an inner existential core and is morally obliged to act in accordance with it, otherwise one is acting in 'bad faith'. Psychoanalyst Winnicott holds that True Self is built upon 'the inherited potential which is experiencing a continuity of being, and acquiring in its own way and its own speed a personal psychic reality and a personal body-scheme.' Whether or not this potential will be realised and how well True Self will develop, he suggests, depends on the 'good-enough' mother's 'management' of the baby's interaction in its stage of first object relationships.[6] However that may be, here in this book the more modest claim suffices that we observe that at least a number of people can be seen to be like this, having an inner existential core, and that to such people it is vital to act upon it.

3 Spiritual True Self

Vignette 12, the autobiography of a psychology student, shows a striking similarity to vignette 13, the woman with the handicapped baby. Here again something keeps resurfacing despite rational rejection and despite rigorous unmasking of self-deceptive, indoctrinated or superego motivations. Something in the depth of the personality keeps calling for acknowledgement and commitment. This is what I call '*the existential aspect of spirituality*'. Spiritual awakening and spiritual consciousness, at the level of Self, involve an 'I-am' experience largely analogous to the True Self experience. There are differences as well. Spiritual consciousness is more complex than the existential because God is involved as well. It indicates a True Self-awareness of a deep longing for God (or however one conceives the transcendent Being) and also an awareness of the existence of a divine reality. It is a broader concept than existential consciousness, because it is not restricted to self-knowledge: it is the awareness, too, of an 'object': God. That is the cognitive aspect, which will be discussed in Chapters 15 and 16.

4 Characteristics of the existential aspect

Because of these many similarities between existential and spiritual 'True Self' experiences, they share a number of characteristics which can be therapeutically relevant. I shall now briefly discuss what I consider to be the most important ones.

One characteristic of a dilemma at the existential level of the personality is, that *the person's decision is only 'right' for this one individual*. Its rightness is neither a matter of applying universal ethical norms to the situation, nor can it be generalised into a norm. It is essentially not a matter of morality, although moral issues may be involved. In vignettes 12 and 13, the dilemma of the psychology student is morally indifferent, whereas the dilemma that the mother of the handicapped baby faces is morally ambiguous. Her choice is not between good and bad. Caring for her child is right. Entrusting it to other loving and probably more capable hands is right too. For this particular mother it may indeed be an existential issue that she has to care for her handicapped child, but for the next mother it might be an existential matter to choose otherwise. For still another mother it might not be an existential issue at all, just a matter of weighing the pros and cons against each other. Therefore no one of these three mothers is 'better' than the others, because the existential is utterly personal, a matter of being *this* particular person and of taking responsibility for *that* fact. People often feel very vulnerable when taking this kind of decision because they can offer no other reason than 'this is what I am'.

As another characteristic of the existential aspect, people themselves normally have *difficult access* to True Self. They usually need an extended period of sorting themselves out. This can be seen, for example, in the content of vignettes 12 and 13. Frankl and Yalom discovered that the role of existential factors is not easy for therapists to observe, but the same is true of self-observation. Most of the time we are immersed in daily activities and problems of a more down-to-earth nature. There is then no need to be aware of True Self. Quite often it takes a critical situation for us to realise that our existence as an authentic human being is at stake. A dramatic situation trivialises our daily preoccupations and forces us to concentrate on the fundamental issues right now, before it is too late. This is why in existential psychotherapy and in spiritual direction people are sometimes invited to a guided fantasy of a dramatic crisis situation in which they face their own death. This may help them to identify what is truly vital to their being this particular person. Some kind of 'death' is often indeed involved, as the mother in vignette 13 faced her 'death' as a scientist, as an influential member of society and as a married woman. Heidegger points out this connection between death and True Self, saying, 'Dying is something that every Dasein itself must take upon itself at the time. By its very essence, death is in every case mine, in so far as it 'is' at all… In dying, it is shown that mineness and existence are ontologically constitutive for death.'[7] The same is true for everybody's conscience.

This is also why the great literature and drama of the world may play an important role in existential and spiritual awakening. Daily affairs are artificially minimised there, and the existential aspect intensified. The fundamental issues are convincingly brought to the fore and force the public to become aware of this dimension of human life. In *The Death of Ivan Ilyitch* Tolstoy forces us to identify with someone who only on his deathbed realises that he has never truly lived. Sophocles' *Antigone* shows how being faithful to your True Self may come down to choosing death.

Yet another characteristic of the existential aspect is that *there is a lot at stake*. It is indeed a matter of life and death, even though physical death is not necessarily involved. You cannot deny True Self without damaging your sense of being truly alive. What is happening is not immediately apparent. It makes itself known in a later phase, as a pervasive and elusive quality of emptiness and lack of direction. Some existentialist writers would say such people are suffering from 'existential guilt'. But this terminology is confusing, because what they mean is different from what we normally mean by 'guilt' or 'guilt feelings'. Real guilt, resulting from something you have done wrong, is a hard thing to face and to live with, and one may want to do all kinds of things in order to do penitence and to make a new start. But in a situation of real guilt it is very much *you*, you as a responsible person, who is at the heart of your feeling guilty and your suffering because of it. Indeed you are very far from being an empty shell or directionless ship. In contrast, ignoring True Self does not necessarily involve 'guilt' in the sense of doing something bad or irresponsible. In many cases it means just going on with an ordinary life. The world may not become a different place because of ignoring or betraying this 'True Self'. In most cases it cannot be said that people are guilty in the normal sense of the word. Nevertheless in another sense they *are* guilty: guilty of betraying their True Self – be it spiritual or not – and with it the meaning and direction of their life. Then they may suffer in a peculiar and obscure way. And quite often they feel guilty in a vague form, not being able to pinpoint just what they feel guilty about. In a religious context this may cause an equally vague and pervasive feeling of being an unredeemable sinner. This is the heavy price for betraying your ultimate identity.

5 How the existential interacts with psychotherapy

True Self concerns – be they spiritual or not – interact with psychotherapy in various ways, each way requiring its own approach. There are essentially four different ways in which True Self concerns may influence psychotherapy:

A problem presented in psychotherapy may in fact *be* a True Self dilemma. This happens often when the problem arises in the context of major life decisions, or matters of conscience, or facing death either literally or figuratively. Though it may then *look* like a psychological problem, it is vital to recognise it as a True Self dilemma and to stimulate the process of existential or spiritual awakening rather than treating it as a psychological problem.

In other cases, psychological problems are *intertwined with* True Self concerns. This would be the case, for example, if the mother-scientist from vignette 13 were both existentially motivated and ridden by false guilt feelings, or if the student from vignette 12 were involved both in spiritual self-discovery and in neurotic indecisiveness. Then therapist and patient have to disentangle the two. Both should be worked through, but in different ways.

Sometimes psychological problems are *caused by betraying or fearing* True Self. Quite often people are not aware of this underlying cause, as in the examples of Winnicott where True Self never had a chance because people had to comply with oppressive outside demands from early infancy on. A long and painful process may be needed, sometimes involving deep regression, to face and overcome 'existential guilt' or 'existential fear' and establish identity.

Still another possibility is that psychotherapy may act as a *catalytic agent* for the process of existential or spiritual awakening. To the extent that patients get more in touch with their feelings and emotions, they are more likely to get in touch with True Self as well, whether they realise it or not. This is probably what Yalom meant when he wrote that existential factors play an important but generally unrecognised role in the practice of analytic psychotherapy. In my opinion this sometimes also happens to a whole group as they move to ever deeper involvement. A pointer to this is probably Murray Cox's 'third level disclosure', which refers to what happens when suddenly group communication moves to a depth where therapeutic intervention and interpretation are inappropriate.[8] The priest's communication of vignette 1 and the group's response to it might have been such a third level disclosure, for example. A group's ability to be quiet and silent – just to 'be there together' may also be a pointer to its moving into a more profound level. It is important then to allow such moments to 'be', to stand in their own right, not to disturb them while they last nor to interpret them afterwards.

6 Discernment at the existential level

Whenever True Self issues in a person interact with psychological ones, this can present any therapist involved with an extra complexity. People may need help to sort out the existential and spiritual from the psychological. This is the 'purification' activity the psychology student and the mother from vignettes 12 and 13 were intensely occupied with for quite a long time. Such sorting out has to precede psychotherapy. If the signals of an emerging existential or spiritual awakening occur *during* psychotherapy, such sorting out has to have priority over the continuation of the therapy. Van Deurzen-Smith gives many examples of this, showing how after existential clarification, psychotherapy is sometimes no longer even necessary.[9] Indeed, it may be positively harmful in such a context to use a therapeutic method prematurely. Winnicott makes the same point when discussing how to retrieve a True Self so deeply hidden as to be virtually inaccessible. He insists that at the intake it may be more important to 'diagnose' False Personality (which is his term for the defence mechanisms used to protect and hide a dissociated True Self) than to diagnose the patient according to accepted psychiatric classifications. He, too, emphasises that this should precede analytic treatment because of the danger involved in treating the false self as real, or in 'stealing' the emergence of True Self by a premature therapeutic intervention.[10]

Not only does this sorting out of the existential take precedence over therapy, but also it is *different* from standard procedures used in therapy. Although Winnicott uses the verb 'diagnose' for discovering a hidden True Self, it is clear from his extended case reports that he refers to something different from usual diagnosing. He obviously describes something rather similar to what in spiritual direction is meant by '*discernment*': the sensitive discrimination between psychological and spiritual phenomena which at first sight look similar, but in fact are different strands in the personality and need different approaches. It is explained and illustrated in the comments on vignettes 5 (the bulimic who saw visions and heard voices) and 7 (the autobiography of Tolstoy) and in the concluding section of Part 1.

Why this difference between discernment and diagnosis? It is because the existential, whether in the context of spirituality or not, pertains exclusively to the meaningfulness of *this one individual and unique person's life* as a whole. That is why its phenomena elude any diagnostic systematisation. That is why we need a different kind of sensitivity for recognising existential and spiritual issues than for psychological ones. Existential or spiritual consciousness is not realised in the transference relationship, but in the realm of self-awareness. It is not a superego phenomenon, so it cannot be reduced to introjection of social and ethical norms. As Rollo May puts it,

> To the extent that my sense of existence is authentic, it is precisely *not* what others have told me I should be, but is the one Archimedes point I have to stand on from which to judge what parents and other authorities demand...
> It cannot be said too strongly that the sense of one's own existence, though interwoven with all kinds of social relatedness, is in basis not the product of social forces; it always presupposes 'Eigenwelt', the 'own world'.[11]

Existential or spiritual awakening is not a phase of ego-development either, although it may be a precondition for ego development. Both in modern ego theories and in classic psychoanalytic tradition ego is a part of the personality, whereas the existential and the spiritual both refer to the whole of one's being, unconscious as well as conscious. Neither should it be confused with self-actualisation, or with the realisation of one's highest ideal, in the sense that these terms are used in psychology. Sometimes actions stemming from existential or spiritual consciousness may coincide with self-actualisation, but sometimes they do not coincide and may even involve the sacrificing of self-actualisation or ideals.

To illustrate the difference, Wolters's differentiation between *structure* and *direction* can be helpful. Psychological factors would then apply to the structure of the personality, whereas existential and spiritual factors apply to the direction of the life of this particular person with this particular personality structure.[12] The direction an individual life takes then acts as the *context* in which his psychological make-up operates. Would this context be changed, then the basic psychology does not necessarily change, but other aspects of it may be highlighted or shifted to the background. To quote Rollo May:

> It does not deny the validity of dynamisms and the study of specific behaviour patterns in their rightful places. But it holds that drives or

dynamisms, by whatever name one calls them, can be understood only in the context of the structure of the existence of the person we are dealing with.[13]

If the mother of a handicapped baby in vignette 13 decides to act according to her True Self, this does not mean she will perform her task well or that she is *ipso facto* cured from psychological problems. She may be existentially involved *and* troubled by neurotic guilt feelings *and* not really talented for the job. As Rollo May points out, existential consciousness is not by and in itself the solution to a person's problems, though it may be a necessary precondition for finding a solution. Nor is it to be identified with the discovery of one's specific powers, drives, dynamisms, etc.

No doubt one needs the usual diagnostic tools. But simultaneously there is something that eludes these, something of a different order that needs to be listened to carefully and sensitively.

CHAPTER 14

Psychotherapy and the Struggle for Authentic Spirituality

1 Deciding about spiritual True Self

'But at some moment I did answer *Yes* to Someone – or Something – and from that hour I was certain that existence is meaningful and that, therefore, my life, in self-surrender, had a goal', wrote Dag Hammarskjøld in his diary on Whit-sunday, 1961.[1] He was the General Secretary of the United Nations, who to all the world had always appeared to be an agnostic humanist. So it came as a great surprise to find after his death a diary which he called 'a sort of a White Book concerning my negotiations with myself – and with God', testifying of a long spiritual journey. As a contrast to the psychology student in vignette 12, he never rejoined the church he had left in his youth, nor do his notes show any sign of wishing for it. As he would not take over patterns of belief from others, he had to make his own 'effort frankly and squarely to build up a personal belief in the light of experience'. His diary is still a spiritual bestseller.

True Self-discovery demands an answer. At some time one has to decide whether or not to live up to it. Like all other decisions, this means accepting responsibility for the ensuing actions and their consequences. This is what in ordinary social life constitutes *personhood.* But there is more to it. In a True Self decision you accept responsibility not only for your actions, but also for what you 'found' yourself to be in your heart of hearts. It also covers motivations, attitudes, emotions, drives, etc., even though you never intentionally produced them, even though you may never act upon them. We could say this constitutes inner personhood, a conscience towards yourself. When True Self is spiritual and therefore relational to God, *the decision constitutes spiritual personhood before God.* So the very first step on a spiritual journey is to take such a decision.

Sometimes religious people object that it is not necessary to make such a decision, as it is already decided by God himself. He should therefore just be obeyed promptly and unconditionally. This objection is not justified. The God of the biblical religions asks for obedience not slavery, for trust not blind docility. Even where in traditional mystical literature there is a lot of talk about 'dying to the self', these authors never mean giving up personhood. In the course of spiritual life one will repeatedly be called to make a free and responsible decision. This is the first one. Although it is outside the therapist's province to discuss theology, it is nevertheless worthwhile to prick up his ears at such signals. They are probably an indication of a basic attitude of pervasive passivity towards life itself.

Many people make this decision without a hitch. But because we are focusing on how it may interfere with therapy, I will now pay attention to those people who at this stage get stuck in a vicious and prolonged indecision. These people could easily be undergoing therapy. And their spiritual indecision would certainly influence their psychological problems. To what extent could psychotherapy be helpful to them?

Spiritual indecisiveness has a different structure from a neurotic avoidance of all personal decision-making. Both forms of indecision may cause unhappiness and stagnation, and therapy may be helpful for both, but the former needs a different approach from that needed by the latter. Therefore the very first thing is to look whether this is a matter of neurotic indecisiveness. People who *always* avoid taking responsibility for themselves will do likewise in spiritual matters. If spiritual indecisiveness is just one more symptom of neurotic avoidance, then obviously a therapeutic approach is indicated.

However, many people who ordinarily are not given to neurotic indecision yet cannot bring themselves either to a clear 'Yes to Someone – or Something', or to a clear 'No'. They are simultaneously attracted and deterred by this 'Someone – or Something'. In spiritual matters, this seems to be a rather common response. Otherwise Otto would not have characterised the Holy as 'mysterium fascinans et tremendum', a fascinating and terrifying mystery.[2] And it is striking in how many biblical stories the characters' first response to a divine call is to excuse themselves from responding affirmatively, saying they are not able, or not clean, or too young, and so on.[3]

2 Spiritual self-doubt and ambivalence

In spiritual discernment it is a general rule of thumb to look at what is happening at two interconnected levels: on the one hand, the level of *(un)willingness* and on the other, the level of *insight and doubt*. Applying this principle to such prolonged indecisiveness about the spiritual True Self would mean to distinguish between spiritual self-doubt and ambivalence.

Spiritual self-doubt is a matter of *cognition* because it is concerned with the truth. Is it true that this desire for God is my fundamental, authentic identity? The critical self-examination reported by the scientist-mother, the psychology student, Dag Hammarskjøld and many others, is a cognitive activity. It is healthy and functional – up to a point. Beyond that point, one lands up in vicious indecisiveness. Nobody will ever attain full detailed self-knowledge, nobody can hope to construct a watertight screen between the authentic and the inauthentic parts of himself. At some point in the process one has to act upon 'good-enough' self-knowledge – or one will never act at all.

Spiritual ambivalence is at the level of *(un)willingness*: one is simultaneously willing and resisting. Resistance against true spiritual commitment goes much deeper than the psychological defence mechanisms and is more pervasive. Of course these phenomena abound on the spiritual stage as everywhere else, but in spirituality there is characteristically an underlying unwillingness which is so pervasive and universal that it seems to be part of the human condition. On the other hand, the urge to say 'yes' is also intense and persistent. As a result there is a very painful inner conflict, possibly causing guilt feelings towards God as well.

These two existential issues, spiritual ambivalence and spiritual self-doubt, are usually intertwined. And here is indeed the raw material for an endless merry-go-round: resistance posing as doubt, doubt hiding behind resistance. And guilt feelings thrown in as an extra. Small wonder indecision never ends!

Could psychotherapy be helpful to such people? Indeed it can, provided it is not downright prejudiced against anything smelling of religion. It can help to disentangle the vicious intertwining. Spiritual self-doubt is a cognitive problem, ambivalence is a problem of (un)willingness. Both have to be resolved to such an extent that a decision can be taken. But resolving the one is different from resolving the other. If people are caught up in a too prolonged doubting of their authenticity, a group could be helpful by 'mirroring'. (Foulkes coined this term to describe the way in which the patient can recognise aspects of his own self in others, the others acting as mirrors. An equally important aspect of mirroring is that the person has to recognise how others see him and to work with their perceptions of him. As in the course of time the group's capacities to understand and respond with empathy and insight increase, much of the mirroring can be performed by the members themselves.) Most groups develop a fine-tuned antenna for signals of authenticity. As for ambivalence, a group could help the person see through his games of resistance. After all, dealing with all kinds of resistance is part and parcel of the therapeutic enterprise. And it could give him support as in any other situation where a member draws from group support just that little bit of extra courage he needs to make a major decision – in this case the decision to 'become who you are, now that you know it'.[4]

Even more helpful perhaps is the support a group may give to those for whom the experience appears to be indeed some form of self-deception. It may be very significant if self-deception takes this particular form. This is analogous to the situation in which a patient, at a certain point in his therapy, suddenly falls in love, a love which feels totally different from all earlier loves and indeed often threatens his marriage because 'now this at last is my True Love. This is my destiny.' This, too, may very well be a form of self-deception, but nevertheless there may be an important truth in it, namely that the person is indeed growing into a new and deeper ability to love. If so, it is important to acknowledge it as such. It will encourage the person to grow further towards mature love, initially leaving open what kind of life may result from it. Likewise a self-deceptive call to spiritual life may also signal a similar growth: growth towards a new and more personal level of relating with the Transcendent. Again it is important for the person and therapist involved to acknowledge this and to keep an open mind regarding it, i.e. to allow the emerging spirituality to take its own shape and course.

3 The existential aspect of spiritual change

Turning now to the intentional spiritual change people engage in after their initial decision, it should be noted that the earlier sections already described a first order change. Becoming aware of a fundamental inner conflict, sorting out underlying motives, and deciding whether or not to live authentically whatever the cost, cannot fail to change one's life, meaning of life and behaviour significantly.

'Many times I had to expose a so-called "voice of my conscience" as dependence. Many times I found I should say no to it. *This is a process that is still going on'*, reported the psychology student (vignette 12) fifteen years after the event. The initial self-examination led him to discovery of his True Self as being spiritual. When people decide to commit themselves to their authentic identity, this does not mean these deceptive voices will automatically stop. On the contrary, they may now start adding the most interesting and beautiful pious inclinations to their repertoire! The saying 'no' to everything not authentic must go on if one is to be serious about committing oneself to spiritual life. In the discussion about existential consciousness in Chapter 13, section 2, it was noted that True Self is neither a static 'entity', nor is it something you 'possess' as such once and for all. This is also true of the spiritual True Self. It has to be found or retrieved repeatedly. There are many examples of people who during their lifetime received a different calling from the one they had first become aware of and implemented earlier in life. But this emphatically does not mean that their earlier calling was not authentic. Nor is resistance to True Self solved once and for all either. For most people ambivalence is a fellow traveller till nearly the end of their journey. In between periods of inner peace and being in touch, there are intermittent periods of oscillating between a wholehearted 'yes' and a fierce or fearful 'no'. This is precisely why it is so important to make a clear and conscious commitment at the start.

Once people have started on their spiritual journey, the existential aspect of their change process largely covers what in traditional literature is called *'purification'* (or *'purgation'*) of the self. Apart from critical self-examination it includes ascetic practices, for which the old spiritual language uses terms like 'mortifying the fallen human nature', or 'self-denial' or 'dying to the self'. For psychologically trained ears such terms can sound suspicious, but careful reading shows that this critical reflection and ascetic practice encourage detachment and dis-identification from egocentricity and from what Winnicott would call 'False Personalities'. Later on in the spiritual journey, people may also try to dis-identify from the 'normal healthy ego', as they gradually come to see through it as a hypothetical construct (which of course does not necessarily imply that they are familiar with the term as such) – or, as Buddhists would say, 'an illusion'. This is where indeed the implicit values of psychotherapy tend to diverge from spiritual ones and quite rightfully so. Many people in need of psychotherapy need to build up ego boundaries and ego strength. If so, they are *ipso facto* not yet ready for renouncing the normal healthy ego. Indeed most writings on spiritual direction draw attention to the risks that people with too weak ego-boundaries and ego-strength expose themselves to if they engage in spiritual exercises that are designed for such dis-identification from the ego.[5]

The reason for this tendency to purify and to dis-identify is probably the fact that the very same experience that makes you aware of the inner core which I have called 'spiritual True Self', often makes you equally aware of how deeply you are estranged from it. Therefore a painful experience of an inner split flows from the initial experience. This conflict between your 'spiritual' and your 'fallen' self is known in all major spiritual traditions, mostly under metaphorical names, such as in Christian tradition the rift between the 'child of God' and the 'fallen man', between the 'Christ-in-me' and 'my old Adam', between the 'spiritual man' and the 'worldly man' – not referring to different individuals but to different attitudes within one and the same person. It is analogous to what happens in therapy when a patient painfully discovers to what extent he is suffering behind self-created walls or barriers.

This painful experience motivates the person to try to get rid of everything that keeps him alienated from himself, from God and from others – to 'purify' or 'simplify' himself. Opinions on how best to do this differ between various spiritual main and sub-traditions. Some prefer the hard way of rejecting and suppressing every inclination that would distract from a totally God-oriented life. Others prefer the method of learning to see through the 'false self' (and finally also the 'self') as an illusion built from numerous self-deceptions and constantly defended by ever more intricate deceptions. This insight is in and by itself a way to dis-identify with the false self. Still others prefer the gentler way of patiently exploring ever subtler forms of egotism and self-deceit, and then exposing these to divine forgiveness and love till they are 'sanctified' or 'reconciled': in other words, until the vital energy behind them has become a natural and spontaneous part of a God-oriented life.

Purifying ascetic practices, it must not be forgotten, can be dangerous when performed without spiritual guidance. All too easily self-destructive forces may get the upper hand. Let us look at what happened to a 'spiritual exile' who experimented with purgative practice.

4 'Transcendental' anorexia nervosa

Vignette 14

Marjan is the daughter of rich parents. Intelligent and inquisitive, she was interested from her early teens in such subjects as art, religion, and philosophy. At school she was conscientious and successful, performing as well in mathematics and the natural sciences as in languages and the humanities.

When Marjan was 14 she chose a life of strict asceticism. 'I wanted to become a kind of Tibetan monk by renouncing all desires. I wanted to detach and transcend all earthly things. I wanted a life of purity, of beauty, and of wisdom.' Radical changes ensued: she withdrew from other people and her eating habits changed. At first, she refused to eat all those foods that she considered to be a 'superfluous luxury'. Soon she stopped eating anything she liked. Then, after a few months, she decided to fast rigor-

ously, restricting herself only to what she considered necessary to stay alive. During this period, she began to think and feel differently: 'It was as if I had become non-material. Everything became so intense, so clear. I felt high, sometimes ecstatic, as if all my limitations had disappeared, as if I were able to do anything. I felt no pain, no grief, no tiredness.'

Gradually, however, her euphoria turned to fear: 'I was afraid that my new life would be "stolen" from me. And I experienced this feeling in a very strange way. It felt as if a power outside myself was forcing me to maintain my pure life.' This period was characterised by conflict on all sides. She argued with her parents over her eating habits; she wrestled with her own sexual desires and her longing for affection and sympathy; and she had to fight off hunger nearly all the time.

Marjan continued to perform well in her studies. After leaving high school, she went on to university and studied philosophy. Her isolation deepened.[6] After a while, she became seriously depressed and attempted suicide. It was at this point, when she was 22, that she decided to seek psychiatric help.

Marjan's case history has been written up by Van Outsem, a Dutch specialist in anorexia and bulimia nervosa.[7] He observes that, in the treatment of anorexia, it is of crucial importance to understand *why* a patient has chosen an extreme diet. This is so very important because the strong resistance of the patient against changing eating behaviour often frustrates treatment. Strangely enough, the vast literature has little to offer in this respect: anorexia is mainly approached in terms of the external symptoms or of the existing psychological, sociological and somatic theories, which, when taken together, are often contradictory.[8] It was for this reason that Van Outsem undertook research into the motivation of anorexia patients, both male and female. As a result of this research he discovered four different categories of motivation which he calls the 'obsessive slimmers', the 'de-sexualisers', the 'manipulators' and the 'transcendentals'. For each of these Van Outsem recommends a different kind of therapy.

The most interesting category for us is that of 'transcendental anorexia'. A deep-seated longing for a 'pure' life motivates patients who suffer from this type of anorexia. Their eating habits seem to be part of a disciplining of the whole person to some high and meaningful ideal. Marjan falls into this category. Van Outsem emphasises that the therapist should be fully aware that the 'transcendental anorexics' have much to lose in their therapy! In abandoning their anorexic lifestyle they would also be 'sacrificing an important aspect of their identity, a precious life goal, an effective means of high performance and a source of self-control and self-esteem.' For this reason, Van Outsem advises against behaviour therapy, suggesting instead a cognitive and a non-directive strategy, aimed at restructuring their ideas about 'performance', 'perfection', 'good and bad', etc. He feels it is particularly important that such patients are encouraged not to think in strict dichotomies.

5 Anorexia as failed spiritual change

What would a spiritual director observe in Van Outsem's report on Marjan? He would immediately prick up his ears when hearing her use terms like, 'become a kind of (Tibetan) monk', 'purity', 'renouncing all desires', 'detach and transcend all earthly things'. These terms all belong to the traditional language of purgative asceticism. So Marjan's urge for purification seems a fairly common response to an experience of spiritual awakening. Likewise is her fasting a common practice. There are indications that the quantity and the kind of food intake do indeed influence spiritual openness and clarity of mind.[9] It is also a very real way of learning to empathise with the poor, to give away something that really matters to you, to realise how illusory your autonomy is, how dependent you are for your subsistence, and as a result: how delicious is the taste of the simple food you are allowed! Most importantly, it shows you how very clever and inventive you are in constantly presenting yourself with the most ingenious arguments for breaking your fast NOW.

In fact it does not matter whether you give in or not. From a spiritual point of view fasting is seldom an integral part of the spiritual life. It is an integral part of the learning process, or rather the liberating process. The important thing is through fasting to gain insight into how intent and clever you are with dressing up plain unwillingness as 'oh so reasonable'. Such insight is in and by itself already an entrée into lessening the resistance. In that sense fasting is analogous to group analysts setting firm boundaries between the 'artificial' group system and all other 'natural' systems patients are part of. The alternative system of the therapy group (with its different rules and roles, in which the patient is a shifting nodal point) serves as a kind of wall. Every time a group member bounces against that wall, there is an opportunity to see the stratagems at work with which he tries to survive in his 'natural' surroundings, strategies so habitual that they were never noticed before.

Such are the reasons why all over the world and all through history fasting has been practised as part of the spiritual learning process. The advice given about how to practise it is also rather similar: to do it for a certain period, to abstain from luxury and some specified nutrients but to do so in moderation so as not to harm your health, to give generously to the poor, not to fast in a rigid or legalistic way nor as a performance, and especially: let it first of all be a period of prayer and honest self-confrontation. Certainly some of the famous saints have gone to extremes in fasting and other ascetic practices, but in and by itself this is generally not considered to be a hallmark of their saintliness but rather something suspect which had to be supervised critically – and certainly not something to be imitated by others. Moreover, such extreme asceticism was usually a temporary practice, a period these people felt they needed for further growth in selfless love.

Marjan seems to have intuited that fasting is somehow important for spiritual life – without having any real understanding of this ideal of becoming 'a spiritual being', and equally without much insight into how fasting can be helpful or not helpful for realising her ideal. Her example shows how confusing this situation is, both for herself and for a therapist. Unfortunately hers is not an isolated case. Other people may feel drawn to trying other universal ascetic practices such as, for example, sexual abstinence or silence or solitude. Or they may be even less aware of the spiritual nature of their desire. Marjan at least had some vague notions about wanting to be like a Tibetan monk. But other people, realising even less what they want and why they want it, misunderstand their inclinations, thinking themselves onto the verge of a depression or worse. This has been discussed in the comments on vignettes 6 and 7 (the man with the near-accident and Tolstoy).

This urge to purify and the practice of asceticism obviously carries serious spiritual, psychological and physical dangers. Spiritual direction is meant to help people avoid these dangers and teach them a way to spiritual wholeness. As for cases such as Marjan's, all spiritual traditions would agree that her rushing into premature and self-prescribed asceticism is very dangerous. Although probably spiritually motivated, what she actually practises is aggressively achievement-oriented – which is something opposite to spiritual practice. Even worse is her isolation, because spirituality grows through relationships. This is so even when people seek solitude. Solitude is different from isolation. Marjan is not practising temporary detachment in order to meditate in peace on the divine mystery, and hoping for a personal renewal so that thereafter she would be able to renew her relationships into more truly loving ones. She is not *detaching* at all, she is *disconnecting*, cutting herself off from meaningful relationships.

In short, a therapist cognisant of the dynamics of spiritual change would find abundant reasons to investigate further whether Marjan should not primarily be approached as a case of 'spirituality in exile'. In Chapter 5 I discussed this modern phenomenon of 'spirituality in exile', people who are wittingly or unwittingly seeking a spiritual life, but who have no access to the guidance and models the religions have tried to give through personal spiritual direction, communal instruction and their religious role models, parables and narratives. In that chapter I also suggested that in such cases it is necessary to differentiate carefully ('discern') between psychological and spiritual phenomena. Although they may at first sight look similar, in fact they are different phenomena and need distinctly different approaches. Let us for the rest of this chapter assume that indeed Marjan is such a case of 'spirituality in exile'. Let us use her case as an example of a failed spiritual change process and try to analyse it using spiritual discernment. The question we then have to answer is, *what* has gone wrong in Marjan's process of spiritual development, despite her determination and her sacrifices? Can we find some clues in her story?

6 Willingness and wilfulness in the spiritual change process

In section 2 of this chapter (the analysis of the decision situation) I have shown that one useful approach in spiritual direction is to look at such a problem from two different viewpoints: what is happening at the level of (un)willingness? and: what is happening at the level of cognition? Let us see if this strategy can help us shed some light on Marjan's case.

Marjan made her decision to commit herself to a spiritual change process at the age of 14. She has stuck to it with admirable determination ever since. At first sight she has no problem at the level of (un)willingness. This is true as far as her initial decision goes, and her sheer determination to stick to it whatever the cost. Still, a spiritual director would say that Marjan nevertheless does have a problem that Gerald May has aptly termed the issue of 'wilfulness and willingness'.[10]

Though worded in different terminologies, the issue of 'willingness and wilfulness' is part of every spiritual education, since it is a crucial aspect of the rift between 'fallen' and 'spiritual' man. Within the awakened individual there is an inherent dilemma between the individual and autonomous quality of the willpower on the one hand, and the unifying and loving quality of the spiritual True Self on the other hand. The dilemma is about *how* we engage the deepest level of our lives in a search for spiritual wholeness. In other words, it is about the underlying attitude with which we approach the mystery of life.

In the *attitude of willingness* the person's willpower 'moves easily with the natural flow of the spirit, and at such times we feel grounded, centered, and responsive to the needs of the world as they are presented to us'.[11] Willpower is not extinguished or suppressed – indeed these people may be very resolute –, but willpower is 'surrendered' or 'reconciled' or 'sanctified', as it is put in spiritual language use. The basic attitude of the person is not of giving up willpower, but of giving up self-centredness. The essence of a spiritual True Self is its being intimately related to the transcendent foundation of life itself. That is why self-centredness has to be given up. And that is what wilfulness refuses to give up.

In the *attitude of wilfulness* the person uses his willpower to stay in control of the change process, to chart his own course to spiritual wholeness. This attitude is one aspect of what is called the 'false' or 'fallen' self. It is essentially saying 'yes' on a superficial level, but 'no' on a deeper level.

Staying in control, charting her own course, this is precisely what we see Marjan's wilfulness is doing. This seems to be the trap Marjan has been caught in unawares. As long as she does not see it for herself and also says 'yes' on the 'deeper' level of willing, psychotherapy may only enhance her basic attitude of wanting to remain a detached person and to decide autonomously how to use her energies for her spiritual advancement in terms of the spiritual goal she has set herself. She may be genuinely moved by a spiritual desire. She may have religious experiences. She may occupy herself continually with spiritual matters – but at some point, at some time, her process will stagnate. Genuine progress can occur only if her willpower is used in the process of integrating its energy into the new-found spiritual True Self, which is essentially an 'Other-directed' relationship. In Marjan's story, the relational aspect is obviously lacking.

This type of existential ambivalence, saying 'yes' at one level and 'no' at a deeper level, is a quite common phenomenon with people in a process of spiritual awakening. Nor is it occurring only at the initial stage. On the contrary, in the course of one's spiritual growth it repeats itself at ever deeper levels.

At the beginning of this section I argued that in a case such as Marjan's it may be useful to analyse the existential aspect of her spiritual efforts at the two levels of '(un)willingness' and 'cognition'. At the level of (un)willingness we have observed how at the existential level the resistance against spiritual commitment may result in various forms of *spiritual ambivalence*. Let us now look at the level of *cognition*, that is to say, at the role of existential self-knowledge and spiritual self-doubt in Marjan's case. Notice that there is no clear evidence in Van Outsem's report of a prolonged critical 'self-examination' like that of the mother of the handicapped baby who had to sort out her motivations for taking the care of her baby upon herself (vignette 13) and that of the psychology student who had to figure out the authenticity of his spiritual longing (vignette 12). Maybe Marjan was or was not involved in such a self-examination. Her spiritual awakening happened when she was only 14 years old. I shall not discuss this issue of Marjan's lack of self-examination here because the subject of the 'search for authenticity' has already been elaborated on.

There is, however, evidence of her having another cognitive problem, not of existential self-knowledge but of 'objective' knowledge. In Chapter 12 I pointed out that spiritual consciousness involves not only True Self-knowledge, but also *intuitive knowledge of the 'Someone – or Something'* Dag Hammarskjøld gave his answer to. The next chapters will discuss this cognitive aspect of spiritual life.

To summarise, some people at some time of their lives, most notably in circumstances demanding major life decisions, awake to the awareness of their ultimate identity, their *'True Self'*. With some people, this True Self appears to be a deep and persistent longing for a 'God-oriented' life. I have called this *'spiritual True Self'*. I have also introduced the terms *'spiritual awakening'* and *'spiritual consciousness'* for respectively *'becoming* aware of one's spiritual True Self', and *'being* aware of one's spiritual True Self'.

Manifestations of True Self are *not* to be identified with, or treated as, psychodynamic mechanisms, emotional conflicts, superego, transference, ego-development, self-actualisation, etc., nor as matters of morality, rationality, in-doctrination or idealism. Authentic existential and spiritual concerns *transcend* these. They are at the level of the meaning and direction of one unique individual's life in its totality. *Ignoring, misinterpreting, or rejecting True Self* concerns (spiritual or non-spiritual) may have serious consequences for a person's ability to live a meaningful life. It is usually difficult for the person to find out whether a True Self concern is at the root of his problem. It may take an extended period of *critical self-examination* to sift out the authentic from the inauthentic.

Some people have difficulty in taking a decision to commit themselves to live according to their spiritual True Self. Spiritual *indecisiveness* differs from neurotic avoidance of decision-making. It may be useful as a therapist to approach it as a combination of, on the one hand, spiritual self-doubt (doubt about the authenticity of one's spiritual identity) and on the other spiritual am-bivalence (being simultaneously fascinated and disturbed by one's experience of spiritual awakening). This process of critical self-examination and the struggle for an authentic spiritual life does not stop when the initial decision has been taken. It *continues at ever deeper levels* of the personality.

Within psychotherapy, both the existential and the spiritual may surface in various ways, each way requiring its own approach. A problem put forward in psychotherapy may in fact *be* an existential-spiritual one, psychological problems may be *intertwined* with an existential-spiritual issue, or they may be *caused* by an ignored or feared True Self. In such cases, clarity about what is happening at the existential or spiritual level has to precede psychotherapy as a necessary precondition to the solution of the problem. The existential or spiritual dimension may also *emerge* in the course of psychotherapy as a positive outcome of therapy's increasing depth. In all such cases the therapist needs a sensitive *discernment skill* to distinguish the existential and the spiritual from the psychological.

CHAPTER 15

The Cognitive Aspect of Spirituality

1 God as 'object'?

I have characterised spiritual life as a life that is centred around the longing for, and the realisation of, a personal relationship with God or however the divine reality is conceived. As in any other personal relationship, there are (at least) two partners involved. In Chapters 13 and 14 I have discussed one of these two: the human partner's self-discovery of his spiritual longing. We have seen how some people have to 'purify' their motivations and attitudes till they are sure enough of their authenticity and able to commit themselves. All of this was not too remote from therapy, where self-discovery, authenticity and self-commitment often are part and parcel of the healing process.

This chapter moves to the other 'partner'. For a relationship to exist at all, you need at the very least to know *to whom* you relate, and to be able to *recognise* manifestations of the other partner from everything else. For spiritual life to be a reality, i.e. more than something imagined or a relationship with an internal object, it needs more than authentic longing and commitment. It also needs *knowledge of an 'object', that is, of a God who can be known and communicated with as a reality.* This element of 'objective' knowledge implied in spiritual conscious-ness is what I have called the '*cognitive aspect*' of spiritual change.

As observed in the introduction to this book, it is relevant for therapists to pay attention to this difference between, on the one hand, 'God as object' and on the other hand 'God as subjective experience or as a mental representation'. It is relevant because for *therapeutic* purposes there are two serious drawbacks to the usual therapeutic practice of dealing with religious material as if there is actually nothing more than internal feelings and representations, and of disre-garding the possibility of a *real* relationship between human beings and a divine 'object' existing and acting independently of human empirical observa-tion.

The first drawback of the above practice and its inherent attitude is, that it conflicts radically with the worldview of most religions and therefore of religious patients. That fact alone, as for example Spero has shown convincingly, already influences treatment. The second drawback is that the *inter*subjective aspects of spirituality are systematically kept out of the picture. Yet it is precisely this *intersubjectivity*, this person-to-person communication or 'communion' with a real God, which is at the heart of religion and at the heart of individual spiritual life. To respond adequately, a therapist needs to understand the implications of the fact that the whole point of spiritual life is that there *is* a transcendent reality you *can* know, albeit partially, albeit permanently in need of correction and albeit experienced at various levels of intensity.

M.H. Spero is one of the few theorists who directs attention to this problem and provides an instrument to correct it. In his excellent article 'Parallel dimensions of experience in psychoanalytic psychotherapy of the religious patient' he writes:

> The remnants of psychologism in advanced object relations theory of religious experience may confound the psychotherapist's ability to explore the patient's reality, such that the fullest value of paying attention to the central dimensions of religious experience may never be achieved and the unique relationship between the individual and the Object called God may go unexplored.[1]

He then proceeds to show how important it can be to do just such an exploration in psychotherapy, and provides a model for conceptualising the parallel or conflicting aspects of relating, on the one hand, with a God-representation, and on the other hand with an independently existing God.

In discussing this cognitive aspect we are moving somewhat further away from therapy than when we concentrated on the existential aspect. At first sight, questions about the existence of a personal, communicating God seem to be too intellectual for discussion in a therapy session. Another difficulty is that talk about the 'reality' and 'knowledge' of God inevitably implies theological and metaphysical assumptions which are part and parcel of the plausibility problem discussed in Chapter 7. Indeed, now that we turn to the cognitive aspect of spirituality, we find ourselves anew right in the middle of this plausibility problem. That problem raises the question: is there any good reason why anyone educated in the tradition of empirical thought should take seriously any person's claim that God exists and that we can communicate with him? Or should we consider any report of communication with God to be a priori irrational and illusory if not delusional – and treat it as such?

To shed some light on this matter, this chapter looks into the rather universal occurrence of 'religious experiences' and the research about this phenomenon. 'Religious experiences' are experiences of being in the presence of, or otherwise being in contact with, a divine reality. Of course all reported experience is interpreted experience and there is always danger of distorted reception and self-deception. Nevertheless, might not the striking similarities between this type of experience all through history and in different religious cultures make the idea more plausible for the empirically oriented mind? Or at least understandable? It is worthwhile to pay some attention to this question because this information may help non-religious readers to make up their own mind on this issue. Chapter 16, entitled 'Psychotherapy and illuminative experience', will then discuss the *characteristics* of spiritual cognition and the *problems* patients may have with integrating it.

2 Illumination as intuitive experiential knowledge

In the traditional terminology of spiritual development the acquirement and deepening of this 'objective' knowledge of God is called 'illumination' and is located in the second stage. In Chapter 12, I explained this ancient development scheme, mentioning that in the first stage, called 'purification' or 'purgation' the emphasis is on the person himself. As he gradually needs to pay less attention to himself, he may enter the second stage, called 'illumination'. He then becomes more receptive for spiritual insights and communications. Although this ancient schema and its terminology is not meant for the kind of people we are dealing with in therapy, it is useful for us as therapists when we need to refer to or characterise certain experiences and goal-oriented practices, provided we take care to use it in a loose (i.e. associative) way. In that loose sense the 'cognitive' aspect of spiritual awakening and spiritual awareness is associated with the traditional concept of 'illumination'. Let me first illustrate this with a simple example of an 'illuminative' experience:

Vignette 15

Sitting in the garden one day I suddenly became conscious of a colony of ants in the grass, running rapidly and purposefully about their business. Pausing to watch them I studied the form of their activity, wondering how much of their own pattern they were able to see for themselves. All at once I knew that I was so large that, to them, I was invisible – except, perhaps, as a shadow over their lives. I was gigantic, huge – able at one glance to comprehend, at least to some extent, the work of the whole colony. *I had the power to destroy or scatter it, and I was completely outside the sphere of their knowledge and understanding. They were part of the body of the earth. But they knew nothing of the earth except the tiny part of it which was their home.*

Turning away from them to my surroundings, I saw there was a tree not far away, and the sun was shining. There were clouds, and blue sky that went on forever and ever. And suddenly I was tiny – so little and weak and insignificant that it didn't really matter at all whether I existed or not. And yet, insignificant as I was, my mind was capable of understanding that the limitless world I could see was beyond my comprehension. I could know myself to be a minute part of it all. I could understand my lack of understanding.

A watcher would have to be incredibly big to see me and the world around me as I could see the ants and their world, I thought. Would he think me to be as unaware of his existence as I knew the ants were of mine? He would have to be vaster than the world space, and beyond understanding, and yet I could be aware of him – I was aware of him, in spite of my limitations. At the same time he was, and he was not, beyond my understanding.

Although my flash of comprehension was thrilling and transforming, I knew even then that in reality it was no more than a tiny glimmer. And yet, because there was this glimmer of understanding, the door of eternity was already open. My own part, however limited it might be, became in that moment a reality and must be included in the whole. In fact, the whole could not be complete without my own particular contribution. I was at the same time so insignificant as to be almost non-existent and so important that without me the whole could not reach fulfilment.

Every single person was a part of a Body, the purpose of which was as much beyond my comprehension now as I was beyond the comprehension of the ants.[2]

This vignette is taken from one of the many letters written to the Religious Experience Research Unit at Oxford after their broadcasting a request for reports on religious experiences during childhood. This research institute owns an impressive collection of reports of religious experiences, written by all kinds of people.

This particular letter is from a woman who had this experience at the age of five. Her report is a beautiful example of what twelfth-century Hildegard of Bingen, one of the most talented women Europe has ever known, called 'seeing through the material world with spiritual eyes' – seeing God through an anthill.[3] The metaphor of 'seeing' (and related notions such as 'the inner eye' or 'the third eye') is universally used for this kind of intuitive flash of apprehending a spiritual reality. 'The most beautiful way of seeing is seeing in the eyes of a visible man the invisible God, who has made his home in him like in his temple', says Pachomius, a fourth-century founder of Christian monasticism.[4]

3 'Religious experience' research

'Religious experience' is the technical term in psychology of religion for a great variety of experiences of contact with a transcendent Being, including 'illuminative' experiences such as the experience of the young girl in vignette 15. The term is in use in this sense since William James's classic *The Varieties of Religious Experience* was first published in 1902.[5] In this book I shall also use the term 'religious experience' in this technical sense, although this is a departure from my chosen terminology with respect to 'religion' and 'spirituality' (see the introduction to Part 1). Unfortunately, the use of 'religious' in this technical sense is somewhat misleading, because such experiences have not necessarily anything to do with 'a religion' as such, although many of them do indeed have a religious content. The term is not restricted to experiences of adherents to some religion, nor does the experience happen exclusively to people belonging to some religion. The vignette of the girl looking at an anthill is a good illustration of how the term 'religious experience' strictly refers to a particular kind of experience, which may lead to religious faith, but in her case never did. Nor is conversion to any religion entirely dependent on religious experience, as is illustrated by the psychology student of vignette 12. In his case, the breakthrough of illuminative insight started by reading certain books. As for the Scriptural religions, these put great value in the experiences of their founding *communities* (the ancient people of Israel, the earliest Christian communities) and the trustworthiness of their accounts. In that sense they are indeed based on experience, but not on each particular believer's own 'religious experience'.

I am including these side comments because such unexpected religious experiences are often credited with too much significance. Some communities even propagate the view that having a religious experience is the only valid hallmark of true spiritual awakening. Having a religious experience is one way to spiritual awakening but certainly not the only way. For explanatory and research purposes religious experience studies are however quite useful. Most are remembered as *clearly dated and demarcated events*. That is why so many historical and contemporary reports of such experiences can be analysed and compared. And that is why these studies are so useful for explaining the structure of the 'cognitive' aspect of a spiritual change process.

The girl's experience at the anthill is a clear and simple example of intuitive spiritual cognition. Through this experience, the girl apprehended the concept of transcendence and accepted the truth of its existence. In that respect, it is 'illuminative' in the loose sense explained in Chapter 12. Remarkably, she never in her later life made the connection between her experience and the God of any religion.

Since the end of the nineteenth century, quite a lot of research on religious experience has been carried out. There have also been large-scale researches, critical surveys and meta-analyses of the cumulative outcomes in the whole field. One outcome of such large-scale research is that about one-third of the population of Britain and the USA has had one or more religious experiences.[6] For decades there has been a cultural taboo on talking about them. People were afraid to be thought sentimental or crazy if they reported them. The subject was seldom included in standard academic psychology courses and research programmes. It was thought to happen only to exceptional people like mystics. Now that it is more acceptable to talk about them, 'ordinary' people are more prepared to come forward.

Another interesting outcome of the research in religious experience is that such experiences appear to be happening all over the world, in very different cultures, and to all kinds of people. By far the most research has been done in Western Christianity, of course. Nevertheless, there is now enough material from other cultures to make it abundantly clear that religious experiences all over the world have striking similarities, even though their evaluation and interpretation may vary widely. So a certain openness to such experiences seems to be a rather universal human capacity.

It is relevant for therapists to know about this outcome, because it suggests that some of their patients are familiar with such experiences. It also means that we have to be careful in discriminating these 'ordinary' phenomena from the pathological and the self-deceptive ones. In discussing visions and auditions (vignettes 4 and 5) I have already touched on this matter.

The recurrence of this type of experience raises two questions. The first is, do religious experiences provide evidence for the existence of a transcendent reality, in particular of the Biblical God? The second question is, if the ordinary senses are not attuned to transcendent reality, as the girl realises so well, how is it possible for some people to become aware of it? Do they have extrasensory faculties or what? The first question is concerned with theory of knowledge (epistemology), the second one with cognitive psychology. Though not always formulated clearly, such questions often play a significant role in religious and non-religious patients' doubts. It makes sense therefore to pay at least some, albeit limited, attention to them here.

4 The validity of religious experience

Do religious experiences provide empirical evidence for the existence of God? In other words, are such experiences illusory or cognitive?

Put in this way, this is a typical modern question. In earlier centuries there was no need for *extra* empirical evidence for the existence of God. There was abundant evidence for everybody to see! Was not the existence of the whole created world evidence of a pre-existing Creator, were not the laws of nature testimony for the existence of a supernatural Legislator, and did not every religion possess reports of self-authorised manifestations of its deities to certain trustworthy people like prophets, priests and saints? Certainly, ancient philosophers designed 'proofs' for the existence of God, but it is important to note their purpose. Originally they were neither meant to remove any real religious doubt by offering rational arguments for the existence of some completely unknown entity, nor to offer irrefutable counter-arguments against atheists. They were meant to 'express in thoughts' what affection and intuition had already taught. That is to say, they tried to put the intuitive knowledge implicit in spontaneous religious experience into the form of a logical argument.[7] One famous Greek 'proof' was, for example, Socrates' extensive argument in which he, in view of the beautiful ordering in nature, concludes that there must exist a divine intelligence to bring about this beauty and order.[8] Later on, Christian philosophers undertook the same, adding to it the purpose of expressing in the language of logic what was already known through Scripture, i.e. the superiority and uniqueness of the One Biblical God.

As discussed in Part 2, nowadays it is just the other way round. For example, neither the existence of the natural world, nor its causality and regularity, nor its endless change and diversity – nothing 'natural' is to us unquestioned evidence for the existence of a transcendent Being. And anything 'not natural', like a miracle for example, does not count as evidence either. We just assume that at some time we shall be able to explain it as natural. As a result, God is in a conceptual no-win situation.

But however that may be, do religious experiences provide evidence for the claim that God exists?

In *The Evidential Force of Religious Experience* Davis has undertaken to answer this question by critically analysing *all* the outcomes of the many and varied researches done on religious experience. Each individual experience, however convincing for the person, cannot be sufficient evidence. Neither can the outcome of any single research project. But the whole lot of twentieth-century researches taken together, and the many autobiographical reports over a long period and from a wide range of different cultures, don't they add up to substantial evidence?[9]

In Davis' meta-analysis of research outcomes it appeared that the great variety of researched religious experiences fall into six categories:

1. *interpretative* religious experiences, when one sees some experience as religious, not because of any features of the experience itself, but because it is viewed in the light of a prior religious framework;

2. *quasi-sensory* religious experiences like visions, dreams, voices, light, etc., when taken to be manifestations of the presence of a spiritual being or to be 'images' conveyed by it, requiring a certain amount of interpretation but as such valid sources of religious insight – this is to differentiate these from the many cases of quasi-sensory experiences like light, music, sweet odours, which are not religious in themselves but may occur as a concomitant of religious experience or during an exercise in meditation;

3. *revelatory* religious experiences, when some specific religious knowledge or insight is being conveyed which seems to be transmitted by an external agency;

4. *regenerative* religious experiences, like experiencing new hope, strength, peace, etc., after prayer, and experiences of being guided, forgiven, healed, aided in leading a more moral or loving life, etc. – this is the most frequent type of religious experience, one of the features which make a 'living' religion more than the mere acceptance of a set of doctrines or the performance of some actions;

5. *numinous* religious experiences, in which the divine presence is encountered as the awe-inspiring Infinite One, both terrifying and profoundly attractive, overwhelming the human being with feelings of fear, of insignificance, of imperfection and unworthiness;

6. *mystical* experiences, in which the person may become totally absorbed in an intense love of God, often described as being united with God.

This is what in the ancient systematisation described in Chapter 12 is called the 'union' or 'unification', the highest stage of spiritual development.

These six categories are not mutually exclusive, since one experience may exhibit the characteristics of several categories at once. Indeed, they could be presented as six different aspects of religious experience: how they are seen by the subject to fit into a larger religious pattern, the quasi-sensory element, the alleged knowledge gained in an experience, the affective aspect and its effects, the 'holy' element, and the 'unitive' element. Few religious experiences, however, have all of these characteristics.

The conclusion of Davis' meta-analysis is that only two of the six categories have true evidential value, namely those of the numinous and the mystical experiences. Let us take a closer look at these two.

Numinous experiences, to which Rudolph Otto in his still famous study *The Idea of the Holy* has drawn attention, are experienced and recognised in all religions.[10] They determine the atmosphere of solemnity and reverence in worship, rites, and liturgies, as well as in architecture and other religious art. In them, the divine presence is encountered as 'mysterium tremendum et fascinans' (a terrifying and fascinating mystery), as Otto put it. Such experiences may be profoundly humbling and disconcerting. Being perturbed by the realisation of the insignificance, the fragility, the imperfection of one's existence in the confrontation with God's majesty is in itself not a negative experience. But depending on the vulnerability of their personality and their faith people may be so much overwhelmed by such feelings of unworthiness that they become despondent. In that respect the consequences of such experiences then become therapeutically relevant (see also Chapter 7, section 6, and Chapter 14, section 1).

Mystical experiences are also experienced and recognised in all religions. Religious authorities and doctrines value them differently. Some of them validate only the mystical experiences of acknowledged saints and founders of their tradition, in contrast to others who train all their members in becoming more receptive to them; still others are wary of such subjective experiences and set much greater store by living ordinary daily life in a religious lifestyle. However that may be, mystical experiences characteristically result in a sense of having apprehended an ultimate reality, of freedom from the limitations of time, space and the individual ego, and a sense of bliss or serenity. Stace has made a useful distinction between 'introvertive' and 'extrovertive' mystical experiences.[11] They are called '*introvertive*' or 'unitary' mystical experiences when all external and internal diversity is shut out in order to dive deep within oneself to discover the One. They are called '*extrovertive*' when a multiplicity of external objects is seen as somehow unified and divine, as in the famous experience of Thomas Merton when observing the crowd on a square of Louisville. When looking at the crowd of people hurrying about the shopping district he had a mystical experience that as a human being he was united with, not separated from, the rest of humanity.[12] As another example, some people have been suddenly overcome by a deep feeling of being at one with nature while walking out in the countryside.

According to Davis, the quantity and the universality of the experiences in these two categories, together with the attested sanity and trustworthiness of by far the most subjects, provide *cumulative* valid evidence for at least some religious claims. Taken together, these claims justify a belief called 'broad theism'.

5 'Broad theism'

What is the content of this 'broad theism'? What are these beliefs that numinous and mystical experience support?

First, that the known world of physical bodies, physical processes, and narrow centres of consciousness is not the whole or ultimate reality and in particular, that the phenomenal ego of everyday consciousness, which most people tend to regard as their 'self' is by no means the deepest level of the self: there is a far deeper 'spiritual self' which in some way depends on, and participates in, the ultimate reality. (This links up with what has been discussed about the 'spiritual True Self' in Chapter 13.) Second, these experiences support the claim that the ultimate reality is holy, eternal and of supreme value, and that this holy reality can be experienced as a presence with whom individuals can have a personal relationship, to whom they are profoundly attracted, and on whom they feel utterly dependent. Third, at least some mystical experiences are probably experiences of a very intimate union with the holy. And finally, they support the view that some kind of harmonious relationship with the ultimate reality is the 'highest good' for human beings, the means by which they flourish into a deeply satisfying and meaningful life.

Some theorists hold that broad theism is in fact the 'common core of all religions'. Now indeed most religions would not contradict these claims, but probably would not consider them to be sufficient. What they share does not necessarily coincide with what they themselves consider the most central beliefs. Judaism, Christianity and Islam, for example, would probably consider the evidential value of numinous and mystical experiences as highly valuable and a wonderful corroboration of their teachings. Nevertheless these experiences do not in themselves make up a valid knowledge claim about the existence or the nature of the God of Abraham, Jacob and Moses. To these particular religions the primary source of religious knowledge is the Scriptural self-revelation of God to the whole community, this being the source and the touchstone for everything, individual numinous and mystical experiences included. This is not only doctrine, it is experienced and lived as well, and therefore in principle relevant in therapy. As another relevant factor, it is also a source of frustration for those people who cannot accept that their own, subjectively convincing, experience should need critical examination. It may even cause them to leave their church. This may of course also have been caused by the clumsy way in which such critical testing is sometimes done, but not necessarily so.

We may conclude that in our modern Western culture many people inside and outside the various religions share these broad theistic beliefs, but that in and by themselves these are too broad and general to function as central beliefs for a religion. People who want to relate to spiritual reality in any meaningful way need more cognitive content than this.

Therapists may easily come to deal with people who have come to spiritual consciousness *outside* any religious teaching, such as the girl at the anthill. Vernon's research showed that 20 per cent of his interviewees who gave 'none' in response to a question about religious affiliation claimed that they felt themselves to be in the presence of God![13] And it is striking how well 'broad theism' corresponds to what such people express when they try to explain themselves. It seems to cover rather well what I have coined 'spirituality in exile'. If people are familiar with religious teachings, it is natural for them to relate their experience to the God they know about. But many people who can *not* relate their experience to any religion seem to reach more or less the same conclusions by intuition as Davis does by critical analysis.

6 Extrasensory perception or special spiritual powers?

If the ordinary senses are not attuned to transcendent reality, how is it possible for some people to become aware of it? Do we need extraordinary sense organs for spiritual experience? Special extrasensory faculties?

Some studies investigate whether there are some special capacities involved in this kind of direct religious knowing. If we decide that this type of knowledge of the Transcendent is not a priori to be 'explained away' as projections, illusions, etc., would we then have to conclude that it originates from some exceptional cognitive capacity or mental state, such as the paranormal or the altered state of consciousness? With this question in mind Watts and Williams have investigated how religious knowing from direct experience relates to cognitive psychology. They conclude that such religious knowing is 'cognitive' in the sense that it is reached by normal cognitive processes that are somewhat similar to those by which other forms of human knowledge are reached, particularly the one in psychotherapy.[14] This suggests that it can be looked into and evaluated as a normal cognitive event that could be right or wrong in more or less the same way as a therapeutic statement could be.

The example of the anthill and the giant watcher (vignette 15) easily shows why we do not need any special gifts. The giant transcends the girl's perceptual and conceptual capacities, so the initiative for a contact cannot be hers. But there is no reason why the transcendent giant would not be able to take the first step and to adapt his communication to her capacities. To formulate this in religious terms: man cannot manipulate God, but God is free and able to initiate a communication by whatever means he may choose, through dreams, thoughts, intuitions, imagination, or through the challenges raised by the situations of ordinary life – an infinite variety in fact. These experiences of 'sensing' intuitively the presence of a transcendent Being are viewed by religious people as a grace, a free gift of the Divine. This is to emphasise that they can never be a natural consequence of human effort or human merit. It depends on the transcendent Being to 'touch' human beings or not. But what human beings can do is to train themselves to become more attentive and sensitive in this respect. Many practices and exercises in the various spiritual traditions are designed precisely to train such an attitude of sensitive attentiveness. I have already mentioned how important it is for people to have expert guidance for such exercises because there are numerous examples of people who have become seriously disturbed by them. All major spiritual traditions have always warned of this danger. Stanislav and Christina Grof have introduced the term 'spiritual emergency' to identify a variety of such psychological difficulties, in particular those associated with Eastern spiritual practices that have become popular in Western culture. On the back cover of their book on this subject, they define such emergencies as 'crises when the process of growth and change becomes chaotic and overwhelming'. They report that individuals experiencing such episodes may feel that their sense of identity is breaking down, that their old values no longer hold true, and that the very ground beneath their personal realities is radically shifting.[15]

The question about extrasensory perception is also rooted in the confusion between spirituality and practices such as spiritism and magic. The latter practices hinge on special people having special powers to manipulate good and bad spirits. Since such practices are intrinsically manipulative, they are intrinsically (in the context of spiritual development) potentially dangerous. This is so even if performed with well-meaning intentions. The issue is thus not so much whether there really are such special gifts, or whether there are such spirits, or whether these practices are effective. The real issue is that authentic spirituality is emphatically not about manipulating, whether it be manipulating God or manipulating men. And it is certainly not about making people dependent on other people endowed with special powers.

CHAPTER 16

Psychotherapy and Illuminative Experience

1 The structure of illuminative experience

The experience of the girl at the anthill (vignette 15) is an elementary form of illuminative experience. I call the experience 'illuminative' because it gives her both insight into what transcendence is about and experiential knowledge of its existence. Particularly interesting is her account of what happened just before her awareness of a transcendent presence. In most cases the experience in itself is so exciting that people tend to forget their immediately preceding thoughts and feelings. This girl has remembered them, however. Therefore, I shall use this vignette again, now for the purpose of analysing the structure of illuminative cognition.

At first the girl is just looking outwards, as you would look at any object that catches your attention. But then she mentally distances herself from her own position, imagining what individual ants from their position would be able to see of the whole they are part of. She realises that an individual ant can in no way gain the complete overview of the activities of the colony such as she herself does. Still from the ants' perspective, she then tries to look at herself and realises this cannot be done because her view as a person transcends that of the ants. As a next mental step, she distances herself again and takes a position from which she can compare her actual outlook and that of an ant. This enables her to see why and how her own view is more comprehensive.

Then she shifts back to her actual physical position and again looks outward, but now in all other directions, to the larger scene around her and the infinite sky above her. Again she distances herself from her actual position, and mentally takes a position from where she can look at herself as one small element within this larger scene. From this position she is not that much larger than the ants! Her outlook, too, is too small to have an overall view of this whole and her own place in it. And no more than the ants would she be able to see someone big enough to have such a comprehensive view.

And then she makes a last mental shift. She now moves to a position of a giant who would have an overview of the whole world and herself as a small part within it. From this 'higher' point of view, she can see how and why her vision and comprehension bump against this barrier. From this position she can also see that the barrier is not a property of the universe, it is only a limit of her own capacities. Taking a closer look at her own capacities from this point of view, she then realises that in understanding the existence and the nature of her limitations she has already somehow reached beyond them. Understanding that you bump against something is 'higher' than just bumping against something. And understanding what you bump against and how and why you are bumping against it is 'higher' than just knowing you are bumping. In other words, understanding the non-understandability of the non-understandable is more comprehensive than not understanding there may be such a thing as 'The Non-Understandable' and how and why this would be non-understandable.

This sounds suspiciously like a philosophical statement. Indeed it is one, and a good one at that. How in the world can a little girl get there?

Actually what she is doing *is* very similar to philosophical methodology. As my philosophy professor used to say to his students, 'The most important words in philosophy are "Suppose that".' He meant that the most important method in philosophy is a thought experiment. From Socrates to modern conceptual analysis, philosophy is full of thought experiments that are conducted in a manner as rigorously systematic and reproducible by others as empirical experiments. In natural science, they precede the crucial empirical experiments designed to prove a new scientific paradigm.[1] For gaining this kind of insight, neither psychological nor physical experiment would have been helpful to this girl. Even boarding a space shuttle and looking at the world from a great height would not have yielded her what her 'suppose that' game near the anthill did.

Both the philosopher and the girl use the same cognitive ability and imaginative flexibility necessary for a successful thought experiment. The difference is, of course, that the philosopher uses these in a systematic and purposive way, as part of a methodology. The girl, however, was only playing a fantasy-game with herself, not heading for any specific result. Without intending to do so, and not knowing the word for it, the girl was acquiring the concept of transcendence in essentially the same way a philosopher would.

Then the girl makes another shift, but this one is of a completely different order. From 'I *could be* aware of him' she moves to 'I *was* aware of him'. This is of a different order because it is a leap from the mode of thinking into the mode of experiencing. Her *understanding* is that there *could* be a transcendent Being. Reflection can never take her further than that. Her *experience* is, however, that there *is* such a reality. Presence is not dependent on having the concept, though having a concept may help noticing presence. Without the concept gained from her thought experiment, she still could have experienced some mysterious presence. But she would probably not have recognised and understood it as such.

So this is a real turning point in her story. This is why it belongs to the category of *cognitive* experience, where understanding and perception of a reality come together. In this respect her experience is fundamentally different from for example the psychoanalytic 'oceanic experience'. *That* concept (in the prevailing interpretation of it) refers to subjective experiences.[2] In contrast, spirituality is a thoroughly relational affair, which is why the issue of the 'real' existence of the other party in the relationship is utterly relevant to it. As in other personal relationships, people may need to differentiate between a real mutual contact and one that is imagined or distorted by projection. But unlike in other personal relationships, they may also doubt the very existence of the 'other party'. I shall come back to this point later on in this chapter because, just as at the existential level, prolonged doubt at this cognitive level may have repercussions in other vital areas.

Awareness of the presence of a transcendent reality does not follow naturally from *reflection* on the *possibility* of its presence. It is the result of two entities actually *being in* each other's presence, and of the capacity to *recognise* that this is so.

2 Illuminative experience as a learning process

The 'illumination' of the young girl studying the ants shows a striking structural similarity with how traditional spiritual teachers such as fourth-century Augustine, twelfth-century Bernard of Clairvaux and thirteenth-century Bonaventura describe the process. They teach that part of the way to 'see' God is to turn your mind outwards, then from there to turn it inwards, and from there to turn it upwards – and then the other way round, from upwards to inwards to outwards. The other part, it was taught, was of course reading the Bible meditatively. Much as in the earliest stereoscopic cinema, for which you had to put on spectacles with one red and one green glass in order to see depth, Bonaventura takes his readers simultaneously through a 'looking outwards-inwards-upwards and back' route (one 'glass') and through the biblical creation story (another 'glass'). The latter is not ordinary reading, it is using a specific meditative reading technique to help you to become as it were part of the story while reading. This second glass is conspicuously lacking in the girl's 'seeing technique'. The 'looking outwards-inwards-upwards and back' route is consistent with ancient psychology, in which man was supposed to be a microcosm of the world. His body equated to the physical world, his mind to the spiritual world. Therefore the *mind*, functioning as a mirror, could as it were 'reflect' God. To know God, and to communicate with him, you had to turn inwards and there you would find him. Likewise you could find him in the *material world* because he created it. This is quite logical when the cosmos is conceived as including God. In Chapter 7 I gave a rough sketch of how in the course of history people began to conceptualise an ever increasing gap between God and man, as well as between God and cosmos. As a result, this earlier psychology is not at all self-evident for most people of today. Actually, it is quite surprising to find the ancient methodology used in this girl's account, and to see how it resulted in a spontaneous illuminative experience. By the way, once you know about this classical spiritual 'seeing' technique, it will strike you that many modern movements are using it as well, although they use of course different terminologies and a different 'second glass'.[3] In my opinion this again confirms the observation in Chapter 7, section 4, about spirituality showing a remarkable continuity through the ages.

3 'Illuminative learning' in psychotherapy

This process looks somewhat like the learning process in group analysis. There, too, group members are taught to 'see through' the empirical reality of their interactions by alternately taking a position within it and a position of distance to look at the pattern of the whole. This suggests that some group member may take this one step further and look at it from an even more inclusive point of view, particularly if he is wittingly or unwittingly involved in a process of spiritual awakening. Vignette 16 is one example, though not from group analysis but from a professional training course.

Vignette 16

There was something strange about this group. After the usual uncertainties of the first sessions, it did not gradually develop an increasing openness and mutual understanding. On the contrary, everybody became ever more caught in an oppressive atmosphere of fear, distrust, and hostility. At last nobody dared to say or propose anything. We just sat there with thickened throats and sweating hands. This fear and suspicion were directed at each other, but were directed even more at the group conductor. Whatever he said or did, it was all interpreted as an attempt to manipulate us, as a sign of untrustworthiness or incompetence. His proposals were all brushed aside. During the breaks he was slandered behind his back.

There was also something strange about this group conductor. Although he had an excellent reputation nationally and internationally, the group made it impossible for him to do his work properly. On top of that, he was continually attacked as a person, sometimes openly, more often indirectly but unmistakably. I knew from his reputation that he was a strong personality, yet he did not defend himself. It showed that he was not only suffering but also hurt in his person. At the same time it showed that he loved us. You could see by the look of his face that he was simultaneously suffering intensely and loving intensely.

It looked unnatural and yet it was not. I loved my family and I knew they loved me. But that love was 'ordinary' to me, part of my everyday ambiance. But the love I saw now was not ordinary, and I didn't know how to handle that. I think this man didn't know either.

The group malaise went on week after miserable week. The group simply did not develop as our theory books taught.

One day – I felt completely worn out and sat quietly somewhat apart from the others – the group was particularly mean to the trainer. Then, suddenly, they began to cry and some of them even went to cry on his shoulder. I kept quiet, just looking. It looked as if the group could no longer bear its own meanness being countered with love. Out of the blue, a Bible text came to my mind: 'Strength comes to its full strength in weakness. . . when I am weak, then I am strong'.[4]

I thought, what this man shows is not weakness, it is the incredible courage to be gentle and meek, to stay with your own love in whatever the circumstances. And I thought that this was maybe what Jesus Christ was doing at his trial.

Then something happened that, looking back on it now, I would express as becoming overpowered by the Gospel. I lived in two worlds simultaneously. Right through our collective bungling in the group I was in touch with the awesome power of divine love. I was absolutely surprised and overwhelmed by this direct touch of divine love. It was completely different from what I had ever imagined it to be. Real unconditional love of inconceivable proportions. I, too, was totally different from what I ever imagined myself to be. I saw that my apparently ordinary and decent life was in fact built on fear and corruption. I could no longer live with myself.

The aim of this group was to learn to recognise the group processes that the trainees themselves had already been taught. They were trying to 'see through the empirical world with group dynamic eyes'. Indeed it is very instructive to analyse this group in the light of Hopper's 'Fourth Basic Assumptions Group' and Nitsun's 'Anti-Group' theories.[5] But that is not the issue here. In the context of this book the point of this example is that the author of the vignette at that particular moment must have looked at the sudden break in hostility towards the trainer with 'spiritual eyes' instead of with group dynamic eyes. This triggered off illuminative understanding and subsequent spiritual experience. This is possible because in group analysis (as in many other psychotherapeutic methodologies) we teach a mental flexibility comparable to that which the girl at the anthill used, the ability to alternate between taking a position within the situation and one 'above' it. We provide people with stereoscopic spectacles that allow them to see depth in their own interactions. In doing so, *we train them in the kind of mental flexibility that is also conducive for illuminative experience and understanding.* Therefore it is not surprising to find some participants will transcend group dynamics and move to an intuitive apprehension of the spiritual.

4 Illuminative experience and self-knowledge

Usually illuminative experience such as in the two cases referred to above is informative *simultaneously* about not only the spiritual reality but also about the self in relation to it. In vignette 15, the girl not only discovers the concept and the existence of a transcendent Being, but also discovers (as she herself also reported) that 'I was at the same time so insignificant as to be almost non-existent and so important that without me the whole could not reach fulfilment'. Likewise, the trainee (in vignette 16) draws attention to the self-knowledge with which he had been illuminated: 'I, too, was totally different from what I ever imagined myself to be.' In this respect such experiential cognition is different from ordinary teaching of religious facts and truths. In both the case of the girl and the trainee the knowledge gained is the same as taught in lessons and preaching all over the world: the existence of a transcendent Being and the love of God which transcends any conception of human love. But in illuminative experience the truth is not so much taught as 'brought home'. This is not really surprising when one takes a transcendent point of view to look at the whole and therefore at oneself as part of the whole. Note that this kind of self-knowledge is different from the True Self-knowledge discussed in Chapter 13! Different, but no less important. The fact that in spiritual consciousness both these kinds of self-knowledge are bound up with the apprehension of spiritual reality accounts for the urgency and passion people show in matters that at first sight can appear to be essentially an intellectual (cognitive) concern. Precisely because the 'informative' components of spiritual consciousness are inextricably bound up with the emotional, affective and evaluative aspects of spiritual True Self, they constitute for the patient significantly more than just an intellectual challenge. They challenge the whole person.

It is important to realise that many therapists are inclined to interpret intellectual preoccupation as a screen for emotional things which may be too sensitive to acknowledge. They are of course right to be suspicious, but this may be one area in which intellectual issues may be of legitimate therapeutic relevance.

A principal message is that the process of spiritual awakening and its subsequent process of spiritual change are characteristically informative about the world 'outside' as well as about the world 'inside'. It discloses one's core identity as being intimately and passionately oriented towards God. It also discloses the existence of a transcendent Being (or beings). It discloses too the meaningfulness of the visible and invisible world (including Self) in the light of its relation to this spiritual reality, either as a part of the intuited transcendent Being, or as a creation of it, or both. This may be expressed in various ways, such as being part of a meaningful whole, being a child of God, feeling essentially a spirit belonging to and interacting with a spiritual world, or many other formulations.

5 Positive after-effects of illuminative experience

Turning now to the after-effects of illuminative experience, it is important to recognise that not everybody awakens to spiritual consciousness through a well-remembered 'religious experience' in the technical sense of the term. There are also many people, such as the psychology student in vignette 12, whose process of spiritual awakening is more gradual. In the next sections, I shall again pay considerable attention to the after-effects of sudden experiences, because those people who come to spiritual awareness by way of such an unexpected breakthrough are the ones who usually have more problems with accepting and integrating this new dimension in their lives. Yet this should not be read as if the gradual process were uncomplicated. These people are confronted with essentially the same challenges as the others, and they may also go through a difficult period because of that. Most positive and negative after-effects discussed in the next sections are part and parcel of both the sudden and the gradual process. However, it is a fact that the gradual process is less prone to create a major crisis.

To begin with the *positive* after-effects, an illuminative religious experience usually becomes a constitutive factor in the long-term process of forming a fundamental life orientation and a lifestyle reflecting this orientation. Generally its long-term effects are, first, a religious life characteristically expressed in personal terms and strengthened by an increased depth in prayer life. Second, the experience serves as a reference point in the life of the person who has experienced it, in the sense that there is a certainty and awareness of an underlying unity and transcendence in life which was not there before. This certainty and awareness from then on can form the basis of the 'alrightness' of life even when things underneath do not feel immediately all right. It is also experienced as a reference point capable of telling you that the Presence is there and this is where you are located in relation to it. Still another effect is that the experience can be recalled and re-approached in meditation, worship or quietness. By re-approaching the original experience one can bring the insights and at-oneness of the original event back into the here and now.

The letter about the girl's illuminative experience with the ants (written about fifty years after the event) provides us with a powerful example of this re-call and re-approach and of its effect in a subsequent paragraph:

Sequel to vignette 15

I was enchanted. Running indoors, delighted with my discovery, I announced happily, 'We're like ants, running about on a giant's tummy!' No one understood, but that was unimportant. I knew what I knew.

It was a lovely thing to have happened. All my life, in times of great pain or distress or failure, I have been able to look back and remember, quite sure that the present agony was not the whole picture and that my understanding of it was limited as were the ants in their comprehension of their part in the world I knew.

Such uncomplicated adoption of a transcendent view on self and the world gives one an inner sense of security and place in the scheme of things. There is little reason to expect such experiences as the one reported above to become an issue for discussion in a therapeutic situation. If raised at all, the important thing for a therapist is to acknowledge that the matter concerns a central point of meaning and stability, so that the person involved feels free to communicate his experience and can expect it to be taken at least seriously if not immediately understood. This woman's letter also shows how important this can be:

Sequel to vignette 15

This inner knowledge was exciting and absorbingly interesting, but it remained unsaid because, even if I could have expressed it, no one would have understood. Once, when I tried, I was told I was morbid.

As a child, she cries 'We're like ants, running about on a giant's tummy!' Understandably, her mother does not understand. Life being what it is for mothers, her mother was possibly at that very moment simultaneously stirring the soup and explaining sums to another child, while the baby cried and the doorbell rang! But as an adult she could not make herself understood either, although she obviously has a good command of language. Unfortunately, this is not uncommon. Although this particular woman (the writer of this letter) stuck to her own conviction, it can obviously do great damage to a person's inner sense of security and place if such a central and significant experience is called or thought of as pathological or escapist by significant others.[6]

6 Negative after-effects of illuminative experience

The aftermath of an experience of spiritual awakening can also be a period of confusion, of doubt, of disturbance, even of psychosis, for some individuals. This is not surprising, because it often undermines one's most fundamental certainties. Such spiritual disorientation is a complex phenomenon. A number of different factors following this awakening will now interact and support, or aggravate each other. Some of these will be characteristically spiritual factors and others nonspiritual (but personally important) factors.

In the first place, if spiritual awakening happens through such a sudden breakthrough experience, people may feel both alarmed and overwhelmed by the experience itself and the intense emotions evoked by it. As a result, the person involved may go through a major *personality crisis*. One's personality structure, therapeutic experience suggests, may account for an unfavourable predisposition in that respect.

Second, such a sudden spiritual awakening may also be followed by a period of *spiritual hypersensitivity*. It is as though some inner door has been opened, and now unwanted visitors also find their way through it to the person's inner self. It may take some time to learn how to manage the lock of this inner door. Sometimes these phenomena of hypersensitivity may be relatively mild, like for example a telepathic hypersensitivity for other people's thoughts or emotions. But others are quite frightening, such as feeling haunted, or overpowered by destructive impulses, or intrusion of one's inner self by demonic forces. Such side-effects of overwhelming religious experiences sometimes look like a depression or a real demonic possession. But there are characteristic differences. There are usually no physical symptoms, and most people are able to continue to do the things they have to do. Characteristically, they feel that deep down there is essentially something *positive* going on. Furthermore, the phenomenon is definitely temporary, and one's prayer life is not seriously affected by it. An example of this is a man who had a religious experience together with his father-in-law. Although both were lifelong church members and sincerely religious men, they felt shy and guilty about it. During several months after this experience he suffered from strong self-destructive impulses for which he sought psychiatric help. He was prescribed some antidepressant. Intuitively he put the medicine on his bedside table but did not use it. He decided to pray whenever he felt on the verge of being overwhelmed by suicidal impulses. Then after a while the feeling faded away and he never suffered a relapse. It was years afterwards that he told about the experience and its aftermath – and was quite amazed to hear that both his experience and the 'depressive' period afterwards were not as uncommon and eccentric as he thought them to be, and that his intuition of how to act upon them had been well-founded. Usually such hypersensitivity gradually fades away, the only lasting effect being a more sensitive intuition both for other people and for spiritual insights. It may be enough to tell the person these are temporary side-effects and advise him to pay little attention to them but to concentrate on prayer.

Another negative effect of spiritual awakening is for the person to become *over-fascinated* with the experience and to try to anchor it instead of allowing it to become an integral part of an ever developing spiritual life orientation. This *'retention phenomenon'* may show itself in a need to keep talking and thinking excessively about the experience, or in a spiritually unhealthy and false preoccupation with what is going on within 'my oh, so interesting soul', or in trying re-peatedly to re-create the experience. This is an egocentric way to handle the experience and leads inevitably to frustration and shallowness. Such experi-ences cannot be repeated at will, and even if they repeat themselves they are spiritually of little value if they do not stimulate the person to developing an ever-deepening love for God and creation. For example, one man, owner and manager of a large company, once had to take an extremely difficult business decision with rather heavy ethical implications. While agonising about this, he saw a light in the corner of his dark bedroom and at the same time he felt a Presence, and then he intuitively 'just knew' what decision to take. Not being a religious man, he was much surprised, but he took the decision in accordance with the experience. The apparition of light never repeated itself, but it stimu-lated him to a fundamental and lasting change in lifestyle and business ethics. As a contrast to this, another man, an accountant, had a similar experience of seeing light in the corner of his bedroom, every morning for over seventeen years, after which it stopped. This repeated occurrence is curious and even really amazing. But it was even more amazing that it never stimulated him to any personal commitment or change. One had only to observe him and listen to him for a very short time to discover that he was a very egocentric and cold man.

The temporary hypersensitivity and the over-fascination with an illuminative experience to which I have drawn attention in the last pages may get dangerously out of hand when the person involved starts *manipulating his state of consciousness*. People may even become psychotic as a result. Obviously both psychological and spiritual factors are involved in such cases. People then need both spiritual guidance and therapeutic help to deal with their love of sensation, self-aggrandisement, narcissism, and the like. Sects that encourage the unscrupulous cultivation and exercising of paranormal gifts are particularly dangerous for people who experience such a period of hypersensitivity and over-fascination. The major world religions all insist that any genuine spiritual experience has to be considered as a gift, and therefore something which cannot be merited, demanded or fabricated. It is also emphasised that one should not cling to this gift when one is given it. When spiritual practices are advised, these are certainly not aimed at producing more experiences or trance-like states. The purposes of such practices would then be aimed at inte-grating the newfound spiritual understanding in the person's new orientation to life and ensuing lifestyle.

Still another negative effect may be the risk of *prolonged doubt and ambiva-lence about the truth* of an illuminative experience. When this happens, it is actually the unwanted outcome of something that in itself is very positive and important, namely, the search for integrity. So we will first take a look at that.

7 The struggle for intellectual integrity

At the actual moment of an illuminative experience, the person concerned is usually totally convinced of its content and the truth of its content. The girl contemplating the anthill (vignette 15) is not at all exceptional with her 'I knew what I knew': this absolute certainty is characteristic for the majority of such cognitive experiences. It is only afterwards that many people start questioning the truth of their experience.

To *religious* people an illuminative experience may be new and surprising but not contradictory in its substance. Since its substance confirms their already established beliefs, it enhances them by a real life experience of the Transcendent Being and deepens their understanding of these beliefs. Yet vignette 16 (the trainee who had an illuminative experience right in the middle of a dysfunctioning group) illustrates how such an experience can surprise even religious people. He wrote, 'It was completely different from what I had ever imagined it to be.' And in Chapter 22 I shall present a case (vignette 19) where a professional theologian discovers the meaning of the central doctrines of Christianity to be quite different from how she had always understood them. She acknowledges that before that discovery she knew them 'with her head, not with her heart.' This element of surprise and contradiction is because most children and adults *start* conceptualising God and any properties ascribed to him as a continuum with human properties. Thus God is taken to be good, powerful, etc. in the way people may be good, powerful, etc., only much more so. Characteristically, transcendent experience shows him to be *dis*continuous with what we already know. It often shockingly belies such religious imagining and conceiving. This is why people already involved in religion are generally surprised by illuminative experience, and this is why it is sometimes called a 'second' conversion. Such cognitive discontinuity indicates a kind of watershed between two modes of religious understanding and involvement. It is often expressed as a surprise about something quite familiar: 'I had read or heard it hundreds of times, but then I suddenly realised I had never really understood it.'

To the *non-religious*, illuminative experience contradicts their beliefs by definition. Some of them have little trouble in changing these beliefs. Some will even report that to them the moment of spiritual understanding, however new and unexpected this understanding is, paradoxically feels as if subconsciously they have always known it. And yet afterwards many of them report that they start doubting. Questions such as 'Does God really exist?', 'Is the universe indeed a meaningful whole?' and so on confront and trouble them. There is of course nothing wrong with thinking carefully about these questions and seeking answers to them. In fact, it is the responsible thing to do. Knowledge gained by an intuitive cognitive experience is not necessarily superior to knowledge gained in other ways and through other channels. Prominent anthropologist Jan van Baal writes that as a prisoner during the Second World War he had an experience that testified to the presence of an all-encompassing Mystery:

> It is surprising how simple the things of a confused and entangled world can become, when you withdraw from it and give yourself over to the unbroken silence and darkness of a long night. You find yourself alone with the mystery of an existence that has become fragile and has separated itself from all the things that tradition and convention has brought with it over the years. What remains is a 'simple self' confronted with an impenetrable world which at the same time is your world. One night the mystery came over me, in a way that cannot be expressed in words. It came as pure power outside, over and inside of me and in no way anchored in any tradition. A mystery that was penetrating me with the certainty of the presence of that which is called 'God' and that which no single word can really describe. An hallucination as a result of being so hungry? I asked myself immediately as the experience receded.

It took Van Baal many years of careful reflection and critical investigation before he was able to confirm his conclusion and to support it by his observations made during his life as an anthropologist. In this way he kept his intellectual integrity.[7]

Likewise the French philosopher Simone Weil reports that she needed a period of intellectual doubt:

> In my arguments about the insolubility of the problem of God I had never foreseen the possibility of that, of a real contact, person to person, here below, between a human being and God... Yet I still half refused, not my love but my intelligence. For it seemed to me certain, and I still think so

today, that one cannot wrestle enough with God if one does it out of pure regard for truth.[8]

Now Weil and Van Baal were talented people, already established scholars before they had the illuminative experience that changed their lives and their views. They had the courage to face the challenge that their experience presented to what they previously thought to be true and therefore irrefutable. They were trained to use their intellect for doubting and for reconsidering very critically all kinds of assumptions, including fundamental ones. And they were clearly flexible enough to re-orient themselves at this most fundamental level. But it is not surprising that other people, less talented, less trained and less flexible, have much more difficulty, despite the gift of insight they have been given, in managing the cognitive conflict their new understanding may create, and in finding the courage to stand up for their new-found beliefs.

It is important to realise that the *cognitive implications* of spiritual awakening can be for some shocking and threatening. Paradoxically, the better one has integrated Western social and cultural values such as individuality, autonomy, assertiveness, competitiveness, the more one's feelings of security, meaningfulness, and self-worth can be threatened. It can hardly fail to do so, even to those people who at the moment of their spiritual awakening respond positively, with joy and a feeling of 'This is IT!' Some will eventually leave such a period without outside help. Others get caught up in endless indecision or become disoriented. They will need help. Such help in principle should come from the church, but for the 'spiritual exiles' and those who have rejected their church this is usually not a realistic expectation. The question then arises: if such a cognitive conflict interferes with or stagnates therapeutic process, could psychotherapy then provide help to such people? Obviously, a therapy group is an appropriate place for acknowledging and exploring a strong *subjective* feeling. But is it also an appropriate place for evaluating the *truth* of spiritual knowledge? Would that not inevitably introduce endless theological and metaphysical discussions? The answer is yes and no. Yes, we *can* give substantial help to people struggling with such a cognitive inner conflict, and no, giving such help would *not* necessarily introduce intellectual discussions into the therapeutic interaction. But as with the existential aspect, *discernment* is needed to succeed in this. In Chapter 13 I have already pointed out that existential and spiritual concerns need to be sorted out from the psychological and that this often has to precede therapy. This also applies when the spiritual problem is whether or not to accept the content of illuminative experience. Therefore let us consider how spiritual discernment can be applied whenever a patient needs to solve an inner spiritual conflict at the cognitive level before he is able to proceed with his therapy.

8 Discernment at the cognitive level

In the context of a group therapy, when a group member is over-preoccupied with 'intellectual' matters, this is likely to be interpreted as a symptom of resistance to therapy. Yet in cases of prolonged indecision or disorientation as a result of an illuminative experience, it makes sense to distinguish ('discern') between resistance to therapy on the one hand and on the other an inner spiritual conflict.

In Chapter 14 I discussed such discernment at the *existential* level. I have explained there how, as a result of spiritual ambivalence and self-doubt, patients can become entrapped in a prolonged state of indecision about committing themselves to spiritual life. This is a major concern they need to solve before they can give their full attention to their therapeutic process. The therapist's interpretation of their preoccupation as resistance to therapy is decidedly unhelpful then. A comparable impasse may occur at the *cognitive* level. People then become entrapped in a prolonged state of indecision about whether or not to accept and integrate the content of their *illuminative* experience. As long as they have not resolved this problem, they are too preoccupied with it to become fully involved in therapy.

In such cases, it is often useful to apply the same strategy from spiritual direction as I suggested in Chapter 14 to do with existential indecision, i.e. to look at what is happening at the two interconnected levels of (un)willingness and cognition. In analysing the inner conflict about the acceptance of the content of illuminative experience in this way, we can distinguish between (at the level of cognition) doubt about the truth of the intuitive insight gained in illuminative experience ('*spiritual doubt*') on the one hand, and on the other hand (at the level of (un)willingness) a reluctance to give up established beliefs ('*resistance to spiritual truth*'), which is quite different from resistance against therapy. Or it could be *both*, i.e. resistance to giving up established beliefs reinforcing spiritual doubt by demanding ever more 'proofs' of ever more religious truth claims. When in tandem with an inner conflict at the *existential* level as discussed in Chapter 14, the two together make for quite a formidable source of spiritual resistance. 'I am willing to acknowledge that my longing for God is authentic, but I cannot take any action upon that because I cannot believe he really exists!' And so on, in many variations. In this way you can keep yourself endlessly undecided – and unhappy.

In the *initial* phase, such spiritual doubt and spiritual resistance are inherent in the process of spiritual awakening. They should be taken as a sign that the person involved in them is seriously seeking personal and intellectual integrity. If however the person is entrapped in a *prolonged* spiritual indecision of this type, particularly in the context of his needing to enter psychotherapy, then equating his preoccupation with spiritual knowledge with resistance to therapy may in fact divert attention from the real problem. Then it has to be taken as a sign that solving this indecision should precede therapy, just as existential conflicts quite often need to precede therapy (cf. Chapter 13). This brings us back to the question of how to deal with these types of prolonged after-effects of illuminative experience while staying within the competence of a therapist and while avoiding theological discussions in the context of a therapy session. With this question in mind, let us now consider spiritual doubt (a matter of cognition) and spiritual resistance (a matter of (un)willingness) separately.

9 Spiritual doubt

For dealing with spiritual doubt, a therapy group is obviously not the place to have discussions about the truth of illuminative experience. But if the person experiencing doubts about some spiritual insight he has intuited in an illuminative experience has no other place to turn to, a therapist could give some helpful suggestions. The key is, to acknowledge that it is quite sensible to doubt, that it is a matter of intellectual integrity, that it is much more sensible than either offhand rejecting one's own intuition or impulsively jumping aboard the first religious boat that happens to pass by. An example of the latter is the student of vignette 3, who impulsively joined a religious sect that took his passport away. At the very least, this sort of intervention could take away embarrassment about their preoccupation with such matters. Perhaps the information about 'broad theism' as a defendable conclusion from universal and cumulative experiential evidence could be supportive, showing them that they are not alone in this, and that belief in a spiritual reality is not necessarily subjective, irrational or arbitrary. And one could explain why a therapy group is not an appropriate place to figure this out, but encourage the person to talk about it with some good friends or a spiritual director or to read some good spiritual books.

Furthermore, the sensible course in such matters is to take the cognitive problem seriously, but not *too* seriously. It could help the patient if the therapist were to point this out. One does not need full-blown metaphysics and theology, nor absolute certainty. As in most change processes, many things simply cannot be known beforehand, because you lack the perspective that will result from the change. A spiritual journey has often been compared with climbing a mountain: starting in the valley you are not in a position to see what you will see from the top. But you will never see from the top unless you start at the bottom. What is needed for the initial decision is to know how strong and authentic your desire is, to know the general direction of the change process, and to decide about the general trustworthiness of your intuitive cognition. Certainly one needs some time for reflection and critical examination, but only to a certain extent. Beyond that it is an excuse for indecision.

10 Resistance to spiritual truth

After analysing the problem of prolonged spiritual doubt at the level of cognition, we shall now see how it looks at the level of (un)willingness. The question then becomes, if and to what extent the person in question is *resisting* the acceptance of spiritual truth. Such resistance has *psychological* sources and as such is relevant to therapy. The same mechanisms are probably at work in other areas as well. If it is really a case of spiritual resistance rather than intellectual doubt, then a therapy group could help the person to work it through without engaging in metaphysical discussions.

One such source of resistance is *fear of others*. Will they attack or ridicule me when I openly acknowledge it as true, when I decide to change my beliefs and my life accordingly? This fear is quite legitimate if people indeed risk losing their family and friends, in some cases even their jobs. Above anything else such a person needs support and a safe place to deal with his fear. Church members should be better off than unbelievers because they have accepted a religious worldview and are part of a religious community. But unfortunately teachings and culture in some of the churches are unsympathetic to individual religious experience. And not without reason: all through history the churches have known their share of dubious characters claiming to be in direct contact with God – sometimes with disastrous results.

Another common source of resistance is *rigidity*. Psychologically, the inner conflict is one of cognitive dissonance. Cognitive dissonance happens when one is confronted with evidence that contradicts one's firmest and most cherished beliefs, and that therefore is indeed difficult both to accept as true and to reject as untrue.[9] Accepting such evidence means rejecting these beliefs, which may be so threatening that people prefer to ignore the evidence or reject its validity. Cognitive dissonance is induced as a *therapeutic* method in feedback sessions. The person then receives information that contradicts his established beliefs about himself. This is very threatening, but in a therapeutic session he feels protected and knows that his acceptance of the evidence will be rewarded, so he can muster the courage to see whether it is true. His subsequent working at integrating this information may be an important step in his therapy.

The cognitive dissonance inherent in *spiritual* awakening, however, cuts much *deeper* than the one evoked in feedback sessions. The scope of the challenged beliefs is much broader. Beliefs about our own ultimate identity, about the physical world we are part of and deal with, and about the existence of a transcendent God communicating with us, sum up to our most fundamental orientation in life. A challenge to these beliefs puts into question everything one used to be certain of. Moreover, in illuminative experience the 'evidence' is not provided by other observers, but only in one's own momentary 'subjective' experience of illuminative insight. And for non-religious people there is not even a community of other believers to help evaluate this experiential insight. Later on, after people have committed themselves to spiritual change, they will be confronted again and again with such challenges to prior beliefs about self, about reality, about God.[10] But then it is probably less of a shock than the first time. Once they have found good spiritual direction, they will gradually learn *not* to identify with cognitive schemata, useful and necessary though these may be as pointers and stepping-stones to spiritual understanding. For growth to occur, it is vital to remain open to the dynamic unexpectedness of self, of life and, above all, of God.

Let me now summarise the discussion about the cognitive aspect of spirituality. For a spiritual relationship to be real and meaningful, at least *some* genuine knowledge of a real Transcendent Other is necessary. Therapists who are inclined to take distance from, or be dismissive of this 'object focused' character of spirituality may risk leaving their patient's core spirituality unexplored.

The analysis of illuminative religious experience shows that the processes involved in gaining spiritual insight are not as mysterious as they may first appear. Nor do they require, as this same analysis has shown, extrasensory or other extraordinary powers. The cognitive processes involved in spiritual development and in psychological development in therapy are surprisingly similar. In fact, the insight oriented psychotherapies involve fostering the same kind of mental flexibility that is conducive to illuminative spiritual experience and understanding. It follows from this that psychotherapy can (but may not always) catalyse illuminative spiritual learning and vice versa.

Given that the above is so, it can be relevant for the therapist to be deeply aware of which effects of religious experience can be positive and which negative. The positive ones include: strengthening and deepening of one's spiritual life, the finding of inner certainty and peace and the establishing of an inner touchstone that serves as a core of reassurance in periods of trial and even darkness. The negative ones include the emergence of: a personality crisis, a period of spiritual hypersensitivity, a too indulgent fascination with the religious experience *per se* or a too prolonged struggle for intellectual integrity before some decision is made or change committed to.

In principle, psychotherapy practice that has integrated this knowledge of both the positive and negative effects of religious experience can do so without tresspassing too deeply into the spiritual domain nor wandering too far away from the domain of psychotherapy.

Concluding Part 3

The basic argument in Part 3, 'Existential and cognitive aspects of spirituality', has been that the conditions created in therapy groups are conditions not only for *therapeutic* change, but also for *spiritual* change. In other words, group analysis may trigger off a process of spiritual awakening that may enlighten religious or non-religious participants. The same is true of other psychotherapies that create comparable conditions. If spiritual awakening indeed manifests itself in and through psychotherapy, then people within their particular therapeutic process are struggling with the major change and decision processes inherent in spiritual awakening. Once they become aware of what is happening to them in regards to these processes in the therapeutic setting and have committed themselves to some decision or change, they will be better able to understand and make their longing for spiritual life a reality.

Although learning and change in the world of spirituality does not always nor completely mirror the learning and change that ideally manifests itself in the psychotherapeutic process, it does so to a significant degree. In cases in which a 'religiously oriented patient' is involved, it can be important for the therapist to recognise in what respect there is a match and/or a mismatch between the two processes. In the interests of the patient and success of his therapy, he must be able to recognise in what aspects the spiritual and therapeutic processes do and do not parallel each other. Only then can he make valid interpretations of what he observes and hears. Only then can he, if it is necessary to do so, clarify for the patient what it is that deep down and albeit often confusedly he (the patient) is really seeking.

These differences are mainly caused by the fact that a spiritual involvement transcends any therapeutic endeavour. It transcends therapy in two ways. First, it is *contextual* to therapy. One's spiritual orientation determines what will count as a problem, as well as what kind of problem it is considered to be and what kind of options are available to solve it. Second, it transcends therapy because *struggling with the great questions of life is in and of itself not a symptom.* On the contrary, it is normal and worthwhile to engage in it. It could as easily be a signal that therapy can be terminated in the near future. The decisive question

193

is *how* people engage in it. It is important for a therapist to realise this and to understand what such people are after and how this may converge or diverge with therapy.

The preceding chapters have been rather elaborate about the struggles for *authenticity and intellectual integrity* that may follow the first stirrings of spiritual awakening. This is especially because these first stirrings may occur in the group and are therefore relevant. Moreover, in this very early stage people are likely to be both confused about what is happening to them and confusing to others as well. Besides, the non-religious generally are not yet ready at that stage to seek spiritual guidance.

The chapters have also elaborated on the 'change tasks' necessary for a wholehearted and realistic *commitment*. One of the most important tasks both for religious adherents and for 'spiritual exiles' is to take a well-considered decision whether or not to commit oneself to spiritual life. Some people have little or no problem in accomplishing this. For others it is an uphill battle. But evading commitment or getting blocked in indecision will have a negative impact both on therapy and on further spiritual development. It makes people more vulnerable for manipulation by dubious religious leaders, too. Moreover, an authentic and well-considered commitment is needed because, although spiritual life is experienced as deeply meaningful, it is generally not an easy life. Without a serious commitment, one will not be able to make sacrifices or to take a stand for the sake of one's involvement.

PART 4

Relational Aspects of Spirituality

Introducing Part 4

The chapters on existential and cognitive aspects of a spiritual change process focused only lightly on the learning and change that follows the decision of personal commitment to spirituality. But there is more which needs to be said about what follows after the initial struggle. Ideally the initial decision is followed by a lifelong relationship with the Divine. I have called such a relationship '*a spiritual relationship*'.

How people deal with their lives, what options are open to them for solving problems and conflicts, depends largely on *how they conceive and enact such a spiritual relationship*. This of course can vary significantly between individuals, and moreover may well change in substance and intensity during their lifetime. As the spiritual relationship is in fact a relationship with life itself, it has an enormous, though often unobserved, impact on how people relate not just to the Divine but also on how they relate to each other.

The next chapters now turn attention to *envisioning, creating and implementing a dynamic spiritual relationship between a particular person and God* and pose (implicitly or explicitly) questions on: what kind of relationship is this? How do people interpret their real life experiences in the light of how they relate with the Divine? What kind of care, affection and conscientiousness is put into it? And above all, in the context of the thesis at the heart of this book: where and how can such a spiritual relationship contribute to or detract from progress in a therapeutic setting?

In order to prevent misreading of the chapters which follow, I first want to highlight a difficulty one cannot avoid when one wants to approach spiritual life as a relationship.

Thinking about relationships, be they spiritual or not, has through the ages suffered from the Aristotelian presupposition that there are only two sorts of reality: substances and attributes. This kind of conceiving reality is also applied to human beings and has resulted in a persistent tendency to characterise human reality in terms of selves (substances) and attributes of selves.[1] In classic psychotherapeutic theory, as an example of this, this persistent tendency has prejudiced theorists into assuming that mental illness is an attribute of individuals. As a result, the focus is mainly on conflicts *within* the individual, caused by intrapsychic factors. Nowadays it becomes ever more clear how one-sided this approach really is. Bowlby, for example, points out that the idea that the adult need for others is a sign of individual regressive dependency is one of the most dangerous ideas promulgated by modern psychiatry.[2] Hassan, as another example, describes how this same conceptual conditioning has led to tragic misunderstanding of Holocaust survivors' needs.[3] Even the object relations theorists, who made relatedness prominent in their theories of human development, mostly designed their relational concepts to fit a model of development toward separation and individualism. Every day it becomes clearer, however, that in a very fundamental way we 'are' relationships or rather, we create our identities as we co-create relationships in combined interaction with others.

This inherited presupposition and its influence is reflected clearly in the literature on the subject of religion and spirituality. This accounts for the still current tendency to characterise spirituality as a feeling, or as a particular mode of experience, or as a disposition, or as an attitude, or as a special state of consciousness – in short, as an 'attribute' of a 'self'. My own view is that spirituality exists as a very special relationship – a personal involvement with the Divine. Stated formally, my position and point of departure is that the personal involvement with the Divine *can best be understood if we view it as a relationship that is continually co-created in the flow of intention, action, and response between people and God.*

Nevertheless I have to deal with the same inherited difficulty: in our language use we talk about a relationship as something you 'have', for example, an expression in which the inherited prejudice *is* already implied. That is why I am making this preliminary remark and why I ask you to keep this in mind when reading the chapters of Part 4. Otherwise the text is easily misread and misinterpreted.

CHAPTER 17

The Analysis of Spiritual Relationships

1 Spiritual and therapeutic relationships

At the outset of this discussion, I want to borrow a useful distinction from Hans Cohn. In his *Existential Thought and Therapeutic Practice*, he distinguishes between 'relatedness' and 'a relationship'.

'Related*ness*' he understands as an aspect of existence, because 'being' is always 'being-with-others': 'We are always in a relational field, in a state of intersubjectivity.'[1] It will be clear from reading the sections on 'foundation matrix' in Chapters 8 and 9, that group analytic theory is quite familiar with this idea.

On the other hand, 'a relation*ship*' is something specific that links people to each other. It can be present or lacking, it can be nourished or allowed to wither away, it can change because a change in one partner of the relationship can trigger change in the other(s) and vice versa.

When we apply these concepts defined by Cohn to characterise how people relate to the Transcendent, the concept of *spiritual relatedness* refers to our being in a state of intersubjectivity with the Transcendent, whether we realise it or not. And the concept of a *spiritual relationship* in this context then applies to the particular way in which individuals and communities construe their involvement with the Transcendent. The *connection* between 'spiritual relatedness' and 'a spiritual relationship' is that people first have to *become aware of their spiritual relatedness* before they are in a position to enter into a spiritual relationship. Spiritual relatedness and spiritual awakening are thus preconditions for *any* particular spiritual relationship. The psychology student's autobiography used in Chapter 12 (vignette 12) is a good example of this. He ends his notes with 'Now my longing for God has evolved into an intimate personal relationship.'

If we look at the chapters of Part 3 with this distinction in mind, the processes of self-discovery and illuminative cognition discussed there come down to *becoming aware of spiritual relatedness* and its implications. The decisions described there mark the transition from relatedness to *entering into a spiritual relationship* of one kind or another. The chapters of Part 4 are about the ways in which people implement this 'one kind or another', in other words, how they conceive and enact *their particular relationship* with the Divine, and how this may influence their therapy.

Implicit in this approach is the assumption that there *is* a God (a divine transcendent reality) and that there *can* be a spiritual relationship between God and humans. This also implies that intrapsychic phenomena like transference, internalised object relations, etc., though actually occurring in and sometimes interfering with a spiritual relationship, are *not* sufficient to describe it. These remarks are not to be read as downgrading the brilliant work on the development of internal God-representations done by object relations theorists, in particular by Rizzuto.[2] My point is that in psychotherapeutic *practice* it is necessary *not to restrict* oneself to internal representations. From a spiritual point of view these are indispensable for spiritual growth, but only because – and in so far that – they pave the way for getting to know, and to communicate with, God himself as he manifests himself in the Eucharist, in his self-revelation in the Scriptures, in prayer or otherwise. This may be contrary to what a therapist as a trained psychologist believes to be true, but here the point is not what therapists believe. The point is that this is the key to *understanding* spiritual people and to discerning in what ways *their* relationship with the Divine may be supportive, confusing or obstructive to their therapy (see the discussions of this subject in the Introduction and in Chapter 15, section 1).

Let us first look again at the message of the earlier chapters on the existential and cognitive aspects, but now from a relational point of view. These chapters discuss authentic longing for communion with the Transcendent Other, intuitive sensibility for the reality of his existence, and self-commitment to re-orient one's life accordingly. In *human* relationships, these constitute preconditions from which a profound personal relationship may develop over time. Whether this really happens, however, depends on the quality and mutuality of the subsequent interaction. Likewise in *spiritual* life such authentic spiritual longing, illuminative understanding, and sincere self-commitment as described there may give rise to a profound spiritual relationship. But again, whether this actually happens depends on the honesty, the receptivity, the respect, the care, the affection, the persistent devotion, and other such qualities people bring to the spiritual relationship. As in human relationships, it takes time and effort to cultivate such capacities in a spiritual relationship –as it takes time and effort to 'unlearn' (or 'purify from') psychological obstacles like self-centredness, possessiveness, manipulation, and so on. In other words, a crucial part of the relational capacities people are supposed to learn and to practise in a spiritual relationship overlaps what patients need to learn and to practise if they are ever to have satisfying human relationships.

Because of this sort of overlap, what is relevant to furthering the progress of spiritual development can be equally relevant for furthering progress in and for success of therapeutic intervention. Learning to relate more authentically and with more intuitive understanding of the other in human relationships can transfer to the spiritual relationship. And vice versa. This is equally so when considering the negative influences on progress in either. For example, things of negative influence in a human relationship can transfer to the spiritual relationship (potential or actual and at whatever stage it is) and be of negative influence there. And vice versa. Awareness of what such positive or negative influences are and how they operate in the context of relationships, is an important asset in a therapist's 'discernment armoury'.

We may thus conclude that it should not be too difficult for therapists to accommodate for spiritual concerns in their own therapeutic work – that is if they believe it is important to do so and if they want to do so. As an example of how this can be done in a simple way, they could, after having worked through dysfunctional ways of relating to each other, encourage their patients to ask themselves whether the same dysfunctional mechanism which they had just explored could also be operative in their personal relationship with God. If it should be so then reflecting on that question could lead to quite a fruitful turn in one's spiritual life. If it is not, raising the question and reflecting on it could at least have the advantage that patients know that spirituality is a normal subject to raise in the context of a therapy. And after all is a therapy not pre-eminently the place to put forward self-reflective questions?

Yet the relationship with God is only *in part* comparable with interpersonal relationships. There are also differences between the two and in these other aspects the two relationships diverge. It is important for therapist and patient to be aware of such differences, for example when in the context of their spiritual relationship people are trying to learn humility or self-denial, whereas in that particular phase of their therapy it is essential for them to learn to stand up for themselves. When a patient as a part of his spiritual practice makes every effort to learn humility while at the very same moment the therapist assumes he must learn the opposite, the only result is likely to be confusion on both sides. Vignette 14, the 'transcendental' anorexic, for example, could easily have caused this type of confusion if her therapist had not been aware of her spiritual motivation.

To make matters even more complicated, some types of spiritual relationships are downright opposite to therapeutic goals. Then there is a conflict. This type of conflict will be discussed in the next chapter.

In short, in so far as the relational goals and aims of therapy and spirituality converge, both activities are mutually supportive. In so far as they diverge, they are likely to cause confusion in therapy unless they are discerned as such and appropriate attention given them. In the rest of this chapter I shall explore the implications of such convergence and divergence. Starting with convergence, the next three sections will look at three important relational qualities people need to learn *both* in human and in spiritual relationships: receptivity, inwardness and trust.

2 Learning receptivity

Caroline Garland in her article 'Group-analysis: taking the non-problem seriously' suggests that change is a necessary precondition for therapeutic change.[3] She proposes that if, and only if, change has been initiated in the individual, therapeutic method may be able to make any such change into a change for the better. This is why it makes sense to analyse the therapeutic process in terms of two coexisting factors: the producer of change and the therapeutic transmutation of this change into change-for-the-better. In group analysis this initiator of change is, in her view, the substitution of the 'non-problem' for the 'problem'. Each individual has qualified for therapy because of a serious problem, and is initiated into group membership by presenting this problem to the others. Yet in a surprisingly short while this problem is dropped and replaced by passionate involvement with the shifting roles, relationships and behavioural communications that make up the system of the group itself. This is what Garland means by saying that the person's problem is exchanged for the non-problem of becoming absorbed in the here-and-now of the group itself. According to her, this process alone, that of becoming totally wrapped up in the group, is sufficient to effect change, that in turn is the foundation stone upon which therapeutic change is constructed.

This element of becoming totally engrossed is equally important for a spiritual relationship. True involvement in the other demands the capacity to withhold, at least temporarily, your own preoccupations and interests in order to pay full attention to the other or others. This is also true in the relationship with God. Therefore one precondition for relating to the Transcendent is to develop the ability to pay full and open attention to its manifestations and communications. In the Christian tradition '*contemplation*' means a wordless prayer, in which you 'forget yourself' because you are paying full attention to God as he manifests himself at the actual moment to such an extent that you may become totally absorbed in it. It grows on the art of 'forgetting' current preoccupations while paying full attention to the Other. This kind of prayer is the exact opposite of any prayer in which God is seen as a background for one's own concerns. (When reading Christian spiritual literature, one has to keep in mind that the term 'contemplation' often refers to a comparable practice to what is translated from Buddhist spiritual literature as 'meditation'. 'Meditation' in a Christian spiritual context usually refers to prayer with the aid of words and symbols or to meditative reflection on scriptural passages; see also Chapter 7.)

Spiritual change is partly a matter of learning this kind of patient dedication. Most spiritual traditions have developed methodologies to train people to turn 'outwards' in this sense. Many exercises and practices are designed to develop this capacity to become fully attentive without interference or distortion by personal worries, dreams, interests, even by your own spiritual longing. The training for such a receptive attitude usually starts very simply. For example, it may begin with some receptive activity people already enjoy, such as listening to music, using that as a stepping stone for gradually acquiring the capacity of paying full undivided and unrestricted attention to what envelops you right now.

By training such spiritual receptiveness one gradually learns to recognise the many subtle signs by which God communicates himself – in nature, in people's hearts, in Scripture, in liturgy, in the events of one's life history – everywhere. The change people undergo in their spiritual life ('transformation' in traditional language use) is partly the result of this learning process on the person.

Because it is so basic, training for receptivity can be found almost universally in otherwise divergent spiritual traditions. The practice of silence and solitude is one example of such a training technique. The use of the mantra as a tool for training receptivity in Hindu spirituality is another example. Orthodox Christianity has a comparable practice, the 'art' (as it is traditionally called) of the Jesus prayer. It is to repeat the name of Jesus or a short and simple formula including the name of Jesus, always with inner attention and concentration, but at the same time without any sense of strain – no self-induced intensity or artificial emotion! Gradually the simple attentive saying of the word(s) grows more interior, till the person 'stands before God' with 'his mind in his heart'. To put it in modern terms: till the whole personality is fully open and receptive to God.[4]

As receptivity is also basic for human relationships, therapy and spiritual direction have parallel interests in it. In fact some therapies have borrowed and adapted techniques from spiritual traditions, and vice versa. And as far as group analysis is concerned, the meaning of spiritual terms like 'self-forgetfulness', 'self-surrender', 'losing yourself', 'emptying yourself' or 'becoming absorbed' is strikingly similar to what Garland says about total involvement in an all-important relationship as it is lived here and now, and 'forgetting' all other preoccupations – among which the one that made you enter psychotherapy.

3 Learning inwardness

A complementary capacity needed for any enduring intimate relationship is the ability to *let yourself be known by the other*. Again the key is the ability to pay full attention, but now to what is going on *inside* yourself. This is essential for an intimate relationship: you 'give yourself' to the other, that is, your most intimate feelings, thoughts, dreams, and so on. Sharing your inner self is what it takes to make a relationship intimate and meaningful. Such sharing presupposes *noticing* and *expressing* yourself as much and as honestly as possible. In the context of spiritual learning this emphatically includes noticing and expressing how one responds to God. Paradoxically, religion may be an obstacle in this. Many people are taught that only certain attitudes, feelings and responses are appropriate when expressing themselves in prayer. As a result they tend to suppress or reject as sinful any 'indecent' feelings or 'disrespectful' ways of expression. But it is well known that any withholding of a 'secret' impedes relationships, even if the secret is quite trivial. This is also true in the spiritual relationship, even though God is supposed to know everything about you. The point is not about *informing* God about your secrets, it is about the *degree and quality of sharing* you put into the spiritual relationship.

This paying full attention to what is going on introspectively has yet another critical function in the spiritual change process: uncovering ever-new forms of resistance. In Chapters 14 and 16, I pointed out that at that initial stage there is often as much willingness as there is a simultaneous *un*willingness to commit oneself to spiritual change. In the analysis of vignette 14, the case of the 'transcendental anorexic', we have also seen how giving up resistance at one level does in fact shift the resistance to another level without the person being aware of it. Actually dealing with spiritual unwillingness is to be compared to peeling an onion: removing one layer exposes the next. The 'skins' of our souls are much more multi-layered than onions, so the job seems to be endless. By far the best way to detect the many subtle and shifting forms of self-absorption and self-protection is paying attention to the ongoing drama of feelings, emotions, dialogues and intrigues in your internal theatre – and to the self-descriptive stories you tell other people, which are more often than not defensive and concealing instead of true self-expressions. Before you realise it, your prayer becomes nothing more than telling God and yourself these very same defensive stories!

It is by no means easy to learn the contemplative attitude towards your inner life, which is needed for discerning ever deeper and subtler forms of unwillingness. Honesty and courage are required, of course, but also the art of detaching yourself from your feelings, thoughts and emotions. You have to give full freedom to your responses, but at the same time not allow yourself to become fully absorbed in them. Otherwise you will not be able to 'see' yourself by simultaneously scanning the whole intricate scene without switching off the painful and the unexpected. Many spiritual exercises are designed to train this capacity. Many teachings are meant to create a safe mental space for self-confrontation, emphasising, for example, that God already knows and has pardoned any shameful things that may surface, that human nature is created essentially good, even God-like, and through grace can be restored to this state, so that cowardice, deceit, egocentricity and the like are never the ultimate truth about self.

Any group analyst knows how important it is to register his own inner reactions to what is going on. His own inner response is a powerful means for gaining insight into what is happening in the group. He also knows how difficult it is to develop this means. It requires rigorous honesty to recognise and acknowledge one's uncalled for responses. It also requires a long training to learn how to become fully involved in the group while simultaneously being fully aware of your responses, and to recognise which of your responses are actually signals from the group unconscious. *Mutatis mutandis* this is also true of the other analytically oriented psychotherapists. This is very similar to what spiritual traditions try to teach and train.

Another building stone for spiritual change is: paying the same kind of attention to what you are *doing* and *how* you are doing it. Nothing is exempted from that attention, nothing is too trivial. More often than not everyday routine activities like peeling potatoes are examples of the thoughtless, loveless way you deal with life itself, precisely because you take such activities so much for granted. The very way you hold the potato and the knife may speak of a very small world, with you in the centre and in control, every meaning restricted to what is useful to you. How much irritation, having to do such chores, is there in your cutting? How much of a self-evident birthright is it to you to be fed? If you try to change from this narrow perspective to the larger one, the perspective of the whole you are part of, how does that change the way you handle the knife, hold the potato?

Thomas Merton points this out in an essay about spiritual direction and meditation. Emphasising that the spiritual life is the life of the *whole* person, however simple that life may be, he quotes an anecdote about a Russian *starets* (spiritual director) who was criticised for spending time seriously advising an old peasant woman about the care of her turkeys. The *starets* denied that taking care of turkeys is irrelevant for spiritual life, and answered the pious faultfinders, 'Her *whole* life is in those turkeys!'[5]

In this respect, too, spirituality and therapy run parallel: therapists are also paying attention to the language of action. They pay attention to what is said and done, to how it is said and done. They try to see the perspective it expresses, and how this relates to the whole. However, in therapy certain areas are selected, depending on the therapeutic goal, whereas in spirituality *nothing* is excluded because everything expresses one's fundamental attitude.

4 Learning trust

The most crucial factor in any personal relationship is mutual trust. Without at least a minimum level of trust you will hold back and not fully share yourself – which comes down to not being fully trustworthy yourself, as well. Therefore it is a vital issue both in psychotherapy and in spiritual change. Just as one has to trust the authenticity of one's own spiritual True Self, one also needs to trust God, if the courage for total commitment and openness to him is to be found. In religious language use this spiritual trust and trustworthiness is often expressed in terms of 'having faith' and 'being faithful'.

This trust has to have a certain quality too. Blind trust, for example, would not be a sound basis for establishing a loving relationship. Examining the other's trustworthiness is important, whether the other is human or divine. This is why, for example, the Bible is so full of stories establishing the trustworthiness of God in and through the history of Israel. Another quality the trust has to have is that it should be unconditional and non-manipulative. 'I only trust you if...', or 'I trust you because you have the power to...', does not indicate the kind of trust a personal relationship flourishes on. Relational trustworthiness is rooted in the intrinsic qualities of each other.

We know from therapy how many people have psychological difficulties in trusting others. They probably have the same difficulties in trusting God, particularly in the early stages of their spiritual relationship. Or it may be the other way round: a basic distrust in God may easily cause a person to distrust others. So for a therapist this is another area where discernment is required, and where it may make sense to allow the underlying spiritual conflict to emerge.

You cannot 'examine' the trustworthiness of God directly, as you can test an employee's honesty. As people advance in their spiritual development, they may experience his trustworthiness personally, but in the earlier stages they often need the help of reliable people who are willing to tell them about their own experiences or have written these down. However, Churches, and even Scriptures, have lost their self-evident credibility, even much of their intelligibility. For many people raised on the religious teaching of the trustworthy Biblical God, it is still difficult to trust him wholeheartedly. To a large extent this is a cultural problem, as tragic historical experience has made us wary of all authorities and ideologies claiming to be pre-eminently trustworthy. Too many leaders and movements, all promising spiritual happiness, have proven to be disastrous. So we ask ourselves, whom can we trust for conveying reliable information? In spite of all their mistakes, I personally still think the major religions are the best sources. They are based on the cumulative experience of a multitude of reliable witnesses confirming the basic trustworthiness of the Transcendent. When people say they trust the God of Abraham, the God of Moses, the God of Jesus or the God of Muhammad, they do more than to consider that Abraham, Moses, Jesus or Muhammad are reliable persons. They *also* put their trust in the cumulative experience of this God, documented by numerous reliable witnesses through the ages.

In the capacity to trust, we find again a common precondition in psychotherapy and spiritual learning. This is thus an area where both may affect each other. In psychotherapy the basic attitude of mistrust is often a personality problem based upon experiences of betrayal by significant others. One such significant other may be God, or rather, an immature or naïve image of God. Or the significant other may be a real father, and the distrust of him transferred to God the Father. As a patient's ability to engage in a trusting relationship increases, this may increase his trust in God as well. In the same way a block to trusting God may be the underlying cause of a block in establishing a trusting therapeutic relationship.

5 Convergence between therapeutic and spiritual change

A spiritual relationship needs at least a minimum of the same personal capacities that are needed for establishing and maintaining satisfying personal relationships. It depends for its growth on the continual development of these capacities. In this respect, therapeutic and spiritual progress have much in common. Both depend on nurturing one's ability to commit oneself to meaningful, honest and trusting relationships. Any spiritual practice or exercise aimed at developing these capacities is in principle relevant for aiding therapeutic progress and vice versa. Equally so, defence mechanisms resisting change in one of these worlds are likely to be present and contribute to resistance to change and progress in the other. Nor is it difficult to see that the capacities needed to give more depth and meaning to a personal relationship with God are the same capacities needed to foster and improve a meaningful relationship between two or more persons at the psychological level. A preparedness to listen to the other, a willingness to express and share one's inner thoughts and feelings, awareness of each partner of the positive and negative factors operating in their interactions, a readiness to trust and be personally trustworthy, and being committed to change are all 'personal attributes' that spiritual practice and therapeutic practice are designed to engender.

Just as in the course of psychotherapy your clinging to another person for selfish reasons may change into perceiving and loving him as the person he is in and for himself, so an ego-centered attitude towards God may change into loving him for what he is. And this is what Christian spirituality is all about. As Jeffner puts it, 'the essential point [of the doctrine of salvation] is that the goal of salvation is *spiritual communion* - communion with God. This communion is characterised by mutual love and corresponds to our relations to each other in ordinary life'.[6] We should therefore not be too surprised when psychotherapy acts not only as a trigger for spiritual awakening (as we saw in Part 3), but also as a catalyst for further spiritual learning, just as it may be a trigger and a catalyst for a change from immature to mature love and altruism in human relationships. So there is reason to suppose that growth in psychotherapy will have a positive impact on spiritual growth, and that spiritual growth will have a positive impact on psychotherapy.

There is much more to say about the convergence between the learning processes in the context of psychotherapy and those in the spiritual change process. I shall return to the subject in Chapter 22.

6 Divergence between therapeutic and spiritual change

The important overlaps between therapeutic and spiritual change sketched above should not obscure the fact that there are also crucial *differences* between therapeutic improvement and spiritual change. At vital points the goal of spiritual maturity diverges from the goal of psychological health as it is viewed in most psychotherapies. There is nothing wrong with that; it has to do with the fact that the aims of institutionalised professional psychotherapy do not coincide with the spiritual aim of a life in communion with God. Moreover, the relationship with God is also significantly different from human relationships, which implies that people also need to learn different relational capacities from those sought after in therapy. So it is quite conceivable that, at a certain point in their spiritual change process, spiritual people are trying to learn relational capacities, for example self-sacrifice, which are contrary to what would be the responsible thing to learn at that point in their therapy, for example to stand up for themselves. Unless this difference in learning goals is recognised and talked through by both parties, such a situation will be utterly confusing. Even more confusing are people who use the group interaction to exercise these capacities. They are then not sincerely expressing themselves, but rather using the group as a training ground for their spiritual aspirations.

In what respects are spiritual relationships different from interpersonal relationships and therefore requiring different relational capacities?

One obvious difference with a human relationship is that *God is holy, sacred.* Personal and intimate as your spiritual relationship may be, you do not deal with God as with a school friend you knew when he was a child. You communicate with him in an atmosphere of reverence and worship. Moreover, your communication with him is not restricted to moments of verbal prayer. Your whole active life is a life 'with God', or 'before God' as well. Because a spiritual relationship is the overall context within which people live their lives, even the most ordinary actions get a flavour of sacredness and carry an extra spiritual meaning.

This has consequences for the way people relate to others. All dealings with other people acquire an element of sacredness as well. Not that as you spiritually grow you start worshipping or idealising others, but you treat them more conscientiously and respectfully. Even if you don't, you are at least aware you should. In itself this need not be a problem in a therapy group, but what may cause confusion is that in a life 'before God' *the standards are much higher* and people *worry much more about it.* For anybody using 'ordinary' standards, the former seem to 'overdo' it. Their behaviour is therefore easily mistaken for neurotic perfectionism. Which indeed in specific cases it may be, but not necessarily so. In a sense one could say that in a group therapy context God is an extra member in the group, introducing an extra voice to the complexity of multiple relationships already present. *Mutatis mutandis* this can also be said of individual psychotherapy, where the therapeutic dyad can become essentially a triad. Sometimes this extra voice makes itself heard to all of those present, for example when we sense the sanctity of the other person, or when the group itself takes on an atmosphere of reverence.

Another effect of the ambition to live 'with God' is *a preoccupation with morality.* Spiritual people understand the meaning of their lives in the light of the way they relate to God. Ultimate meaningfulness consists in being in the right relation with God. This relationship is disrupted through sin. One fundamental religious issue all spiritual people have to face is to be honest about sin, and to do their very best to restore the relationship whenever it is disrupted. Therefore they feel a much greater responsibility than ordinary life requires. One element of spiritual practice is to keep your conscience alert by examining your behaviour and intentions on a daily basis. One learning goal is increasing and refining your moral sensitivity. *This creates a continuous concentration on how to deal with guilt and guilt feelings, remorse, penitence, punishment, reconciliation, and forgiveness.* This outlook in spiritual practice is contrary to a tendency in therapeutic thought to consider such worries as the demands of a domineering superego. But the superego is precisely a mechanism from which one needs to be 'purified' if spiritual growth is to happen. This is why traditional theology has again and again opposed the ever-emerging 'theology of merit' (the idea that you can achieve your own salvation by a high output of good works), which feeds the superego (cf. Chapter 21, section 3). God is definitely *not* superego. He is rather a loving and compassionate transcendent Other to whom the person responds from his heart. The risk of neurotic scrupulosity is always present, of course, but it should be carefully distinguished from the inherent moral seriousness of spiritual life.[7]

Another difference has to do with *dependence.* Any intimate loving relationship makes your own happiness to a large degree dependent on the other partner. But in a spiritual relationship you are not only emotionally dependent on the other. You are dependent for your very existence, your survival, your humanity, your spirituality. In that sense, the relationship with the Divine is infinitely more asymmetric than any asymmetric human relationship. Moreover, it not only requires acknowledgement of this dependence as a matter of fact, but also requires you to be ever more willing to *become ever more dependent*. I have already discussed this aspect in the section about wilfulness and willingness (Chapter 14, section 6). Here I mention it only because people who are practising or *training to develop* capacities such as dependence, surrender, obedience, humility, 'dying to the self' and self-sacrifice, are confusing in any therapy that implicitly advocates the opposite. They are likely to be interpreted as resisting therapy, whereas in fact therapy unwittingly thwarts their legitimate spiritual learning efforts.

The last difference I want to point to here is *coping with suffering and evil*. Engaging in a spiritual relationship makes sense only if you believe God is good. Expressing gratitude for his goodness is one ever-recurring element in religious prayer, hymns and liturgy. But how are you to express gratitude in the middle of human misery and evil? Understandably, this creates an area of enormous tension. Pargament has written an excellent overview, based on extensive research, of how people cope with this tension: to avoid hypocrisy and artificiality, spiritual people need to work at *(re-)interpreting their spiritual relationship* in such a way that it does not contradict the goodness of God. To them, this is an integral and indispensable part of their working through trauma and crisis. Such (re-)interpreting, too, can easily be misinterpreted as rationalisation or resistance.[8]

7 The need for discernment

In cases where the above parallels and differences between spiritual and therapeutic learning look like a possible source of confusion, a critical thing is to avoid or resolve any misunderstanding between therapist and patient. For this the patient and the therapist need to become aware of the underlying difference between their aims and purposes and bring it into the open. This is not always easy, but even if it is clear what the patient is seeking, a therapist may still need sensitive discernment to assess whether or not the patient is using his spiritual process to resist therapy. The above sections are there to provide the therapist with some insights that can be helpful for this type of discernment. Let me now give just one example of how ambiguous such a situation may be, both on the side of the therapist and on that of the patient:

For their research on religious coping with grief, Cook and Wimberley selected a sample as homogeneous as possible. Their subjects were all parents who had lost a child as a result of either cancer or blood disorders. Most of these couples were white, married, employed, Protestant, had a high school education or more, and lived in the same geographical area. Yet their religious responses varied widely. Some parents believed that they would be reunited with their child in heaven, others that the child's death was a punishment for their own sins (cf. vignette 11), still others that the death of their child served a noble and divine purpose, and so on.[9] In Chapters 19–22 I shall return to this variety of spiritual relationships; here I want only to point out that each one of these interpretations and subsequent convictions is compatible with the religion these people shared. Furthermore, none of them is in and of itself *inadequate* for religious coping with grief. This is even so in the case of the punishment variant which at first sight would look particularly questionable. (NB: In Chapters 9 and 10 I commented on this conviction in the context of explaining how *metaphors* function or actually dysfunction, *here* I use this conviction for another purpose, i.e. showing how many ambiguities can be involved in *discernment* in the aforementioned cases.) The conviction that the loss of a child is a punishment for real or imagined sins *may* easily be a rationalisation of neurotic guilt feelings. Yet it could as easily be that these parents are honestly facing their *real* guilt 'before God' because of *real* sins they have committed, and are trying to restore the broken relationship with him. Then they need to be helped to separate their dealing with their mourning from their dealing with remorse and penitence, as discussed in the commentary on vignette 11. If however people are not rationalising neurotic guilt feelings, but are sincerely preoccupied with wanting to do penance for their sins, then their motivation could *again* be ambiguous. It could either be a tranquilliser to alleviate guilt, or an expression of true sorrow and a genuine desire for restoring communion with God – or both. Similarly, the other two variants in this example from Cook and Wimberley's research (hope of reunion and noble acceptance) may equally be motivated by an effort to deny the pain as it may be an expression of real hope and meaning right in the epicentre of real suffering.

The major difficulty for conducting this type of discernment is that therapeutic theory has never developed *criteria* for evaluating spiritual motivation, interpretation and re-interpretation. Since Freud, therapeutic thinking tends to view *all* religious motivation and interpretation as rationalisation and a flight from reality. Any *re*-interpretation in order to integrate major life crises is then automatically labelled a further proof of this. In this way of thinking critical assessment *within* this area would be superfluous. But this is to overlook the difference between rationalisation and what Smith coined '*living reason*'. 'Rationalisation' means: *mis*using your rational capacity to avoid pain or shame. 'Living reason' means: using your rational capacity to integrate your life experiences. We tend to think that 'rational' means: to start with what is universal, common to many people, and from there to proceed by logical thought to a valid conclusion. All the rest is considered to be irrational, or misuse of reason as in rationalisation, or – at best – intuition. However, this is to overlook 'living' reasoning which in fact all of us use frequently (therapists in particular), and which is a vital cognitive process both in psychotherapy and in spirituality. Such reasoning starts with one's own direct experience and proceeds from there by tracing out the patterns implicit in it, all the while living in and through that experience. The whole self is engaged in this type of thought, which is more configurational than linear. That is why its conclusions persuade and convince the whole person. In Chapter 9, for example, I mentioned that some people make sense of their lives by regarding themselves as prisoners. It is rarely if ever helpful to use logical arguments to get them off this track. Much more helpful is to help them ask reflexive questions about their own direct experience, encouraging them to seek for other patterns in their own experience. In doing so, they use 'living reason'. If in the course of therapy such a patient changes that view into a healthier one, this is the result of essentially the same process as when religious people seek for a valid religious re-interpretation to make sense of their experience. Rationalisation may happen, of course, but it is not rationalisation *per se*. It is to be hoped that they are instead using their 'living reason' as honest and whole persons.[10]

8 Finding balance in therapy and spirituality

Turning now to the question how these aspects of spiritual learning relate to therapeutic goals, I think these tensions are rather a matter of balance than of real contradiction. Take the issue of dependence, for example. Of course therapy should encourage independence when confronted with overdependent patients. So it is quite understandable that working towards more independence has become a valid therapeutic goal. However, too much independence is also dysfunctional. Dependence is an undeniable fact of life we all have to come to terms with. So the proper therapeutic goal is rather finding the right balance between dependence and independence. But a therapist by definition has to deal with people who in all kinds of respects cannot find the right balance. Moreover, being over-dependent usually causes more trouble than the other way round. So it is obvious that a therapist will have to deal more often with too much dependency than with too much independency. On the other hand, spiritual people indeed need to learn to be dependent on God, but that does not imply that they should act equally dependently toward other human beings. On the contrary, Jesus and the great prophets are examples of God-dependent and man-independent characters. In other words, both psychotherapy and spirituality seek the same goal, i.e. to find the right balance, to know when it is appropriate to be dependent and when not. And most important: to know which situations you may use for training dependency and which not – among which is the therapeutic situation.

To sum up, the areas of convergence and divergence discussed above are vitally important issues in spiritual life. Therapists who want to understand spiritual people need to know about their struggles and conflicts with these issues. Insight into such struggles and conflicts is also indispensable for discernment. For example, are patients in the context of their spiritual change process in reality trying to develop *other types of* relational capacities than those advocated in therapy? If so, are they doing that adequately or neurotically? Or are they using spirituality to resist the demands of therapy? Or are they using therapy to resist the demands of spirituality?

   To be more precise, the therapist needs to discern between the following:

1.   behaviour that is authentically motivated by the ideals of spirituality, ideals which are generally much *higher* than the ideals in everyday relationships, and which are in part *different* from therapeutic ideals;

2.   behaviour motivated by the authentic wish to *train* for attaining some high spiritual ideal such as, for example, learning to sacrifice oneself on behalf of others as Jesus sacrificed himself on behalf of the whole world, or learning to detach oneself from all 'worldly' concerns (as long as someone is *training* one is not behaving spontaneously, therefore training of such behaviour does not belong *per se* in a therapy group where the intention is to have everybody behaving and responding spontaneously and to work with such spontaneous manifestations);

3.   behaviour motivated by escapism, manipulation, resistance, etc., which has nothing to do with spirituality but everything with *using* spirituality for one's own ends;

4. behaviour of people who are not involved in a personal spiritual relationship with God but at the *existential level* authentically express the same high ideals, for example sacrificing themselves on behalf of a handicapped child like the scientist-mother in vignette 13.

CHAPTER 18

Spirituality as a Negative Therapeutic Factor

1 Conflict between therapeutic and spiritual change

After concentrating on how the learning goals of spirituality and of many psychotherapies may converge and diverge, we now turn to the fundamental conflicts between the two. In the preceding chapters I have already discussed quite a few conflicts and tensions. Let me summarise these before turning to those I want to discuss here.

Essentially, the conflicts discussed earlier fall into two categories. The first category consists of conflicts between (sub)cultures with different plausibility structures and mutual prejudices, stereotypes and ignorance. Examples are vignette 2, a patient and a therapist who were both afraid that such a conflict would happen in the therapy group; vignettes 4 and 5, people seeing visions and hearing voices, illustrating how secular culture makes people suspicious of conversion experiences, visions and messages from God, which a spiritual framework often accepts as legitimate or even normative; and vignettes 6 and 7 about the businessman and Tolstoy illustrating how easily spiritual darkness may be mistaken for a depression. Part 2 discussed the cultural character of this category of conflicts. Its chapters explained how the spiritual and the secular-ised modes of experiencing, conceptualising and communicating can be viewed as (at least) two subcultures, each with its own plausibility structure. They also drew attention to the influence of root metaphors and to phenomena of metacommunication and metatransference which may easily occur in such conflict situations. The basic approach to conflicts of this type is, in my opinion, to bring the cultural background of such a conflict out into the open whenever it actually occurs, so that it stays connected to the form it assumes in a real therapeutic situation.

The second category consists of conflicts originating from childish, rigid, egocentric or manipulative traits in the person's spiritual life. Problems originating from restrictive metaphors that have been made absolute and thereby become closed systems are also in this category. Vignette 11, the woman who interpreted the death of her child as God's punishment for adultery, was used to illustrate this. The cognitive habits and the attitudes involved in this category are quite probably pervasive and therefore part of a person's interpersonal problems as well. Whenever this is indeed the case, problems of this category can be approached at the interpersonal level. Afterwards, a well-chosen open question may confront the person with the possibility that he may do exactly the same things towards God as he does towards himself and others. To discern problems of this category and to find adequate interventions, I suggest a therapist ask himself about the underlying attitude rather than about the content of the patient's spirituality, using questions such as:

1. How does the person *construe* his religion and/or spirituality? As a closed or an open system? One-sided or balanced? Rigid or flexible?

2. How does the person *use* his spirituality in his approach to *others*? Positively, for example, trying to be as loving or as fair as he can? Or negatively, for example, manipulating others or allowing himself to be manipulated by others? Or assuming a 'holier-than-thou' attitude? Concentrating exclusively on the salvation of his own precious soul?

3. How does the person *use* his spirituality in his approach to *his own problems*? Positively, for example, by coping effectively with his problems? Or negatively, for example, by misusing it as resistance against therapy?

Let us now carry the discussion further to a third category of conflicts, namely conflicts in which not the underlying attitudes, but the *content* of a person's theology is obstructive to the aims and goals of psychotherapy. To what extent and in what way would it be helpful to take a relational view on such problems? Let me introduce the problem with an example.

2 Who is afraid of theology?

Vignette 17

The war between Sandinistas and Contras in Nicaragua in the 1980s resulted in more than fifty thousand deaths and seventy thousand invalids in a population of less than four million inhabitants. Many non-invalid survivors are still war victims because they are unable to cope with their war memories. Consuela Ruiz, one of the psychologists trying to help these people, says these victims are not always easy to recognise as such. Most traumas show themselves indirectly: mothers suddenly getting psychosomatic complaints after their sons' deaths, men who start drinking, demobilised soldiers prone to violence against their own families.

When treating victims of war it is striking that male patients have much more difficulty in talking about their experiences than females. According to Mirna Rocha, another psychologist, this is caused by the indigenous culture of 'machismo'. Another observation is that Protestants have more trouble in coming out with their war memories than others. This is probably due to the so-called 'cheerful theology' popular with Nicaraguan Protestants. Consuela Ruiz: 'In therapy we often meet this "cheerful theology", which can considerably obstruct a patient's coming to terms with his traumas. This is why more often than not we start our psychotherapy with a number of Bible studies in which other theological views are offered. For many patients it is quite a surprise to discover that Jesus also had feelings and emotions, that he could become mad, or sad, and that he complained on the cross. Another surprise may be that the God of the Bible is not only revengeful, angry, or almighty, but also loving, compassionate and empathic. It may be an unorthodox way to start a therapy, but we have obtained good results with it."

Think about this for a moment. Would you, as therapist, introduce Bible studies in your sessions under such circumstances? Why would you do that, or why not? And if not, how then would you deal with this situation?

The Nicaraguan situation is exceptional, but what to do in ordinary heterogeneous therapy sessions? How to approach, for example, an incest victim believing the Bible demands absolute obedience to her father? What to do once you discover their particular theology is a major obstruction to therapeutic progress? Take your hat off to her belief because one has to respect other people's religion? Write such patients off as untreatable? Try to change their theology? Refer to their pastor who in fact may be the very person who preaches these obstructive ideas all the time? In such situations, what is the meaning and the function of the unwritten agreement to respect every group member's religion? This is a serious dilemma. On the one hand, criticising or correcting other people's theology is outside the province and competence of psychotherapy, while on the other hand, it may at any given moment appear to be particularly helpful to therapy to do just that. Since the dilemma may arise at any moment, whether the therapist acknowledges it or not, it seems wise to think about such a religion-related problem beforehand. This is especially so if you are open to the idea of allowing spiritual concerns to be expressed in your therapy groups or, as DSM-IV suggests, even of treating problems related to religion and spirituality.[2]

In my view a therapist need not be caught in the above dilemma. I would suggest that even in these difficult cases he can offer substantial help by concentrating on the *relational qualities* implied in the theology that appears to be the source of the problem. But before turning to issues of therapeutic strategy, let me first explain the connection between a spiritual relationship and some specific theology.

3 What is the connection between a spiritual relationship and a specific theology?

For acting meaningfully and appropriately in human relationships, we all depend on background information as well as on a conceptual framework. This is true for all meaningful action, and no less true for action as part of a spiritual relationship. Therefore, when people commit themselves to a spiritual relationship, they are inevitably confronted with many more, and much more specific, questions than those discussed in the preceding chapters. What is the nature of a relationship with God? Subservience? Friendship? Judging and punishing? Educational? Magical? Does this transcendent Being want me to do some specific things, or to live according to certain principles? May I expect some special favours or powers in return? And what about this unique real-life situation I am in right now, with all its nuances and ambiguities? To translate such questions into meaningful actions, that is to say, to implement a spiritual relationship, people need a theology: not necessarily a well-thought-out theological system, but 'good-enough' interconnected conceptions that help to see how real-life situations relate to spiritual meaning and translate into meaningful action.

Up to this point this chapter has presupposed one particular spiritual relationship, one of mutual love. Such a relationship can be practised only within a corresponding theology, i.e. one with a personal and loving God at its centre. We have to acknowledge that this is not by far the only theology operative in our culture, even if we leave aside the recent influx of non-Christian religions. Teachings and practices of religions diverge widely, even within the confines of the Christian theologies. Still more divergent are the 'theologies' that individuals construct for themselves. Please note, I am not talking here about the idiosyncratic interpretation systems operating in religious psychopathology. These matters are not a subject of this book. What I want to discuss here is the basic conceptual framework in which ordinary people enact their spiritual life (influenced by, but not coinciding with, the efforts of academic theologians to construe coherent doctrinal systems), and how in some cases these may present a problem in therapy.

Each theology implies a certain type of spiritual relationship. Or, the other way round, different types of spiritual relationships will automatically call forth different types of theologies. Each type of spiritual relationship in its turn requires people to develop different relational capacities. In this chapter we now turn to theologies which for some patients can be quite problematic for their therapy. From a therapeutic point of view, a given theology can simply be *not* 'good-enough'. It is neither supportive nor helpful then, because it implies spiritual relationships and relational capacities that are oppressive or restricting. We must recognise in fact that from the viewpoint of both spiritual and therapeutic progress, theology is a mixed blessing. Some kind of theology is necessary for spiritual life. But every theology, however adequate it may be, always runs the danger that people will forget its inherent limitations. Whenever this happens, even the best theologies have the potential in particular cases of restricting people's spiritual (and psychological) growth instead of fostering it. The latter is not the prerogative of theologies. Exactly the same is true of all other conceptual frameworks that non-religious people consciously or unconsciously use to guide their lives.

The question then becomes, what can a therapist do about this problem without overstepping his competence? As a first move, he would be wise to make two preliminary questions very clear to himself: what are his *own criteria* for assessing other people's theologies? and: where does he himself draw the role borderline between the areas of responsibility of, on the one hand, psychotherapy and on the other hand pastoral counselling and spiritual direction?

4 What are your own criteria for evaluating other people's theologies? A preliminary question

Obviously, we first have to look at ourselves. What are in fact the criteria you use yourself? Theoretically, a therapist has to maintain a neutral stance but that is only true as far as it goes. One cannot make decisions about strategy, interventions or interpretations without at some point taking a stand. So what is your own outlook? Exactly what makes *you* think someone's spiritual relationship and its concomitant theology is obstructive or potentially obstructive to therapy? Obstructive in what way and to what? This question has to be the first one, because the 'obstructiveness' may be in the eye of the beholder. Moreover, it is quite natural for a therapist to look at spirituality and its concomitant theology in terms of their *effects* on therapeutic progress. But if you *restrict* yourself to the effects, then you are reducing spirituality to its therapeutic factors.

The problem is minor as long as we are talking about positive effects. However, when we focus on negative effects, we have to be aware of this reductionist tendency. From that narrow point one may evaluate negatively what is in fact spirituality of the highest order, be it of another *kind* than expected. An example of this is the spirituality of Simone Weil, who died in London during the Second World War because she restricted her food intake to the rations the Nazis allocated to her Jewish compatriots in occupied France. This was quite consistent with her radical solidarity with the oppressed, at the cost of her health, both during her time as a communist activist and again during her time as a Christian mystic. Because of this consistent self-denying behaviour she might easily have been therapeutically *mis*diagnosed as anorexic, depressed or even suicidal. Yet her writings have been translated into many languages and are still read widely as major spiritual literature. Another example is the diary of Etty Hillesum, Simone's Dutch contemporary who died in Auschwitz because she refused to go underground, wanting to share the fate of the 'masses'.[3] Other expressions of such 'unworldly' spirituality can be found in many writings both modern and ancient.

Most religions, Christian or otherwise, have spiritual traditions that teach people to practise, in a well-balanced way, what Weil and Hillesum learned in-tuitively. They are trained to abstain from legitimate things and practices that our society considers to be good for one's well-being and well-functioning. The difference between such spiritual self-denial and self-destructive (non-spiritual) behaviour can best be illustrated by an incident Carlo Carretto tells in one of his *Letters from the Desert*. At some time of his life he wanted to join the order founded by Charles de Foucauld. These 'little brothers' live among the poorest of North Africa, sharing with them 'that abject poverty in which the proletariat of all races and peoples lives, for whom labour is a daily torture, a labour not freely chosen, a filthy and badly paid labour.' From the point of view of a European wanting to help others, what these brothers do is quite dubious and ineffectual: they bring no money, they teach no technical or agri-cultural skills. Without any money and clothed as Arabs they just immerse themselves in the nameless mass of poor Muslims in the alleys of the Kasbah. When Carretto went to Africa for the first time, he stayed as a guest with an old friend. He was in an inner turmoil about his vocation. That same afternoon he saw a long queue waiting at the entrance of a fortress-like building. Each one held a food bowl. Then he saw the door open. It was the hour of the daily almsgiving, and a sister in an immaculate white habit started to hand out soup and bread to the poor. Carretto felt torn. What should he do? He had the means to organise food and education and medication for these poor people. Would that not be a much more sensible way to serve the poor? In his imagination, he looked around for the place Charles de Foucauld would have taken in this scene. In his mind he saw Charles standing at the very end of the row – very small, very humble, food bowl in hand, smiling shyly, as if to apologise for his making things even more complicated by his presence there. At that moment Carretto became sure of his vocation, but he also understood that the sister and Charles represented two different vocations to serve the poor, both equally authentic. They represent two different types of spirituality, *not* a difference between healthy spirituality and self-destructive behaviour, even though Weil's, Hillesum's and Carretto's type *can* lead to suffering and death.[4]

People of the stature of Weil, Hillesum and De Foucauld would be unlikely to have needed the help of a psychotherapist. But their less talented, less perceptive and less confident brothers and sisters may very well do so, particularly the 'spiritual exiles'. They may have a natural propensity for this type of spirituality but, unlike Weil, Hillesum and De Foucauld, could be muddling along intuitively without quite realising what it is they are seeking. The anorexic Marjan from vignette 14 seems to be such a one. So too could be a significant number of the people who nowadays are experimenting with altered consciousness techniques in a misguided search for mystical ecstasy. As therapy cases bear witness, they may end up in deep trouble. This does not mean their individual spiritual longing is less authentic and less vital to their finding inner happiness and peace. But such cases show how an emerging or badly guided spirituality may sometimes lead to a psychotic-like state called 'spiritual emergency'. But note that their trouble is rather in their choosing the wrong means than in choosing the goal of an otherworldly type of spirituality.[5]

In short, in cases where the theology implied in a patient's spiritual life comes into conflict with his therapy it is important for a therapist to *examine his own criteria for assessing other people's theologies and not to apply them unthinkingly.* One reason is that spirituality is *contextual* to therapy. As such, it may have either positive or negative effects on the therapeutic process. But assessing a contextual factor by its effects only, as a therapeutic factor, is probably too reductive to be adequate. Another reason is that the usual therapeutic criteria may be fundamentally at variance with otherworldly spiritual frameworks. A finer-tuned 'discernment' may be needed to distinguish these from the many destructive or escapist 'theologies' that do indeed haunt the contemporary spiritual scene as well.

5 Where to draw the line between psychotherapy and spiritual direction? Another preliminary question

Exactly where would you draw the boundary of psychotherapy? There is an overlap, certainly, but where does it begin and where does it end? Which problems qualify for psychotherapy, which do not? This is a question every psychotherapist has to answer for himself, but let me explain why it is particularly important to do so when he wants to integrate the spiritual dimension into his methodology.

Let us take another look at the example from Nicaragua, now from the viewpoint of coping with war trauma in a Christian context. Everybody at some time of his life has difficulty in coping with seemingly senseless suffering and evil. It is one aspect of being alive, or rather, of being human. For religious and spiritual people, this is one of the problems that they tend to feel much more intensely about than others, because it seems to contradict the faith in the inherent goodness of transcendent Being. Therefore the issue of how to make sense of suffering and evil is right at the heart of all major religions. The way you make sense of that determines the way you can cope with it by endowing it with meaning. Crucial to this is the view of the human body as part of the material world, a seemingly endless discussion all through the centuries. This is because our body is the fundamental locus of our life and our experience – and of our suffering. In a sense we are our bodies. But in another sense we are not our bodies. They are also objects for us, with their own needs to which we are inevitably subject and of which we are only partly aware. They have power over us and through it others have the power to make us suffer or die.

How to deal spiritually with these inherently restricting and threatening aspects of bodily existence? And with the apparent contradiction they can present to the goodness of the Creator God? Quite a few spiritual traditions, Christian and non-Christian, try to work this tension away. This can be done in various ways. One way is to *deny the role of God*, for example by denying that he has created the physical world or by denying that he possesses the power to intervene. Another way is to *justify God*, saying, for example, that our suffering has some ultimate value and will be rewarded after death or that it is to test our faith in adversity. Still another possibility is to *deny reality*, for example, by denying the reality of the physical world (and thus the reality of our bodies), of our physical identity (saying our true identity is in our immortal soul) or of our suffering (declaring it to be an illusion or explaining it as a problem of our ego and not of our real selves). The possibilities seem to be endless.

Most tenets of these three types have a long history. In so far as they deny the role of God and/or physical reality, they are not accepted by mainstream Christian teaching. Yet for many centuries the particular exclusion of the body and the focusing exclusively on the spirit has been very influential in Christian spirituality. This view can be problematic from a genuinely spiritual and thera-peutic perspective, because it has the dangerous potential to alienate people from themselves, from the world and from society. If you accept only part of yourself, the rest automatically becomes 'non-self', or 'illusion', or 'just matter', and so on. Identifying your 'real self' with your immortal and pure spiritual soul (as some movements persuade you to do) encourages a tendency to escape your humanness, a tendency to be at least in *one* respect divine-like, namely as infinite as God. In the Western world this view retains its influence, for example through some New Age movements, although contemporary mainstream Christianity has developed a much more positive view on the body.

The alternative to the above views (at least within the biblical religions) is very difficult to accept. It is to accept fully that we are restricted by our bodies, that we can suffer from them, that we can make each other suffer and can oppress others through their bodies, and that we will actually die; in short, that in this world this bodily existence is our reality. It is to accept at the same time that we are created by a good God and that his creation is good, even though it is finite and even though it is *not* divine. In the light of what people do to each other, this is hard to believe. To hold on simultaneously to this apparent contra-diction is paradoxical and creates a nearly unbearable tension. This is why the issue of suffering and evil is such an intense and ever-recurring one in Christian history. This view offers neither a clear-cut solution nor an escape. Instead, it tells you to go ahead right into the middle of the profound tension thus created. Right there is where you develop your humanness, your solidarity and your faith – where you will find God and his goodness. Your own vulnerable body and finite life are precious and indispensable in a spirituality that wants to be there for and with the other.[6]

How people deal with suffering and evil is at the very heart of therapy, too. The various options outlined above diverge between the different spiritual tra-ditions, and the one a person chooses has a fundamental impact on how he will cope with physical and psychological trauma of whatever kind. People involved in spirituality, be it of a life-affirming type, an otherworldly type, or an escapist type, may all at some time in their lives be unable to cope and therefore qualify for psychotherapy. But does psychotherapy qualify for helping them? As has been explained, spirituality and religion are the contextual frames *within* which people make sense of and direct their lives. But would a therapist be able to provide help in making sense of overwhelming experiences of suffering and evil *within* each one of the above ways? Even if he is, *should* he do so in cases where the spiritual framework runs counter to the ideals of psychotherapy?

Returning to the example from Nicaragua, I think what those therapists did was very appropriate. After all, the main thing in therapy is getting good results, and they certainly succeeded. But should it be called psychotherapy and be provided by institutes for mental health care? Is it not in fact offering spiritual guidance without saying so? I find it confusing, particularly with so many different spiritualities active nowadays, and with DSM-IV including religious and spiritual problems.

This is why I think it makes sense to reflect on boundaries. Should psychotherapy include part of what is traditionally the job of a pastor or a spiritual director? If so, which part? Could one do that in all sincerity? And what about the variety one can expect in heterogeneous therapy situations?

6 Back to the main question: how to deal with counterproductive theologies?

The Nicaraguan situation is both exceptional and yet relatively simple. After all, 'cheerful' Protestantism is a life-affirming religion. Now let us consider more difficult cases, for example such ones as Manlowe writes about: cases where three themes are interconnected, sexual abuse, a negative body image resulting in eating disorders and a theology derived from a patriarchal religion. Even though such patients may be genuinely devout people, their religion quite often itself is a second cause of trauma. It allows them to spiritualise their past and their symptoms, or to justify such with texts from Scripture, reading these as affirming that a relationship with God is one of helpless victim and omnipotent Father. Such people are not exceptional, and neither are other cases of such destructive interconnections.[7]

What help can be given in such difficult cases, given the fact that most therapists have little or no pastoral expertise? I can offer only some very general suggestions and considerations.

As a first and obvious suggestion, a therapist would be wise to consult the person's pastor or recommend referral to a pastoral psychotherapist. Another useful procedure is to let the patient work at a specific spiritual issue in a series of sessions with a pastor. After that, both the patient and the pastor report back to the therapist. Unfortunately, such help is not always available, particularly in such cases as we now have in mind. Sometimes the pastor, or the community itself, is the source of oppressive or debilitating theologies, as in vignette 3, the student who had joined a fringe religious sect.

If no adequate pastoral help is available, then a therapist has two options. He can approach the individual person's spiritual relationship either *indirectly* or *directly*.

The *indirect approach* is by intent not allowing theology to be discussed in the group. While confining analysis to the psychological and interpersonal level, one hopes that new insights at these levels will stimulate the patients involved in spirituality to ask themselves questions also at the spiritual level. This approach is indicated in cases where in a direct approach to their spirituality the chances are that therapy will not catch on because the patient feels it runs counter to his faith, or in cases where the therapist feels the group as a whole is not open to the subject of spirituality. Becoming involved in the 'non-problem' of group interaction, as Garland put it, may in the end feed back upon, and thus affect, the 'non-debatable-problem' of the interaction with God (see Chapter 17, section 2). It can be, however, that such feedback will not happen, either because it simply does not occur to the person that his newly won insights on something like his dysfunctioning in human relations could also be relevant for spiritual matters that are of concern to him; or because he is too defensive in regard to his spiritual life. The spiritual is then in danger of being split off. Despite the negative opinion of that particular theology from the therapist's point of view, for the *patient* it may be well worth protecting. For *him* it is quite often simultaneously a vital lifeline to the Transcendent, and/or to the community into which he is socialised. In such a circumstance it is more urgent than ever that religion and spirituality do not split off as separate realms. But what can be done to prevent a split-off from arising when the therapist for a good reason has decided deliberately to move away from approaching a theology issue directly? Maybe moments of silent reflection could be made a standard procedure in each session? After analysing and working through whatever has occurred at the psychological or interpersonal level, the therapist might then insert an integrative phase. In that part of the session, each individual group member could be invited to consider silently whether what has just happened in the group sheds light on how he personally relates to others *outside* the group, God included. In that way integrating new insights into the spiritual realm will not be something special, but a natural part of the process.

The alternative is to use the *direct approach*. This means dealing with a problematic theology openly despite the lack of theological expertise and authority. In my opinion, it is indeed possible to do this without transgressing the boundaries of psychotherapy. To explain how, let us first see how a pastor or spiritual director might deal with this type of problem. In spiritual direction, as in therapy, the aim is to help people gain sufficient insight and confidence to make their own decisions. In both practices, this is usually done by asking relevant questions and suggesting illuminative interpretations. In spiritual direction, unlike in therapy, the questions and proffered tentative interpretations relate to the person's relationship with God. In the cases we are discussing now, they would aim at helping people to re-interpret, in a way that is both relevant and adequate for them, the particular tradition into which they have been socialised. Such re-interpretation is in fact a second-order change, which paves the way for other changes.[8]

This is essentially what the Nicaraguan therapists did. The Bible being the pre-eminent source for all Protestant denominations, these therapists conscientiously stayed within the Protestant tradition when they stimulated these groups to reflect on relevant texts. In doing so, they helped them re-interpret their theology in such a way that they could acknowledge their suffering and yet remain faithful Protestant Christians. Their 'cheerful' theology was unhelpful because, as William James put it, 'the evil facts which it refuses positively to account for are a genuine portion of reality; and they may after all be the best key to life's significance, and possibly the only openers of our eyes to the deepest levels of truth.' Pargament draws the same conclusion from his empirical research, 'A religious frame of reference that fails to face and respond to the negative side of life cannot sustain the individual through the most painful of life's experiences.' He illustrates this with an example from his own practice in which he, as part of the work of therapy, had to encourage an abused woman to develop a more differentiated religious framework.[9]

Such re-interpretation is the basic spiritual strategy for the more difficult cases we are now discussing. Fortunately, most traditions allow for more than one interpretation. Only if the person's own tradition offers no chance at all to reach a more adequate interpretation, and therefore the person's theology is irrevocably 'counterproductive', only then could alternatives be suggested.

The reason for this is threefold. First, a transition to a quite different type of religion nearly always causes estrangement from one's social milieu. Second, people usually strongly resist changing their religion. To most it is their last resort. Pargament's research also confirms this: 'Typically, the individual has engaged in many coping strategies before he or she is willing to even entertain the thought of a drastic departure in living.' He observes that radical change become a serious possibility only after all other efforts have failed, and failed repeatedly and convincingly.[10] Third, even the most oppressive theology quite often contains some positive elements which are a virtual lifeline to the person. An example of this is an incest victim who from early childhood on had been raped and battered by her father, a Protestant minister. She was thoroughly indoctrinated with a cruel patriarchal theology. Her father had taught her that God thought her a bad child, a whore who deserved to be punished, because 'Whores are bad, the worst there is, it says so in the Bible!' Yet she prayed to that same God to send somebody to help her. And she loved the story of the lost lamb: how dirty and lost you may be, Jesus still loves you.[11] Various therapists of the regional mental health institute tried to help her with the usual approach for incest victims. It was all in vain. In the end she found a religious therapist who used the story of the lost lamb as a crucial turning point in her healing process.

Back to the therapeutic situation. The question was, how to approach a problematic theology openly without transgressing the boundaries of psychotherapy? How can we help such people extricate themselves from a destructive theology and yet nourish their authentic spirituality?

As in spiritual direction, the analytic therapies also use the same basic strategy of asking questions and suggesting tentative re-interpretations, both aimed at moving the healing process forward by gaining relevant insights. The only problem with the kind of cases we are discussing now is, *what* questions and interpretations, aimed at *what* insights? The usual psychological ones would be inadequate here. For example, exposing the 'helpless child/omnipotent Father theology' mentioned above as a product of a dysfunctional family is too reductionist. Questions aimed at gaining that insight are likely to be rejected as an attack on the Christian faith. Even if accepted, this interpretation cannot nurture spiritual life. Moreover, it is not a relevant insight. *In theological and ethical matters, the point is not how you get such insights. The point is whether these are valid or not.* You may, for example, have become an honest person because as a child your parents bullied you into honesty, but that does not mean that your conception of honesty is invalid. You should reject the bullying, not the honesty resulting from it. That goes for a theology too.

7 Assessing spiritual relationships

So how to design more relevant and acceptable questions? I suggest taking up the relational point of view again. The quality of the spiritual relationship is the area where therapeutic and pastoral competence overlap. Earlier, the discussion was about a spiritual relationship characterised by mutual love. Now the focus is on some kind of destructive or debilitating relationship, which nevertheless is a vital one. By analysing the metaphor on which the particular spiritual relationship of this particular person is modelled, a therapist could assess its *change potential*, that is, the space it allows for change in the direction of more inner freedom, more perspective, more mature ways of relating to self and others. I suggest a therapist should consider *directing his questions and other interventions to the change potential of this particular relational metaphor*. The insights gained in this area are likely to be both relevant and acceptable to the person. Because the relational metaphor functions as the organising principle, the questions and insights are within the person's overall religious framework. Therefore they offer the opportunity to remain faithful to what is felt to be positive and to change what is obviously negative.

To succeed in this, a therapist would need answers to the following questions:

1. *Which* relational metaphor is at the centre of the person's theology (for example father, judge, ruler, teacher, avenger)?

2. How is this metaphor actually *implemented* by this particular person in his particular spiritual relationship, and what aspect of it is *responsible for its apparent negative effect* on the person's psychological problem (for example submission to tyrannical father, despairing about eternal damnation)?

3. Can I assess the *potential for change* of that root metaphor? That is, could it be implemented in such a way that it offers more possibilities for developing a spiritual life with more freedom, more perspective, more self-respect and love (for example, the 'father' metaphor has the latent possibility to change from 'a relationship between a strict

father and a naughty little child' into 'a relationship between a wise father and his adult and responsible son or daughter')?

The outcome of this analysis may then direct the therapist's thinking on how to help the person involved to gain the relevant relational insights and relational quality, and to integrate these into his spiritual relationship.

8 Three relational categories

A helpful instrument for finding an answer to the above questions is Brümmer's division of interpersonal and spiritual relationships into categories. In his book on the spiritual metaphor of mutual love, Brümmer points out that, despite the enormous variety in human relationships, it is possible to categorise them in *three identifiable basic types*. These three basic categories are *impersonal (or manipulative) relationships, agreements about mutual rights and obligations (or contractual relationships)* and *mutual love (or fellowship) relationships*.[12] He then proceeds to show how these three basic categories of human relationships function as root metaphors (or 'key models' as he prefers to call them) in the various prevailing theologies. In other words, if you analyse a theology, you will find that the relationship between God and man it implies is modelled as an analogy to one of these three basic categories. Thus these three basic forms can be recognised in the great variety of different theologies. This insight is very helpful for bringing some order into this variety: there are obviously large *differences* between the manifold theologies, but there are also significant *correspondences* between theologies in so far as they imply the same view on the *kind* of relationship between God and man – that is, in so far as they fall into the same basic category of relationships. Brümmer also discusses what it would mean to break and restore a spiritual relationship in each model, and what potential each has for human beings to develop self-esteem and maturity. In his earlier book *What Are We Doing When We Pray?* he analyses how prayer necessarily differs within each category, and what this has to do with personal *identity*, with exercising *freedom* and with assuming *responsibility*.[13]

Brümmer's categorisation is helpful because it gives a systematic account of the dynamics of different spiritual relationships. Each category can be examined as to which relational capacities are to be learned and practised if people are to construct what is a meaningful spiritual life. Each category can also be examined as to what are the immature or restrictive ways of constructing spiritual life that in the context of that particular type of theology are likely to be encountered. Such a comparative analysis of latent positive and negative possibilities will provide *a key to assessing the potential for therapeutic change* via someone's theology.

In the next chapters I shall demonstrate this type of analysis. In dealing with each category I shall first summarise what Brümmer has to say about each category and thereafter explore its usefulness for assessing the latent possibilities for helping people change *within the context of their own theology* in a direction that from a therapeutic point of view is less obstructive to their healing.

CHAPTER 19

Impersonal
(or Manipulative) Relationships

1 The category of impersonal (or manipulative) human relationships

This is the first basic form of human relationships Brümmer distinguishes. In such relationships, relations are 'impersonal' in the sense that only one of the partners (A) is his own agent. The other (B) is treated *as if* he were an 'object', a thing, a non-person. Such relationships are *asymmetrical* because one partner in the relationship (A) has complete control over the other partner (B). This control is not necessarily exercised for selfish purposes. It could be beneficent and exercised to B's advantage. Nevertheless A *treats* B as an object rather than as a person, because he forces or manipulates B instead of asking or convincing him.

In such a relationship, what does *love* look like? As a personal agent, A is the only one who can love in the full sense of the word. He can be both emotionally involved in B *and* commit himself to act for the good of B. But can A make B return his love? At best he can manipulate B's feelings and emotions, but he can never manipulate a commitment, because only free personal agents can commit themselves to a course of action. If B would commit himself to love A in the full sense of the word, which implies a commitment to act for the good of A, *then* this *ipso facto* proves that he is *not* an 'object' but is also a personal agent. Unfortunately for him, as long as the relationship remains impersonal and manipulative, such evidence of being a person and his own agent will not stop A from *treating* him as a non-person. Please note that it is *types* we are discussing here: a categorisation of *basic* forms that can be recognised (apart from other characteristics) *in* concrete relationships. A pure and unambiguous example of an impersonal relationship as characterised above is rarely found to exist between human beings. In reality, most forms of impersonal relationships are mixed with elements of other types of relationship. If impersonal relations in their

232

pure form are found, such as for example in the Nazi concentration camps, then this is generally condemned as inhuman. Slavery at first sight also seems to be an example of a 'pure and unambiguous impersonal relationship'. But the study of ancient Roman culture, where the juridical position of slaves was indeed that they had no legal personality and were considered as objects in the ownership of their master (and where slavery was just assumed and its moral justification seldom questioned), reveals an implicit but perpetual conflict between the view that the slave is a chattel and that a slave is also a person. And the development of Roman economic life, to which slaves contributed considerably, gradually enforced a recognition of their personhood.[1]

2 Impersonal or manipulative spiritual relationships: magic and determinism

A theology modelled on this kind of relationship sees either the divine or the human being as the one in control. An example of man being in control of the divine partner is in the use of magic. In religions based on magic rituals the human being is in control in so far as it is believed he is able by performing certain magic rites to force the gods to do his will.

A spiritual relationship is also impersonal if God's action is thought of as being the *direct* cause of everything in the relationship and the non-divine partner the direct cause of nothing. In this sort of relationship, the human partner is totally dependent for everything, even though God may use his power in the best interest of man. Theologies modelled upon this type of human relationship are *determinist*. They teach that ultimately man has no free choice either to accept or to reject whatever good or bad that God allots him. An extreme example is the ancient belief in fate found in Greek and Roman literature. Oedipus, for example, however hard he tried to prevent this, could not avoid killing his father and marrying his mother as the oracle had predicted this would be so before he was born.

In such a spiritual relationship, what does *prayer life* look like? Prayer is the way to communicate heart-to-heart with the Divine. In such a causal, impersonal spiritual relationship as the sort referred to above, prayer can become no more than a way to come to accept the inevitable. At best it can be 'therapeutic' prayer, that is, prayer which gives inner peace because it changes the attitude of the praying human into accepting whatever it is that God gives him. Or it can be therapeutic in the sense that it increases our spiritual strength to undergo suffering and so helps us to become better able to cope. The source of such strength is not necessarily a personal God who answers prayer. Such strength may, for example, be siphoned off by a meditational technique or a magic ritual from some universal spiritual level of reality in which all our minds unconsciously participate. Nor is the result necessarily a purely subjective affair: there may be a real increase of strength through absorption of such spiritual power, or the increase may be the psychological effect of the activity of praying as such.

Another aspect is, how can this type of spiritual relationship *go wrong*, and how can it be *restored?* Because the passive partner (B) is treated as an object and therefore not his own agent, the active partner (A) must be held responsible for what goes wrong. The same is true for restoring it: the active partner is responsible for restoring the relationship. In a theology based on this manipulative model all credit for restoration of a broken relationship ('salvation') goes to God. There are no grounds whatsoever for claiming any of it for ourselves. Divine grace is the exclusive and sufficient cause of salvation.

3 Exploring the potential for therapeutic change in impersonal spiritual relationships

Turning now to the therapeutic analysis, a spontaneous and immediate response could be to consider the *whole* category of impersonal manipulative spiritual relationships as destructive to mental health. Religions based in magic, at the one extreme of this category, threaten to aggrandise the desire to control one's own and other people's fates into cosmic proportions. At the other extreme of this category are the deterministic religions in which people are subjected to an all-powerful God who treats humans as non-persons. This seems to lead inevitably to a passive and dependent attitude to life, and to shifting in principle all responsibility to the broad shoulders of God. And how can the other variant mentioned earlier, i.e. not a personal God but an impersonal spiritual power, whether beneficial or not, inspire and support people's efforts to become loving, righteous and responsible persons?

But the judgement implied in this rhetorical question is too facile. It is simply not true that all those involved in impersonal manipulative spiritual relationships are necessarily unhappy, unbalanced or shirking responsibility.

As for the one extreme, *religion based in magic*, it undoubtedly creates fear and encourages spiteful people to use witchcraft against their enemies. But it is not necessarily destructive. Studies of tribal religions show that, in general, cultures with religions based in magic do not produce overly unbalanced or irrational people. Life is just structured in this way for them and they usually deal with it as a matter of fact. Despite its obvious potential for misuse and deception, magical practice is not by definition and *per se* detrimental to mental health.

As for the other extreme, *deterministic religion*, numerous peoples live and have lived in a deterministic religious framework – one in which the Divine is seen as the direct cause of everything and in which free will does not exist. Undeniably this is conducive to a basic attitude of passivity and fatalism. But that does not make them automatically patients or robots. Actually, it may also engender inner peace by liberating people from constantly struggling to control their fate.

In section 7 of Chapter 18, I stated that it can be useful to assess the *change potential* of dysfunctional spiritual relationships, i.e. the space the spiritual metaphors involved allow for growth towards more inner freedom and more perspective. The search for the potential for therapeutic change in the theological framework of patients is about finding and enhancing counterbalancing elements *in* their spiritual relationship. To explore the actual potential for change in individual cases, one needs to know more about the *particular* characteristics of the spiritual relationship that is under scrutiny. The reality of the need for this spiritual exploration with a particular patient can never be over-emphasised. In this book, we cannot deal with specifics since these are necessarily patient-bound, but some general indications of what to look for can be derived from the characteristics of the category to which the relationship belongs. The remaining sections of this chapter will discuss the three most relevant of these general indications of where to find latent possibilities for therapeutic change in the context of an impersonal (manipulative) spiritual relationship setting. These three foci of change potential are:

1. Even determinism still offers *inherent opportunities* for spiritual and therapeutic growth (section 4).

2. Most religions contain elements in their philosophy and theological reasoning that *counterbalance* extreme determinism (section 5).

3. By far most human and spiritual relationships have a *composite* character, and these elements from other types of relationships can provide an entrée for therapeutic change (section 6).

4 Latent possibilities for spiritual and therapeutic change within determinism

If it is true that even deterministic theologies still offer possibilities for spiritual growth, what *kind* of growth is possible in such models?

To answer the above question, let us first consider the gloomiest version of determinism that we can think of and see what it has to offer. In human relationships, the most pessimistic and deterministic form could be, for instance, something like being imprisoned by a cruel and capricious tyrant exercising absolute power in some Kafkaesque atmosphere in which it is a foregone conclusion that you are doomed and doomed for no clear reason. At first sight, such a scenario seems to offer no room at all for developing spiritually and therapeutically positive qualities. Nevertheless, even though in such extreme circumstances people are treated as worthless (non-person) objects, they *are* not 'objects'. In even the most desperate situations, many individuals have in fact resisted the tendency to identify with their oppressor's view. History tells us that even in the context of extremely deterministic religions, in which the relationship with the deity or deities is very like such manipulative human relationships, there have always been people who have developed inner strength, peace and compassion, who adhered to the values they held high, and who found the courage to accept their fate without self-pity or vindictiveness. In antiquity, the Stoics even systematically developed such an attitude of inner freedom and strength within their strictly deterministic view of the world. In short, even if you are not in a position to *act* as a free and responsible person, either in a tyrannical human situation or in an impersonal spiritual relationship with the Divine, you have still the freedom to *choose a certain attitude and develop the inner qualities it requires* – that is, the *inner* freedom of being a person. In spirituality of this type, one possible choice is for a radical surrender to the Absolute in obedience and humility, without any demand for special favours or extraordinary experiences in return.

As a conclusion, the relational capacities that would help people change in a positive direction *within* the impersonal framework are obedience instead of servitude, the humility needed to accept being part of an unknown greater design, giving up the urge to be rewarded for your good deeds, and other such virtues. These still are not congenial to many of the usual therapeutic ideals. In part these can be such points of divergence between therapy and spirituality as have been discussed in Chapter 17, section 6. When confronted with patients who relate to the Divine as to an impersonal and unchanging power, it may be worthwhile to reconsider these points of divergence, and to find ways to approach and integrate them as valuable in their own right. As drawn attention to in section 8 of Chapter 17, it could after all be more a question of finding balance than of real divergence.

As a last remark, the *issue of control and dependence* is part of everybody's spiritual relationship to whichever relational category it belongs (impersonal, contractual or mutual love). I have already discussed that subject in the context of a personal spiritual relationship: in Chapter 7, section 6, I mentioned the well-known experience of the terrifying fear of losing oneself completely in the overwhelming encounter with God, and in Chapter 14, section 6, I discussed the continuing struggle between willingness and wilfulness throughout the spiritual change process. In an impersonal spiritual relationship it is clear that the human partner is aware that he has no control over the divine other partner. But in personal spiritual relationships this recognition is also necessary. In spiritual as in human love the urge to manipulate is most often dictated by fear: love requires that we voluntarily give up autonomy and acknowledge our dependence on somebody else. This is a threat to our sense of security, whether true or false security, which tempts us to manipulate the other into returning our love. That is why the realisation that we are *not* in control of God is necessary both in personal and in impersonal relationships with the Divine.

5 Looking for counterbalancing elements in a manipulative spiritual relationship

As a second aspect, a therapist in search of the change potential of a manipulative spiritual relationship can look for elements that counterbalance the effects of extreme determinism. Determinism in the extreme pessimistic form such as sketched above is rare. In the course of their history, many religions have known long and heated discussions about determinism. But generally these religions have succeeded in counterbalancing extreme determinism one way or another. Indian religion, for instance, offers a spiritual way to escape from Karma. Islamic orthodoxy holds that man is neither free nor unfree. Originally, Christianity was not in character a deterministic religion. Yet there is a tendency, from early Christianity on (and still operative in conservative Roman Catholic and Protestant theology), to interpret God's perfection in a 'static' way. For many centuries there has been a strong tendency among the intellectual elite to portray God as being eternally unchanging and unchangeable, as not subject to feelings or emotions or suffering, and as foreknowing and predetermining *everything*. One typical conclusion based on this interpretation of the perfection of God is that it is impossible to change God's mind. All change has to be *on the part of the human partner in this relationship*. This view is a theological *dis*couragement to try to manipulate God, and a theological *en*couragement to trust him and his promises unreservedly. For centuries people were taught to read the Bible with this static view on God's perfection as a presupposition. Passages picturing the Biblical God as angry, as repenting, as changing his mind, were usually interpreted beforehand as being symbolic of something else. This static concept of perfection is the main cause of the deterministic tendency in Western thinking.[2] Yet such as it may be, this Christian version of a deterministic theology is not totally modelled as an impersonal relationship. Christianity has always *also* modified and counterbalanced its static and deterministic tendency. For example, the earliest hymns and prayers already express God's genuine relationship and response to us.

I shall discuss the Christian variant of deterministic thinking in the next chapter more extensively, because on the one hand it is still rather influential, while on the other hand it tends to put people in a spiritual 'double-bind' which can be a negative therapeutic factor.[3]

6 Composite relationships

A third aspect a therapist could look into when trying to assess the potential for therapeutic change in the context of a predominantly impersonal spiritual relationship is whether the particular relationship under consideration is combined with elements of the other two basic categories of relationships, i.e. agreements and love relationships (see Chapter 18, section 8). By far the most spiritual relationships and their concomitant theologies are mixed with elements of the other types, and these elements may provide a handle for change in a positive direction. Moreover, people are hardly ever fully consistent in their thinking about such matters. This is true at the general level of the traditions in which people are socialised. It is also true at the level of the unique relationship each individual person creates from elements picked up from religious education. This is even true of the destructive spiritual relationships of severely disturbed patients. Sensitive observation often exposes how individuals unexpectedly express traces of an 'affective personal spiritual relationship' in the very middle of despair and fatalism. This is one reason why it always makes sense to ask how they pray: this 'affective' quality of their spiritual relationship is often expressed in spontaneous prayers. An example of this composite character can be found in the story of the incest victim described in section 6 of Chapter 18: in her prayers she clung desperately to the story of Jesus' compassionate love for the lost lamb.

CHAPTER 20

Predestination and Double Predestination

1 Predestination as a theoretical problem

As noted above, *total* determinism is very rare in Christian theology. Yet a kind of qualified deterministic thinking has played a major role in the *shaping* of complex and multifaceted contemporary Christianity. Therefore, if you meet people from 'conservative' churches or congregations (conservative in the sense that they stick to teachings that originate from roughly the period between the fourth and the eighteenth century) they are likely to explain everything that happens to them as determined by God from the beginning of time. Within Christianity their spirituality comes closest to the category of impersonal spiritual relationships because the human person is seen as powerless to change anything, even himself. This is also the form of Christianity that for a non-religious psychotherapist is the most difficult to understand. Let me first briefly explain the historical background, because it is still an important key to understanding the inner world of patients who are brought up in this way of thinking and feeling about God and their relationship with him.

As a result of the age-long influence of Greek philosophy, there has been a tendency in early theological thinking to project a rather static image of God: an image which suggests that the dynamics of a relationship with him is more impersonal than personal. This is connected with a particular interpretation of the concepts 'omnipotence' (God is all-powerful), 'omniscience' (God knows what is to happen from the beginning of time) and 'perfection', qualities that in Platonist type philosophies were held to be the essential qualities of the One Deity and were transferred to the Christian God. Any *change* in what the omniscient God knows and wills beforehand (from the beginning and until the end of time) would deny the perfection of God himself. *Ipso facto* what is preordained has to be.

This rather 'static' view of God has created a problem: a relationship with a God conceived in this way gives the human partner no room to change anything whatsoever, including man himself. And it suggests that God countenances and is also responsible for all sin and evil, which is an idea totally inconsistent with the notion of his perfect goodness. It is also inconsistent with the central ideas Christianity *also* developed in the first centuries of its existence: that God became incarnate in the historical person of Jesus without diminishing his Godhead, that God not only acts upon but also interacts with and 'dwells within' man whom he has created in his likeness, and that the Trinity is supremely dynamic, personal and relational. Later on, the Reformation gave a new impetus to counter this 'static' view of God by stimulating people to read the Bible with its many stories in which God changes his earlier decisions. This dynamic and relational biblical view of God is virtually irreconcilable with the static one. The tension between the two has never been resolved once and for all.

As a *philosophical* problem the dilemma is logically unsolvable. But unfortunately it cannot be discarded with that observation, because it is not just a philosophical problem. In the context of a living religion, it is also a spiritual problem. And as a *spiritual* problem, it touches on one of the most delicate issues: the issue of God's guidance in spiritual life and the role of human will and freedom in it.

In history, theologians have again and again tried to resolve this inner inconsistency, for example by stating explicitly that on the one hand God is omniscient and governs all things so that in this world nothing happens without his ordinance, while on the other hand God despite his omniscience is neither the author nor has he any responsibility for the sin committed by man that does and shall exist. The responsibility for such is the responsibility not of God but of the human partner in this type of relationship with the Divine. Understandably, solutions such as this one in their turn created new problems.

The doctrines of *predestination* and its variant *double predestination* are two such attempts to resolve this inner inconsistency. Predestination differs from determinism in that this term exclusively refers to the divine predetermination with respect to the eternal salvation (spiritual happiness and fulfillment) *of the individual human soul*. In contrast with determinism and fatalism, it concerns life itself and the living relationship between God and man – what I have called 'the spiritual relationship'. It sees spiritual life as founded in God, and as such the notion of predestination belongs to spiritual life, not to philosophy. As such it has survived the outdated philosophical reasoning.

Predestination is based on two considerations: first, the believer knows that he will find his salvation only in God and as a free gift of God, and second, God's will manifests itself in everything and everyone, with everything and everyone and despite everything and everyone. Predestination is often, though not necessarily, also connected with a belief in *original sin*. The latter is a concept from Augustine who since the late fourth century up to the present day has had an enormous influence on the Roman Catholic church and on most churches of the Reformation. The term 'original sin' refers to the belief that all human beings are born in a state of sin, which they inherited from Adam and Eve. In this way of thinking, sin is more than doing wrong: it is also a permanent and pervasive state of corruption that all human beings find themselves in. Salvation here is not primarily reconciling a relationship broken by some specific act, but salvation means here also: being freed from this inborn state of corruption exclusively by the action of God. The human being is the passive object in this. Furthermore, there is a difference between 'election' and 'rejection'.

Election is *directly* connected with spiritual life: the believer acknowledges that, if he has found God and the others have not found him, this is not the result of his own doing but exclusively due to God's grace. The 'good works' the believer does are not the means to earn that grace, they are rather the results of that grace and the signs of that grace. But, being *human* actions, they have also their doubtful aspects (as psychotherapists know all too well). Non-salvation, according to this doctrine, means that you will be left in that overall misery in which you have put yourself by ignoring the message of the Gospel.

Rejection is *indirectly* connected with spiritual life, that is to say, it is believed to be an analogy or a consequence of election: if the believer has *not* found God, then God has not granted him this grace. But that does *not* imply that God equally elects the one and rejects the other. In other words, it does not lift man's responsibility and guilt. The term *'double predestination'* refers to the belief that not only election, but *also rejection is predestined*. Because rejection is thought to be also predestined, the variant 'double' predestination is the gloomiest of the two. It makes quite a few people feel simultaneously 'helpless but guilty', as A. Schilder has put it in her study about religiogenic depressions with people adhering to this 'double' variant of predestination.[1] The concept originates from Calvin (the sixteenth-century founder of the Calvinistic Protestant churches) and raised such furious controversies that half a century after his death it led to deep and enduring schisms between the churches of the Reformation – and sometimes even between congregations of the same church. The schisms are alive to this day.

Since the late seventeenth century the concept of 'predestination' is no longer in the centre of Western theological thinking, but it is still there. Roman Catholicism teaches an eternal predestination, but preserves the element of human consent and the reality of the divine will that all men should be saved. The Reformers taught different variants of it which are mostly still in the creeds of their churches. The 'double predestination' variant is still very much alive in various conservative Protestant religious movements and congregations in Western Europe, Canada and the USA.

Predestination is and always has been controversial, but despite all differences and controversies its main point is the same, namely that God is the one and only foundation of spiritual life, that we human beings lack the capacities for understanding what he does and why he does it, but that his justice and compassion are beyond doubt. Most contemporary theological thinking is however based much more on the intensely dynamic Biblical God who is obviously prepared to reconsider his decisions and to go to any length to save even rather unsavoury people.

2 Predestination as a spiritual and psychological problem

I am paying so much attention to the predestination and double predestination doctrines here, because both are still influencing many people's spiritual life and are recognised from psychotherapeutic practice as a possible factor in religiogenic depressions. But before we turn to that therapeutically relevant aspect, let me first give a moment's thought to the question: how is it possible that such an abstract and centuries-old theological problem, reflecting the assumptions and debates of an outdated philosophical climate, can still be a factor in 'ordinary' people's depressions?

There are essentially two reasons, and these also apply to other ancient doctrinal formulations. First, the *questions* they try to answer are still vital. In this case, the underlying question is: how can I, given the all-present evil and suffering in the world, believe in the goodness of God who created it all, ourselves included? This is a very real question and the way you answer it considerably determines how you experience your own life. Second, the *conclusions* of important theological thought found and still find their way into the doctrines of the faith of one or more churches. In that form, i.e. as formulated conclusions *without* the underlying assumptions and arguments, they have been and still are passed down from generation to generation of church members. And in that form they 'inspire' the lives of individuals and communities on both a spiritual and a psychological level. Depending on their psychological make-up *and* on the way in which the whole corpus of doctrines has been transmitted and 'embodied' by the individual and his religious community, an unresolved theoretical problem in a theology such as the one referred to above *can* cause some people to get entrapped in psychological problems while others *can* emerge (from wrestling with the same problem) psychologically and spiritually stronger. Still others will not even seem to notice the problem. Moreover, we must not lose sight of the fact that such a doctrinal system *as a whole* also has many other aspects which can be more directly beneficial to a balanced and loving spirituality. Unfortunately, most outsiders are blind to these counterbalancing aspects. It is precisely that element of 'embodiment' – a person's own daily life becoming inspired by it – that makes people experience doctrines not as a theoretical system but as a guide to a spiritually satisfying way of life. In a particular therapeutic session it may be vital for the therapist to be aware of this 'inheritance', its 'embodiment', its 'origins' and not least its 'possible inspiration for living and behaviour'. This is evident in an event relating to belief, spiritual struggles and psychological problems in a wartime incident in Dutch history.

3 Predestination and coping with misfortune

Vignette 18

In October 1944, the Nazis held a razzia in a rather isolated and orthodox Dutch Reformed agrarian village. Their reason was that a high German official had been attacked by a resistance group from another part of the Netherlands. They took nearly the whole male population, over six hundred men, and transported them to a concentration camp in Northern Germany. Less than fifty survived. This was disproportional, even for German concentration camps.

Nowadays if a calamity of this scale happens, the next of kin automatically qualify for psychotherapy to help them cope with their traumas. At that time and for many years after the war, this was out of the question. In due time, psychologists became interested in the question why there had been so many deaths among the prisoners and how the population had coped with their losses. The first studies, dating from the 1970s, stated that their religion (conservative Calvinist, endorsing the 'double predestination' doctrine) had accounted for the deaths among the prisoners. It had prevented them resisting the oppressors and had made them passively accept their fate as the will of God. As for the survivors and the next of kin of the victims, they had obviously not been able to cope: they had been verbally 'flogged' by their ministers, who had preached that the razzia had been a punishment and/or a chastisement from God. This preaching had not made them abandon their religion, which is why these earlier researches considered them to have learnt nothing from their tragedy and to be still in need of psychotherapy.[2]

However, recent in-depth research into the coping process of the villagers shows an opposite outcome, namely that they had not been unresisting and passive and that the survivors and next of kin had essentially done their mourning and coping very successfully. This raised the question *how* they had managed to cope. Another follow-up study, using the 'terror management theory' of Greenberg, Solomon and Pyszczynski to assess how they had achieved this, showed that it was precisely their religion that had enabled the population to cope with their trauma.[3] The preaching about the razzia being a punishment or a chastisement of God answered their question as to the 'why?' Abhorrent as this idea of interpreting this event as God's punishment may be at first sight, it enabled them to give their loss and suffering a place. It also encouraged them to answer the 'why this punishment?' question sincerely, to draw conclusions from it for their future way of life and to open themselves to the realisation that God will give consolation to whomsoever contritely turns to him. The idea of chastisement also offered another metaphor, derived from the book of Job, which allowed them to see their suffering as leading to meaningful insights and a step towards some ultimate good that transcended their own individual experience.

Another element in the preaching was the answer to the question: had the victims 'died in the faith'? – a very important question for them. One minister, himself a camp survivor, had assured the next of kin that his fellow prisoners indeed had done so and he had been able to give them details about how the victims had died. He also told them that many of them right in the middle of their misery found God as a Father who turned their misfortune into a blessing. As explained above, 'finding' God is a grace of God and *the* central experiential issue in predestinarian spirituality. In other ways, too, their ministers had brought real consolation, albeit in religious language that is hard to understand and accept in a secularised culture. Other important coping strategies were erecting and maintaining monuments and having yearly memorial services on the day of the razzia.

Shortly after the war the villagers had also started working on reconciliation and forgiveness, which their belief told them is necessary for living according to God's will. A delegation of the village population and two ministers went to the German village where the victims were buried. The local pastor there acknowledged that the Germans had caused much grief. This visit was followed by a visit from the German pastor a year later, and by many subsequent yearly visits of the villagers to the graves and the German parishioners. Since 1958 the relations between the two villages have been intensified and the visits to the graves in Germany became explicitly intended as working on Christian reconciliation for which admission of sins is indispensable.

The study referred to above concludes that the central issue in this particular religious subculture is to know oneself as dependent on a transcendent existential order of things. These people had coped with their suffering by orienting themselves on this transcendent order, which enabled them to give their suffering a meaningful place within that order, provided them with directions for meaningful actions, and allowed them to regain a positive self-evaluation by the standards of their own religious culture.

I have also tried to compare this outcome with the items of Pargament's (evidence-based) positive and negative styles of religious coping. Pargament *et al.* discovered that in religious coping with loss and trauma there is not one particular factor that accounts for either a positive or a negative outcome of the religious coping process, but rather a pattern of interconnected factors. That is why they use the term 'coping *style*' instead of 'factor'. The positive style of religious coping consists of: (1) seeking spiritual support; (2) collaborative religious coping; (3) spiritual connection; (4) religious purification; (5) benevolent religious reappraisal; (6) religious forgiveness. The negative coping style is characterised as (1) having spiritual discontent; (2) punitive God reappraisals; (3) interpersonal religious discontent; (4) demonic reappraisal; (5) reappraisal of God's powers. It seems to me that these villagers achieve a high rating against the criteria from Pargament's positive coping style.[4]

Comparing all this with the material presented in the earlier chapters of this book, it immediately strikes me that what these preachers did is in sharp contrast with the woman of vignette 11 who was convinced the death of her child was a punishment from God and had made the punishment metaphor absolute. The ministers of the Dutch village used the punishment metaphor, but they obviously did *not* make it absolute. They used it to help their parishioners confront their own reality and to show them the way to renew their lives. They also added other metaphors, i.e. the chastisement metaphor, which suggested they should seek for new insights, and the metaphor of Job, which suggested that the events were a meaningful part in a greater cosmic plan that transcended their understanding. In this way they counterbalanced the punishment metaphor and put it in a wider meaningful context. They also counterbalanced the inherent deterministic inconsistency (of being powerless to change anything whatsoever while at the same time being guilty and responsible for their sins) by emphasising God's compassion, forgiveness and willingness to grant them the grace of 'finding' him in their hearts. Analogously to what the Stoics did in their strictly deterministic framework, they also taught their parishioners to transcend their acceptance of unchangeable *external* fate by putting ultimate value in *internal* peace and strength –which in their religion they find in the unitive experience they call 'finding God' (cf. the next section of this chapter and Chapter 12).

In short, they did *not* turn their religion into an ideology, a closed system (which they would have done if they had made the punishment metaphor absolute), they used the positive therapeutic potential present *within* their spiritual relationship, they *counterbalanced* the impersonal element of the unchangeable, predetermining and punishing God by emphasising his goodness and compassion, and they used the *elements of a spiritual relationship of intimate love* that, in addition to the deterministic strand, are also present in their religion.

4 Predestination and depression

In psychotherapy, however, we have to deal with individuals who generally have *not* been able to cope. Usually they have not developed a trustful and loving spiritual relationship, and many are resentful, despairing or fatalistic because of this deterministic strand in their religion. So let us not close our eyes to the spiritual and psychological vulnerability of those who are all the time worrying about eternal rejection, or who are trapped in the vicious double-bind of being 'helpless but guilty', or who, like the woman of vignette 11, are convinced the death of their child is a punishment and a sure sign of their eternal rejection. Most often these patients need both psychotherapy and pastoral care. For a non-religious psychotherapist, patients with this type of religion are the most difficult to understand and empathise with. Such patients appear to confirm the widely accepted notion that religion focused on predestination is a major cause of depressions. Therefore let us look at what recent epidemiology research has to say about this.

'Double' predestination indeed seems to be a factor in spiritual despair and religiogenic depression, or at least with certain people. Research among the older population in the Netherlands shows a correlation between belief in this type of predestination and the occurrence of depressions. *But it is not clear how this correlation should be interpreted.* On the one hand, research evidence proves that the conservative Protestant communities holding this belief show a much higher percentage of depressions than the Dutch Reformed and Roman Catholic communities. But on the other hand, the *non*-religious population shows the *same* high percentage of depressions as these conservative Protestants![5] Be that as it may, for a therapist it is relevant to know that this belief in 'double' predestination is still deeply influencing some religious subcultures. The ordinary church member may not be familiar with its theological line of reasoning, but the whole community has been exposed to its implications for many generations. As a result, it has often become a pervasive and persistent spiritual condition. Whenever this leads to depression, the spiritual factor needs to be recognised because dealing only with psychological factors is in most cases probably not enough.

5 Predestination and prejudice

However, the example of the terrorised village is also an illustration of still another problem we should not close our eyes to. The earlier studies indicate that the psychologists involved all too easily hypothesised that this religion *must* have led to passivity and lack of resistance to the oppressors which in turn *must* have been the cause of so many deaths under the prisoners. They also obviously concluded all too easily that the acceptance of the preaching about punishment and chastisement by the survivors *must* be a sign that they had not managed to cope with their loss and trauma. Not that they were alone in this view: it was the general consensus of the rest of the Dutch population too. This is understandable because it is indeed very difficult for an outsider to assess the value or non-value of such ideas as a razzia being interpreted as a punishment or a chastisement from God. It is obvious that the criteria used in the earlier studies were dictated by the tacit assumption that accepting a calamity as a divine act can have *only* negative results and that the obvious way to cope in such circumstances is to abandon that religion. But is abandoning one's religion really the answer?

And they all too easily *assumed that psychotherapy is the one and only possible way to resolve their problem.* But is psychotherapy really the answer? With the latter's emphasis on autonomy and individuation instead of on radical and trusting dependence on a transcendent order?

That is why I think it is absolutely necessary for a psychotherapist to reflect carefully on the two preliminary questions I have asked in Chapter 18: what are your own criteria for evaluating other people's theologies? and: where to draw the line between psychotherapy, spiritual direction and pastoral care?

CHAPTER 21

Mutual Agreement (or Contractual) Relationships

1 The category of mutual agreement (or contractual) human relationships

This is the second basic category of human relationships that Brümmer calls attention to. It consists of relationships based upon an agreement or contract between two persons each of whom accepts certain rights and duties towards the other. In contrast with impersonal relationships, agreement relationships are *personal and symmetrical* in the sense that each partner acknowledges the freedom and responsibility of the other as well as his own dependence on the other for maintaining the relationship.

The agreements may be specific and restricted to a certain period or area of life, as in an agreement in which the rights and duties between employer and employed are specified. Or they may be general and open-ended, as in a marriage in which the partners cannot possibly know beforehand exactly what demands their future together will make on them. The agreements may be formally agreed upon, or they may be informal and perhaps never explicitly agreed upon. In short, there is an enormous *variety* of relationships in this category, and this is also true for the analogous spiritual relationships.

In such a relationship, what would *love* look like? In contrast to impersonal relationships, both partners *can* love in the full sense of the word. Both *can* be emotionally involved *and* commit themselves to act for the good of the other partner. Yet this also contrasts with Brümmer's category of mutual love or fellowship relationships, where people enter into the relationship because they are interested in this unique other person. People basically enter into agreements because they *both benefit from it.* Therefore, the other partner as well as the relationship itself have primarily *instrumental value,* and as such are replaceable by any other means. Love may be an important reason to establish an agreement or contract, and love may be an important factor all through its duration. But *not necessarily so.* Many contracts and agreements, marriages included, are entered into for other reasons than love. Loss of love does not automatically result in ending the mutual obligations. Good and fair fulfilment of the mutual obligations rather than love determines the quality of this category.

Another aspect is, how can this type of relationship *go wrong*, and how can it be *restored*? Such a relationship breaks down when one of the two partners fails in his obligation. He then has forfeited the right to call on the other's obligation to him. Restoring the relationship comes down to restoring the balance between rights and obligations. This may be done in essentially three ways: the offender can *apologise* and quickly still do his duty or an equivalent of it; or the wronged partner can *punish* the other by in his turn suspending his own obligation; or the wronged partner can indirectly *condone*, i.e. accept what the other has done by waiving his right to the obligation that has been neglected.

2 Spiritual relationships of mutual agreement

Let us now turn to *spiritual* relationships modelled as analogies of mutual agreement or contractual human relationships. The fundamental difference between impersonal or manipulative relationships on the one hand, and on the other hand the two categories of mutual agreement and mutual love relationships, is that the latter are *personal.* Transferring this characteristic to the spiritual relationship means that, despite the fact that the human being and God are obviously fundamentally different, both acknowledge each other as partners, and both are responsible to each other for the maintenance and quality of the relationship. This difference between the personal and impersonal categories can have a major impact on people's spiritual lives. Let me give just one example here: how people envisage the *will of God.*

In the *impersonal* model, where the human being is the 'object' of divine power, the will of God is something that simply *overcomes you* and in which you have no say. When people meet some misfortune, they consider its ultimate cause to be the will of God, and may respond with anger, disappointment or stoicism, depending on their personality structure. In the *personal* model, however, people are likely to see the will of God as something *to be done.* Whenever they meet some misfortune, the question to ask is, 'how to *do* God's will in these circumstances?' Their emotional response to some misfortune may also be one of anger or disappointment, but the main thing is to do his will, either from a sense of obligation as in agreement relationships, or from the heart as in love relationships.

This is but one example, but it is one with which anyone can easily empathise by trying to remember as vividly as possible some critical period in one's own past. Now try to imagine first how you would feel and act if your main concern was about who or what is *doing this to you* and why. Now step back and imagine how you would feel and act if your main concern was, how can I *do the right thing* in these circumstances? Now you will probably have felt a little of how different your experience and the course of your life would be in either an impersonal or a personal model of relating to God. This exercise may help you understand how the various theological positions I am explaining, dry and theoretical though they may seem to be, are in fact cutting deep into people's emotions, feelings, attitudes and life decisions – in short, into their whole lives.

What is the basic goal, form and intention of *prayer life* in this category? Prayer in such a contractual relationship can neither be a way to force God by causal magic, nor a form of 'therapeutic' prayer. It can either be a way to oblige God, or to remind him of his obligation to act in accordance with the agreement between you (or you as faithful member of your religious community) and him. It can also be an attempt to negotiate some new conditions, or a reaffirmation of the agreement, or an expression of gratitude for being invited into this relationship, or a protest that under these particular circumstances the required duties are too difficult to perform, or a request for the moral strength needed to perform them, or an act of penitence for failed obligations, etc. In short, the communication with God is in principle much richer than in the impersonal spiritual relationship. On the other hand, it may reflect a lack of depth and purity when we compare it with the prayer life of someone who in the context of an impersonal spiritual relationship is trying to surrender himself radically to the Absolute without *any* demand for reward. It may equally reflect a lack of depth and purity when we compare it with prayer life in the context of a mutual love spiritual relationship, where spiritual depth and purity are the results of unconditional love which is its own reward.

There are many religions in the world that are contractual in the sense inferred above. People perform their prayers, rites and other duties in order to receive, for example, good harvests and other things that they need. If there is a drought or an epidemic, they try to find out in humility what obligations they have failed to honour and for this failure are intent on making amends.

Theologies using this kind of relationship as a root metaphor are definitely *not* deterministic. They assume that *both* the divine and the human partners are *personal agents*. In respect of exercising control, this type of theology also presupposes that God, like man, is *vulnerable* in the relationship. By granting man freedom and responsibility, God acknowledges that the agreed-upon services are valuable to him. Moreover, he shows that he values human personhood by *not forcing* people to perform, but rather inviting them to *share the responsibility* that the relationship with him implies. But precisely in doing so he accepts the reality of the risk he takes, the risk that he can be disappointed and that his own plans will become thwarted by human failure. Indeed this theme of God being disappointed, angry and his plans being thwarted, is a recurring one throughout the biblical Scriptures.

In the Hebrew Bible, one central theme is that at Mount Sinai God has entered into a *covenant* with the people of Israel. Christianity has taken up this theme and teaches that through the mission of Jesus, God has renewed his covenant and extended it to all humanity. The traditional translation for this covenant is 'Testament', which is why the Hebrew Bible is called the 'Old Testament' and the Scriptures about Jesus the 'New Testament'. Because of this theme of the covenant, theologies that are structured by analogy to contractual relationships have always been very influential, particularly the 'satisfaction theology'. I shall try to explain the latter shortly, because it is still influencing many people, even people who never consciously knew and accepted it. Depending on their personality structure, the acceptance or, even more significantly, the rejection of one or the other version of this 'satisfaction theology' has created subtle (and sometimes violent) disturbance of an individual's happiness and mental state.

3 Satisfaction theology

The Old and New Testament covenants are often interpreted as analogies of an agreement of rights and obligations. In the Old Testament God is said to commit himself to providing the people with both the Promised Land and blessed descendants and in return the people are required to commit themselves to honouring God by living their lives in obedience to his will. In the New Testament God promises eternal happiness to whomever believes in Christ and lives accordingly.[1] Whenever individuals and communities fail to keep their side of the agreement, they forfeit this right to eternal happiness. The relationship is then broken and needs to be restored. But remember I have already pointed out that a broken relationship of this kind can be restored in three ways. First, the offender can repent and quickly make *amends* for his failure. In theological language this is called '*satisfaction*'. Second, the wronged partner can *punish* the other. Third, he can *condone*, i.e. overlook, the offence.

Transferring this to a broken relationship with God, the penalty according to this interpretation would be for God to withhold eternal happiness and bestow eternal damnation as the offending humans' just due. To condone the offence, i.e. simply allowing the offence to pass without punishment, would be contrary to God's *justice*. Moreover, just letting the offender off would suggest that the neglected obligation is not really important to him and does not affect his real goal and interests. In this event, God (as partner in the spiritual relationship) would imply that he does not take human personhood seriously, that he does not take his own entering into a partnership with humanity seriously, which in fact implies that he does not take himself seriously. This is why he cannot *per se* accept rebellion or neglect of duty lightly. The inevitable conclusion of this is that the only way to satisfy the conditions required to restore the relationship with God *and* to avoid punishment is to give him adequate satisfaction for the failure.

So far, so good. But here again we see that the theological discussion is haunted by the problem of 'merit'. The problem is, that if human beings can *earn* reinstatement into the covenant through giving satisfaction, for example by doing 'good works', this implies that by doing such 'good works' they can claim the credit for their own 'salvation'. In other words, a straightforward satisfaction theory leaves the door wide open for a 'theology of merit', which in its turn encourages (as we have discussed earlier) the complementary attitudes of spiritual arrogance and spiritual despair. However, a theology of satisfaction can pave the way for the spiritual dangers of a theology of merit, *only if* sinners indeed *have* the full capacity to make personal and adequate satisfaction. To close that doctrinal escape route once and for always, satisfaction theology stipulates that mere human beings do *not* have that capacity, and that Christ has by his death given satisfaction in their stead. In this way all *credit* for their salvation goes to God and Christ, not to the sinners themselves.

This 'theology of satisfaction' has been very attractive ever since its formulation by Anselm of Canterbury in the eleventh century. One cause of its attraction might be that subconsciously or archetypically it may be associated with the very ancient and widespread practice of having a substitute take upon himself the punishment for the sins of the whole community thereby reconciling the community with the angry local godhead. It was practised by the ancient Egyptians, Aztecs and Babylonians, to mention only a few. In ancient Israel there was, for example, the practice of the scapegoat that on Yom Kippur, the yearly Day of Atonement, was sent into the desert, carrying all the people's sins with him. According to philosopher René Girard, scapegoating and imitating ('mimesis') are still the pre-eminent mechanisms that hold our society together.[2] Be that as it may, a therapist is well aware how therapy groups time after time treat one particular group member as their collective scapegoat.

In Western Christianity, Anselm's theology was particularly well appreciated because it avoids the 'theology of merit' without having to turn human beings into 'objects of divine manipulation'. It explains how we ourselves rather than God are agents of our own downfall. It also explains how the work of Christ is essential to restore the broken relationship between God and man and to save us from eternal punishment. Jesus Christ is the one who brings about the required satisfaction that is far beyond our own human ability to realise.

This teaching has been widely accepted and preached in all mainstream churches of Western Christianity. The fact that it is currently the subject of a heated discussion all over the Netherlands (prompted by the claim of a professor of theology that the 'satisfaction doctrine' has no foundation whatsoever in the New Testament) shows that this subject is still very much alive.[3] Emotions ran so high that considerable pressure was used on the Board of his university to dismiss him on the spot! I think it is important for therapists to realise that such matters of seemingly abstract interest are in fact vital for large numbers of ordinary people in their ordinary, everyday lives. They are vital because they provide a lifeline for people who feel through their own fault estranged from God because they have failed in being good Christians, spouses, parents, employees, or whatever.

For therapists it is important to realise that guilt in a religious context is always a two-edged sword: you have injured another person *and* you have injured God. So you have to make good to both. Satisfaction theology essentially assures people that Christ has made good for anybody who is willing to truly repent. It assures you that there is no need to spend the rest of your life in fear of divine punishment or in endless futile acts of penance, i.e. acts of self-mortification as an expression of penitence. To patients who are neurotically convinced that they are so bad that they deserve to be continually punished, it may be truly liberating and therapeutic if they can bring themselves to believe this. Satisfaction theology has a particularly vital and therapeutic element in it. It provides an opportunity for them to be spiritually and genuinely *grateful*. Trying to do better next time because one is grateful for getting a second chance gives one's whole life quite a different flavour and perspective in contrast to trying to perform better because of what one may gain from doing so – an attitude which you will recall a 'theology of merit' implicitly encourages. Incidentally, another undesirable implication of a 'theology of merit' is that we do not love God for himself alone, but merely as provider of eternal happiness. Then, as Brümmer puts it, 'we value heaven more than God!'[4] The 'theology of merit', with its implications and implicit claim on God to reward, cannot compete in spiritual quality with gratefulness for a second chance. This is why the majority of theologians throughout history have been so busy to counterbalance the 'spiritual counterproductivity' implicit in a theology of merit in their teachings.

In short, it is indeed relevant to know something about these seemingly intellectual and speculative issues. They can (and most times do) make a significant difference in the emotional and spiritual quality of numerous people's lives, and this is why they respond so passionately whenever they feel these are under attack.

4 Contractual spiritual relationships as a negative therapeutic factor

How can this category of spiritual relationships and their concomitant theologies become *obstructive for therapy*?

The category of mutual agreement or contractual relationships covers by far the largest *variety* of interpersonal relationships, each one of which may be used as a spiritual root metaphor. Negotiated mutual rights and obligations in fact structure our whole society. Yet it makes quite a difference whether the rights and obligations are educational as in the teacher-pupil relationship, or businesslike as in a commercial relationship, or judgemental as in a criminal court, or related to negotiating power as in politics, and so on. Within each of these types there is still further differentiation. Moreover, most people are not quite aware of *how* they relate to God. To find out how individuals *actually* implement spiritual relationships of the mutual agreement kind it is necessary to listen and observe very carefully. Much has to be deduced from the way they approach their problems (everyday, religious and psychological) and it may turn out to be at odds with the religious tenets they hold.

Given so many different types of contractual spiritual relationships, how can the therapist discover in what way a *particular* relationship from this category can be or is in fact a negative factor in the psychotherapeutic process? The answer obviously must depend largely on what particular model is being implemented, and what particular life experiences are integrated into it. A knowledge of the general structure of this category can however provide us with some general indications on how to proceed with this discovery.

Both from a *therapeutic* and a spiritual point of view, one conspicuous flaw of the agreement model is that, in any relationship that revolves around rendering services (as in mutual agreements), the partners are in principle *replaceable*. Despite the acknowledgement of 'personhood', each partner is by definition (although possibly not in reality) not valued for who he *is* but for the services he can offer. As such agreements are strictly speaking by definition entered into for the sake of the advantage each party can gain for himself, *the relationship is essentially instrumental and self-serving*. This implies that essentially the co-partner is replaceable by any other self-serving means, provided it is equally profitable or even more profitable.

This is so in interpersonal relationships and equally so in spiritual relationships. But the *effects* of such instrumentality are quite different in each. In social life, people have many different personal relationships. In some of these they are valued for the services they render (and paid or rewarded otherwise for them). In other relationships they are valued for the unique person they are (and loved or respected for being that unique person). And in some other relationships they are valued both for the way they fulfil their obligations *and* for the unique persons they are. As long as they have enough satisfying relationships of these kinds with enough other individuals, there need not be a problem. Agreements or contracts with other persons or organisations can become problematic of course, for example when they are grossly unfair, or if one or both parties are cheating. It could also happen that one or more of the relationships are associated with psychological problems, for example, if the person involved cannot tolerate that he is viewed as instrumental and replaceable in even the most businesslike relationship. In the latter case there is reason for a therapist to look into the psychological problem underlying this vulnerability, but in and by themselves interpersonal relationships in this category are not obstructive to therapeutic progress.

This is different for the *spiritual* relationship. The difference is that spirituality is concerned with only *one* relationship, namely the relationship with *one* God, and moreover this is a vitally important relationship that concerns the person's *whole* life, not just a part of it.

In principle, a theology modelled on an agreement relationship *denies* the unique value of each individual as a person. In that respect, Anselm's theology is consistent with this model: if God values his own honour more than he values me, I am replaceable by anybody else who is able to satisfy his honour. It does not matter to him whether it is I or Christ in my stead who does so, provided his honour is satisfied.

If, as a result of this type of theology, the human individual feels he is replaceable and only valued for the way he executes his obligations in such an important and all-encompassing relationship, this can *damage a person's self-esteem* much more than any interpersonal relationship can ever do. If on top of that the person feels he has failed and therefore lost any value he may have had for God, the result can be a self-despair that is indeed a formidable obstruction to therapeutic progress. Any attempt to help the person to restore his self-esteem by making him feel valued and respected by, for example, other group members will predictably founder on this underlying spiritual damage.

Another therapeutically problematic aspect of agreement or contractual relationships is that they create such a *close connection between failure, guilt and punishment*. Each therapist knows how notoriously difficult it is to help patients who are entrapped in problems of this kind at the psychological level. It is easy to see that therapeutic work will be even more difficult when their psychological guilt feelings are reinforced by a conviction that they are guilty towards God and therefore *deserve* to be punished. I have already touched on that theme in the commentaries on vignette 11, the woman who was convinced the death of her child was a punishment for her adultery. Therefore I will confine myself here to one example: Ciarrocchi writes that, whenever therapy of obsessive-compulsive disorders is not a success, this is quite often the result of the therapist's non-recognition of religious scrupulosity. The patient involved has kept silent about how his spiritual life is poisoned by moral anxiousness. He found that once their spiritual problem is allowed to be discussed in therapy, it appears that even atheistic and agnostic therapists have remarkable success with patients who sometimes have been treated unsuccessfully for many years.[5]

The earlier discussion on the dangers of a theology of merit has already noted that a spirituality that identifies the value of a person with his performance all too easily leads to, on the one hand, arrogance and self-righteousness in people who can and do perform well, and on the other hand to despair with people who forever try and fail. We have characterised satisfaction theology as an historical attempt to prevent people from getting caught in one of these two traps. Despite its longstanding popularity, satisfaction theology's success has been limited. It has introduced a problem of its own: if taken literally and superficially as many people tend to do, then the story emerging from satisfaction theology about God's justice, love and satisfaction is a rather cruel story. What father, divine or not, would allow his son to be put to death in order to reinstate a broken relationship? It then entails a concept of God that is radically defective from a spiritual point of view: if the account of the death of Christ is misunderstood as *divine cruelty*, then there is little chance that the contractual relationship will be warmed and enriched by mutual love, as in a happy marriage in which both partners undoubtedly have justice related obligations towards each other but which they execute from the depth of their hearts.

The idea of the sacrifice of the Son has indeed offended many people. If people tell you they reject God, they may, in fact, be rejecting this or some other cruel *account* of God rather than God himself. They are right: cruelty, divine or not, should be rejected. But for people with an authentic spiritual longing, their rejection of God himself leaves them with an underlying sense of meaninglessness which cannot but impede both spiritual and therapeutic progress. Therefore it is always worthwhile to ask just *what* it is they reject, and *why*. Encouragement for them to say what is *un*acceptable to them may set them thinking about what to them *is* acceptable – which often marks a turn both in their spiritual and in their therapeutic process.

To sum up, everything that may go wrong in interpersonal contractual relationships may also go wrong in spiritual relationships which are modelled in an analogous manner to these, but even more so. And everything that in fact goes wrong in such spiritual relationships is likely to become an underlying spiritual problem that intensifies the individual's psychological problems. Some particularly sensitive areas of this type of inner conflict and anxiousness are: performance versus failure to perform; mature conscience versus scrupulosity; real versus imagined guilt; responsibility versus paralysing fear of it; scapegoating; vagueness about what one is required to do and therefore never feeling secure; never daring to say enough is enough; fair play versus cheating or feeling cheated.

5 Exploring the potential for therapeutic change

The argument in section 7 of Chapter 18 (on assessing spiritual relationships) has been that, in those cases where a person's theology is obviously destructive for his mental health, it is generally a sound strategy to seek for solutions *within* the overall religious framework of the person involved. That is, to seek the space within that framework where the person is open to new and liberating insights without making him feel his faith is under attack or obliging him to let go of the positive aspects of his present relationship with God and his religious community. A valid model of that overall framework can be derived from the *human* relationship that functions as a root metaphor of his spiritual relationship. Chapter 19 (on impersonal or manipulative relationships) discussed how by analysing the metaphor on which the particular spiritual relationship of a particular person is modelled, a therapist can make a valid assessment of the relationship's change potential, that is to say, the space it has for change in the direction of more inner freedom, more perspective, more mature ways of relating to self and others. In that chapter I have suggested that such an exploration of the change potential can be performed in three directions: we can look for possibilities for a more positive implementation that are *inherent* to the relational root metaphor in question, or for elements in the person's theology that *counterbalance* the prevailing negative elements, or we can tie in with the fact that most relationships are *composite* and therefore contain elements from other types of relationships.

Let us now apply this strategy to spiritual relationships (and their concomitant theologies) modelled on the category of agreements of mutual rights and obligations. What latent change possibilities do such spiritual relationships offer? For a real assessment we need of course more specific information about the actual person involved and about his actual spiritual relationship. But some general points can be made, as was done in Chapter 19 concerning the assessment of the potential for change in the category of impersonal relationships and their concomitant deterministic theologies.

First, one could look for the opportunities for spiritual growth that are *inherent* in the category itself. Obviously, a spirituality that is basically self-serving and calculating is less likely to grow in depth and intimacy than a spirituality that is basically other-directed. But that is not inevitably so. Given the dynamics of this category of contractual relationships, people can for example change in the direction of a less strictly self-serving view and a more compassionate practice of mutual rights and obligations with others and with God. Or, to give another example, they can learn how to fulfil their obligations primarily because they are honourable people who *want* to keep their promises, and not primarily because they will get a prompt and proportional reward. As another example, they can learn to accept when they have transgressed that they are really allowed to make a new start, and so on. Such opportunities for spiritual growth are usually also favourable for therapeutic progress. Simply to recognise where the spiritual relationship has become out of balance and how this can be interfering constantly and negatively with their interpersonal conflicts is a significant step in spiritual and psychological growth. Being well acquainted with all that may go wrong in human relationships, it is feasible for a therapist to see the parallels in a God-human relationship and therefore be able as a therapist to figure out where he can look for the positive elements that can be linked in the therapeutic process.

Second, one could look for positive elements in the patient's philosophy and theological reasoning that *counterbalance* any implementations of the spiritual relationship that are therapeutically obstructive. For example, attention has been drawn above to the fact that satisfaction theology was intended as a counterbalance to the negative effects of a spiritual relationship that is strictly construed as an agreement of rights and obligations, and its con-comitant 'theology of merit'. We have noted that the satisfaction theory indeed provides a counterbalance, but that it, in its turn, creates new difficulties. However, what may be theologically unsatisfactory is *not necessarily* spiritually and therapeutically so. People may ignore these disadvantages, or consider them to be divine mysteries that are too deep for them, or, it is hoped, they may conclude that the superficial and cruel interpretation of the Father demanding the sacrifice of his Son *cannot* be right and start searching for a deeper spiritual meaning and indeed discover one. Meanwhile, they may profit spiritually and therapeutically from the support and psychological balance that satisfaction theology can offer them. They may derive their lost or seriously damaged self-respect from their feeling of being acknowledged as free and responsible persons contributing to God's plan for humanity. Fulfilling their obligations in their relationship with God fairly may well lead to a very rewarding lifestyle; falling short in their obligations need not lead to paralysing fear nor to diminishing their sense of God's holiness.

Third, because by far the most spiritual relationships are *composite*, i.e. mixed with elements of the other categories of impersonal and of mutual love relationships, one could look for positive elements in such composite relationships. In *human* relationships, agreements and contracts are seldom *restricted* to the mutual obligations people are supposed to have committed themselves to. In the same way that the Romans were in the long term not able to keep treating their slaves strictly as 'non-persons', we too seem to be unable to keep our contractual relationships strictly businesslike. The difference between my shopping in a supermarket in the centre of Amsterdam and my shopping in the local shop on the next street owned by the same family for generations is, for example, that my personal relationship with the latter is a unique combination of a 'contractual buyer-seller relationship' with elements of 'mutual friendship', created by both them and me in the matrix of this particular family's and this particular neighbourhood's history. Similar processes happen in the *spiritual* relationship, modifying it into a *composite* of obligations and an affective and uniquely personal relationship. The latter is unquestionably relevant for therapeutic change. Satisfaction theology, to reuse that as an example, has consciously created space for such affective elements. Responding to Jesus with thankfulness for his loving self-sacrifice and returning his love may give warmth and depth to a relationship that otherwise might become all too strictly give-and-take in character. Above all, people may experience in their innermost self that they are reconciled with God and healed by his overwhelming and radically renewing love, notwithstanding their shortcomings and failures. This is the spiritual experience such theologies as the satisfaction theory try to safeguard. They are never simply intellectual or speculative theories.

CHAPTER 22

Mutual Love
(or Fellowship) Relationships

1 The category of mutual love (or fellowship) human relationships

This is the third basic category of human relationships that Brümmer calls attention to. It consists of relationships between persons each of whom freely choose the best interests of the other partner in the relationship as their own good. Examples of such relationships are the ideal ones that can and may exist between man and wife, between parents and children or between friends. In his book on love Brümmer argues that *love* is the outstanding paradigm of this category, given that we understand love primarily as a *relationship* between persons and not just as a feeling or an attitude of one individual – although feelings and attitudes do, of course, come into love relationships as they do in all human relationships.

Love or fellowship relations, like mutual agreements, are *personal*. That is to say, they are possible only if both partners freely choose to involve themselves in them, and if each partner acknowledges the freedom and responsibility of the other as well as his own dependence on the other for establishing, maintaining and improving the relationship. But in love or mutual fellowship relationships, unlike in agreements, each partner chooses to serve the interests of the other *without obligation*. Characteristically, both partners value the other (as well as their relationship with him) *for no other reason than that they appreciate each other for the persons they are*. They cannot have quite the same relationship with anybody else because theirs is a unique creation between these two particular individuals. This is in sharp contrast with the former category of agreement relationships, where partners were as partners in principle interchangeable with whomever else could offer the same agreed-upon benefits. In the love or fellowship relationship, the partners bestow personal value and identity on each other and that makes them special and irreplaceable to each other.

In both agreement and love relationship categories the partners make themselves *vulnerable in relation to each other*. Yet there is a difference in the risk in which each relationship involves them. In agreements and contracts, honouring of obligations is critical for the relationship. But in mutual love and fellowship, relationships are entered into and maintained on the basis of a valuing of the other as a unique person. So *you yourself as the loving and beloved partner are at stake*. Love relationships differ from most others also in that they entail a desire for *reciprocation*. This implies that people can hurt each other deeply by refusing or violating the relationship: the one then rejects the other as the person he is and not only as a satisfier of needs and provider of benefits.

How can such relationships go wrong? Relationships of this kind are *open commitments*. There is no specification of rights and duties, and neither is it clear beforehand just how each partner is supposed to act for the good of the other in any future situation. The relationship requires that the partners adopt a lifelong attitude of dedication towards each other. At any given time, such dedication may show itself in unforeseen activities which may share only one thing in common, namely that they are sincerely intended to be in the best interest of the other and of the relationship. Such relationships can tragically go wrong if one partner acts or behaves in a manner contrary to the interests of the other, or contrary to the quality of their interaction. If this should happen, the relationship is marred or even broken.

A broken love or fellowship relationship hurts deeply precisely because the injured partner's value *as a person*, his very identity, has been belittled. How can that ever be restored? Condoning it, i.e. simple acceptance of the fault by the involved party, cannot be enough. This, in principle, would imply that the offended partner denies that he has been really injured. This in turn would mean that he denies that he is really and personally involved in the other. Neither can punishment and satisfaction *per se* restore a personal bond of love, trust and dedication. There is only one way to restore that bond, and that is through the willingness of the injured partner to identify with the offending partner in spite of what he did. In other words, through *forgiveness*. But forgiveness can effectively heal the relationship only if the other *sincerely* repents and desires to restore it. If this was not required, the injured person would resign himself to the other's breaking off the relationship rather than repairing it. Another condition for effective restoration is that forgiveness has to be the *wish and free decision of the injured partner* to come into the relationship again. No expression of repentance and desire for renewal can in and of itself earn forgiveness. The conditions mentioned above must be met by both partners. If this is not so, the result is at best a feigned or partial restoration of the love relationship.

Once real forgiveness is asked for by the offending party and granted by the offended partner, then that very fact causes the love or friendship to become deeper and stronger. Partners now have come to know something new and relevant about each other. The offended partner has shown himself to be a person who is able to forgive the pain of betrayal because he really desires to keep the other as a friend or beloved. And the offender has shown himself to be a partner who values the other so much that he prefers to acknowledge his faults rather than to risk losing the love relationship with him.

2 Spiritual relationships of mutual love or fellowship

Let us now turn to *spiritual* relationships modelled as analogies of human relationships of mutual love or fellowship. In their concomitant theologies some human relationship of this category functions as a root metaphor. In such spiritual relationships, both God and man are vulnerable, because neither can compel, cause or oblige the other to reciprocate. But God is surprisingly the more vulnerable of the two because *he* keeps his commitments whereas *we* humans all too often break or just forget ours. As in human relationships of this type, the necessary and sufficient conditions for reconciliation are not punishment, satisfaction or condoning, but penitence and forgiveness. Nothing more is required than to acknowledge you have damaged the fellowship, demonstrate your sincerity, and express your desire to be forgiven. Unlike in human relationships, God will never fail to forgive the truly penitent.

Christian theologies of this type make a connection between the death of Christ and human salvation that satisfaction theology does not. In the model of love as a relationship, the person who forgives has to pay the price for reconciliation, because he is willing to suffer the consequences of the wrong done to him rather than lose the friend or beloved. The death of Christ reveals the extent of God's willingness to suffer and forgive. Jesus' actively seeking out people whom society considered to be irretrievably lost reveals the same attitude. It shows how precious the relationship with even these objectionable people is to God. Existentially, many people both religious and non-religious respond with deep feeling to precisely this aspect of Christian spirituality. The view that ultimate happiness consists in being in a relationship of mutual love with the transcendent God has been a constant all throughout history. This has been more often and more passionately expressed in spiritual writings, poems, hymns and prayers than in systematic theology, something due to the break-up between spirituality and theology discussed in section 4 of Chapter 7.

Spiritual relationships created by analogy with human love or friendship are potentially very rich because they presuppose both partners to be interested in each other's unique personhood and in the quality of the interaction. In such a relationship, both God and humans are free persons in relation to each other, freely committing themselves to each other not because they expect some profit in return, but rather because the other is precious to them. Prayer in such a relationship is opening up towards God. Implementing a spiritual relationship of this type is *not* simply performing specific actions and that's it. Being an open commitment, it may develop in unforeseen directions. Therefore there is no saying beforehand what particular action in any future situation will follow from your commitment to relating lovingly to God and his creation – which includes your own existence. Most of the time, it comes down to trying to do whatever you do with all the love, care and integrity that you can put into it. In doing so you will be ploughing and sowing in rich spiritual soil.

3 Characteristics and learning aspects of spiritual relationships of mutual love or fellowship

The most important characteristics and learning aspects of spiritual relationships of mutual love or fellowship have already been implied in the chapters of Part 3 (on existential and cognitive aspects of spirituality) and Chapter 17 (on convergence and divergence between therapeutic and spiritual learning and change processes). These chapters took spiritual relationships of this type for granted, but let us recapitulate.

The discussion about the *existential* aspects of spiritual awakening and spiritual True Self is about how the human partner in such a relationship discovers his own yearning for a mutual love relationship and how he needs to 'purify' his spiritual longing from inauthentic motivations. The discussion about the *cognitive* aspects is about how experiential knowledge of the divine partner is needed to establish a loving relationship with him and how such 'illuminative' knowledge needs to be 'purified' from projection, illusion and self-deception. Together, these chapters give an account of how spiritual relationships of mutual love or fellowship *come into being.* Chapter 17 then followed with a discussion of those relational qualities that people have to learn in order to *maintain and develop* this type of spiritual relationship. It also explored some areas in which these learning processes converge and diverge with processes that most therapies consider as being favourable for their patients.

After Chapter 17 the discussion took a turn. The issue addressed was now 'how to deal with patients whose spirituality and its concomitant theology is in *conflict* with the therapeutic goal?' To get a handle on this complex problem, I first introduced the three basic relational categories that function as root metaphors ('key models') for three different ways in which people construe their relationship with God. Each of these, it was pointed out, offers its own distinct opportunities and its own obstacles for the therapeutic effort. The chapters which followed focused on the first and the second of the three types of spiritual relationships: the impersonal and the contractual ones.

In the present chapter I am returning to spiritual relationships of mutual love and fellowship, but now characterising these *explicitly* as analogies of human relationships of mutual love or fellowship. With the introduction of this third category I am therefore linking up again with Chapters 13–17, in which most of the characteristics and learning aspects of spiritual relationships of this type have already been discussed. What remains is the question 'could a spiritual relationship of this type in some circumstances prove *obstructive to therapeutic progress* and, if so, what is its potential for change in a more positive direction?'

4 Spiritual relationships of mutual love or fellowship as a negative therapeutic factor

'Change' in relationships of the mutual love category is not primarily change of behaviour. It is you, your unique self, who has to change, mainly along the lines indicated in Chapter 17, i.e. learning receptivity, inwardness, trust, reverence, obedience, and so on. There is much more, of course, as I have selected only learning aspects that in my opinion are the most relevant for therapists to know about. I have already shown how in principle this kind of change largely converges with therapeutic learning and how the divergent learning aspects are more a matter of imbalance than of real conflict. The structural analysis in the preceding sections now calls for two critical additions. These are: one must learn to *accept forgiveness* and to develop the *capacity to forgive others*, to prefer sincerely to suffer rather than break the relationship with whomsoever has rejected or betrayed you as a person. Both in human and spiritual relationships, accepting and giving forgiveness can be a very painful and demanding process.[1] This is also true of the implied process of 'purifying' oneself from insincerity and, above all, from a *misguided* sense of duty: 'as a Christian I ought to forgive and therefore I am in the wrong if I do not succeed in forgiving.' Such concerns as those mentioned above of course may complicate and delay the therapeutic process, but in the end dealing with them can only prove to be a positive therapeutic factor. *Not* dealing with them will inevitably prove to be a negative factor – both spiritually and therapeutically.

In short, I don't think spiritual relationships modelled on mutual fellowship or love can very easily become truly obstructive to therapy, provided the therapist recognises what his patient is striving for at that particular point of his spiritual involvement.

5 Spiritual non-fulfilment

There is, however, something else that is spiritually and therapeutically relevant and needs to be mentioned. This is the negative effects resulting from a person's disappointment when a passionate yearning to experience divine reciprocity is going *unfulfilled*. In such a situation much suffering is experienced, because divine reciprocity can be one of the deepest longings in an individual's life. As a therapist, you can often sense it behind expressions of spiritual homesickness, bitterness, sarcasm and isolation. The potential for therapeutic change is dependent on the cause of such a deep experience of spiritual non-fulfilment. Quite often the cause in the main is due to a psychological problem and therefore often amenable to psychotherapy. Below are some examples of both some psychological and some spiritual causes of lack of fulfilment.

The most obvious cause of spiritual non-fulfilment is when people's *capacity to love and be loved* has been damaged in the interaction with others. People may not be able to accept or believe they are loved for who they are. Sometimes they cannot even imagine what it would be to be loved at all and consequently cannot be receptive to messages of love. Or people may have been so disappointed or betrayed by their loves so often that they are afraid to trust anybody any more, God included. There is little need here to remind therapists about this kind of damage. Sadly it is encountered only too often. I think the first thing for a therapist to do is to approach the psychological level, work through the patient's traumatic past, let him gradually learn what it is to love and be loved. Before this psychological level is reached, his spiritual yearning will probably give rise to despair rather than hope and fulfilment.

Another common cause of spiritual non-fulfilment is *spiritual 'Schöngeisterei'*, an untranslatable ironic German term for a philosophy of life with an emphasis on the aesthetic and a distinct odour of conceit.[2] Applied to spiritual love, it means something like manufacturing the most lofty daydreams about your beautiful selfless love for God and humanity which have little or nothing to do with reality. It is self-idealising, and maybe God-idealising, but as in human relationships it is hardly a basis for any real reciprocity. A similar shallow idealisation may happen at the experiential level, when the 'Schöngeisterei' applies to having beautiful spiritual experiences. People infer from mystical literature or over-charismatic leaders the idea that expressions like 'union' or 'communion' with God refer to having continual beautiful ecstatic experiences. Such experiences indeed happen occasionally, but all renowned mystics assure us that far more important is just to involve yourself actually and on a day-to-day basis in loving acts. Fixating on one particular kind of experience is destined to make you blind and unreceptive to other communications, including divine reciprocity. Small wonder then that you don't pick these up.

Something very similar to the idealising referred to above is *suppressing negative feelings*. Therapists are only too familiar with patients who from early childhood have learnt to suppress any negative feelings against their parents. Likewise, some people think that they cannot afford to feel angry, disappointed or wronged towards God. Some have even completely repressed any such feelings, but beneath all their sweetness and apparent lack of negativity lurks a terrible anger – with all its potentially destructive consequences for the relationship with God and for the person himself. A Roman Catholic nun, a nice woman and a competent teacher, once told me that she felt guilty because she was addicted to smoking. I asked her how much she smoked. 'Two cigarettes a day.' Most of us would hardly call that an addiction, and even less see the need to feel guilty about it. However, listen to the circumstances. She was not allowed to have money, so she stole cigarettes and money from her pupils. As a nun of that particular order, she was also not allowed to smoke, so she had to do that in the toilet, otherwise her sisters could smell the cigarette smoke in her room. I asked her if she had talked it over with her spiritual director. She had indeed, but he had only answered her that he himself had managed to stop smoking within one week. I asked whether she thought Jesus himself would smoke, had he lived in our times. She said, 'Maybe, but then he is a man and I am a woman.' I probed further. It appeared that she deeply resented Jesus. Being a nun, she was supposed to be his spiritual bride and to love him unconditionally, but when we discussed this in detail, her bridegroom looked rather like a nagging tyrant, enforcing a large number of detailed infantilising regulations upon her, and all the time spying on her to catch her breaking them. She had never allowed herself to realise her resentment. As a result, her authentic religious vocation had never had a chance to develop into a mature loving relationship.

Yet another cause for spiritual non-fulfilment is the *testing of the faith*. Obviously, we humans not only need to *use* metaphors and theologies to engage in a spiritual relationship, but also need to *get rid* of them, otherwise we will just stay at the psychological level of communicating with the 'internalised other' rather than with the other partner himself. In a very fundamental and rather paradoxical way, we have to purify ourselves from our religious thought and imagination, in order to move from 'my God' to 'God himself'. I have already mentioned the important task of religious education and practice to correct the personalised images of God we construe from our own experience, from self-idealisation, and from wishful thinking. Your spiritual goal is that you want to relate with the *real* other, not with an image of him. We have to detach ourselves from *any* image, both of God *and of ourselves*. Although these God-images and self-images do have their function for a while, their function is definitely a temporary one. Ultimately we have to get rid of all of them. They stand in the way of the real encounter that is at the core and is the essence of a real relationship. This process is what the 'testing of the faith' is all about. It is an ongoing process of emptying of the mind, and very painful because it feels as if nothing is left once the metaphors, the theologies, the self-images and the mental God-representations have been stripped away. It requires absolute honesty, not pretending that you understand more than you in fact do, not trying to do more than you are in fact able to do, not trying to manipulate yourself into experiences you do not have, not to identify with anything, not even with your identity as a spiritual person. There are times when nothing is left. You have to stay within that emptiness then, and wait. Some people then experience intense crisis-like periods which in the Christian spiritual tradition are called 'dark nights of the soul'. With others, the process is more gradual but nevertheless intensely painful. In the commentaries on vignettes 6 and 7 (the businessman who had a near-accident and Tolstoy) I have discussed in more detail how a period of spiritual 'darkness' is often a precursor of a person's spiritual awakening, and how spiritual 'dark nights' may occur in the course of one's further spiritual development. There I have also paid attention to the fact (which can be very important for a therapist to be aware of) that this may easily become mistaken for a depression, but that a depression is in several ways of a quite different character. Important too to know is that without such purifying and the ensuing period of spiritual non-fulfilment, the deepening of the spiritual relationship and the growth to spiritual maturity will at some point inevitably stagnate.

As a last example of a source of spiritual non-fulfilment in the spiritual love relationship I want to mention people who *take the analogy with human relationships* too far. This is quite understandable because you do not sit down and think, 'which root metaphor shall I use for understanding and implementing my relationship with God?' Usually you just construe your ideas from your interactions with your family and from literature, film or television, and then transfer them to God and your relationship with him unthinkingly. Thus if the one outstanding loving figure in your life has been an indulgent grandfather, then there is the possibility that you will identify love with indulgence. But if you expect the perfect love of God to be identical with the greatest indulgence imaginable, you will definitely be disappointed. The love of God is anything but indulgent! Your root metaphor is probably in part valid in that there is real mutual love between you and your grandfather, but also in part invalid since indulgence, good intentioned as it can be, is at best misguided love. Religious education is meant to correct such deficient images, but does not always succeed in doing so. One purpose in reading the Gospels is that Jesus represents the love-of-God-in-action, and as such can correct mistaken images inferred from defective and imperfect human loves. And one of the functions of the doctrine that Jesus was fully God *and* fully man is to emphasise that Jesus reveals the love of God in *both* the great cosmic acts of Jesus' death and resurrection through which death is in principle conquered, *and* the 'divine humanity' Jesus displays in the way he acts as one human being among others.

So we are touching again one of those difficult doctrinal formulations which have caused so many to consider religion irrational. Certainly, such ancient formulations can be strange to us. But they are anything but irrational from the viewpoint of 'living reason', that is, the rational processes involved in how people make sense of their own life experiences and direct their actions in real-life situations. I have already tried to show this earlier (in section 7 of Chapter 17), but allow me one more example, just to show how relevant it may be for therapists to be aware of the ideas behind such seemingly obsolete doctrines, ideas that are still vital for spiritual life.

6 Doctrine and spiritual root metaphor

The following vignette is taken from an autobiographical article by theologian Roberta Bondi.[3] Roberta had a very strict father, and as a child she suffered from terrible nightmares because she assumed that her heavenly father was like her earthly father, only more so. One day, while browsing in the Bodleian library in Oxford, she found an exotic book: sermons of an early-sixth-century Egyptian bishop. Thumbing through its pages, one phrase caught her eye. It said monks should treat each other with the gentleness of our heavenly father, who especially loves the ones the world despises, and who is always so much more willing than human beings to make allowances for sin. This because God alone understands our circumstances, the depths of our temptations and the extent of our sufferings. She was astounded. God the Father gentle and making allowances? This was new to her. She then started looking up the names of God as found in the Bible. She found a whole set of names for God she had always overlooked until that moment: 'faithful one'; 'shelter from the scorching heat'; 'wings of a great bird'; 'the one who sides with the outcast against the powerful'; 'mother'; 'creator'; 'quiet voice'; 'light'; 'love'. She writes:

Vignette 19

I was beginning to understand how those names of nurture, life, and gentleness not only modified the meaning of the magisterial names of God, like almighty, king, warrior, and judge, but actually seemed to have turned their meaning upside down. Perhaps, I thought, Scripture turns the meaning of the name 'Father' upside down as well.

Now, for the first time, I could see the point of the orthodox insistence that the Son is not subordinate to the Father... It means, if the human Jesus who is also God does not spend his time bossing around his friends, intimidating or demanding obedience from them, then the Father must not demand our unquestioning obedience, or wish to intimidate us, either... It means, if Jesus' particular concern is for the healing and empowerment of the poor, the widows, those with loathsome social diseases, and the crooks, so was the Father's... Mary and Martha are Jesus' adult friends. Because they love him, they are not submissive or subservient. They are not in the least afraid of him. They are not sullenly, silently angry with him... They tell him they are angry with him, and why. As for Jesus, he does not simply tolerate these uppity women. He values them. He chooses them for his closest friends. He trusts them in their anger with him, and he trusts them with his life.

The amazing aspect of Roberta's illuminative experience is that she is a professional theologian. When she made her discovery about the doctrine of the relationship between the Father and the Son, she had already been teaching this very same doctrine for years. She knew it, but she knew it 'with her head, not with her heart'. Keeping head and heart together is exactly what 'living reason' is all about (cf. section 7 in Chapter 17).

At the end of her article Roberta describes how some time after this new insight, she decided to visit her father from whom she had been estranged for many years. She writes how for the first time she came to see him through adult eyes, not her childhood image of a powerful, mythical father, but rather her real human father. For the first time in her life she argues with him and is amazed to discover that her father wants her just as she is, and needs her friendship. As with the Nicaraguans, the doctrinal correction here is a precursor of the therapeutic effect. It does not just precede it, it appears to have been a necessary precondition for therapy. Strange though the formulation of such doctrines may seem, they point to mature, realistic and truly compassionate love. I think it is worthwhile for therapists to be sufficiently familiar with what the most important ones really have to say, even though they say it in a language and in images that are many centuries removed from us. Just a hint in the right direction may be enough for religious patients to start moving from 'head-knowledge' to 'head-and-heart-knowledge' as Roberta did.

Concluding Part 4

The chapters of Part 4 have focused on the spiritual change process resulting from the individual's conscious participation in spiritual life, either in some traditional form or by figuring out one's own way as Hammarskjøld, Weil and Hillesum did. I have approached this process as an ongoing spiritual relationship between God and man, which operates as the context in which the individual's spiritual development grows and deepens – or stagnates. Because the spiritual relationship, in contrast with human relationships, affects the *whole* life, it also acts as the context in which the individual's *psychological* make-up operates. When this context changes, the basic psychology does not necessarily change, but other aspects of it may be highlighted or put into the background. So it is dependent on one's mental structure whether or not the aspects of spiritual involvement discussed in these chapters actually present or cause a particular problem for any particular person.

Much as in most personal relationships between two individuals, spiritual relationships are complex and unique. Yet it can be important for a therapist to assess whether and in what way a patient's spiritual relationship affects his therapy. In my opinion this can be done by looking at the deep structure of the patient's spiritual relationship. This is in principle possible because the human partner understandably tends to construe his relationship with God as an analogy of the human relationships known to him. In other words, human relationships operate as root metaphors for implementing spiritual relationships.

Furthermore, these analogies have given rise to *theologies* that are still determining the majority of the Christian churches. I have tried to characterise briefly the three types of theologies that are modelled on the three basic categories of human relationships. Possibly the reader will have felt put off by such theological reasoning of the past. Indeed it is far removed from the way of thinking he has been taught in academia. The point is, whether you consider these theologies and their originally underlying reasoning invalid or not, for you as a psychotherapist they are *facts*. That is to say, they are part and parcel of the religious foundation matrix that has shaped the individual's psyche to a large extent. All three types of spiritual relationships, as well as various combinations and modifications of them, have been taught to generations upon generations all over the Western world. As a result, they still have great influence on how people find meaning and direction in their lives. It is important to realise that this meaning and direction *may* be quite a different from what psychotherapeutic theory and practice (mostly tacitly) assumes it *should* be.

When using this analysis, one should remain constantly aware that there is a continual *tension* between, on the one hand, the necessity to use adequate metaphors and theologies for implementing the relationship with the Divine and, on the other hand, the necessity to acknowledge that they are all functionally incomplete and at some point in someone's spiritual growth need to be abandoned. If they are not, then they will in the end stand in the way of relating person to Person.

How to Proceed Further

Given the breadth and the diversity of the subject matter, I have presented a general structure that is meant to help psychotherapists find the most relevant connections between psychotherapy and spirituality. As in finding your way in an unknown city you start your orienting with mapping the main streets, I have offered a sort of map which you as a reader can implement as your understanding and expertise increase through further studies and practical experience.

In the introduction to this book I explained why I have mainly restricted myself to one spiritual tradition, namely mainstream Christianity. Depending on the population in your practice it may be necessary to think through the implications for *other spiritual traditions*, (Christian and non-Christian). Let me briefly indicate the applicability of the chapters of this book to such other spiritual traditions.

The chapters of Part 2 (about plausibility structures, metacommunication and root metaphors) can be applied to a broad clientele. In these chapters I have sketched the dominant attitude in secularised Western culture towards mainstream Christianity. Its attitude towards other Christian and non-Christian religions and spiritualities is basically the same, although for example a Mormon is likely to evoke (or to expect he will evoke) a different set of these (sub)cultural prejudices from a Roman Catholic, who will in his turn probably evoke other responses than a Muslim or a member of some New Age movement. Although currently there is indication of a trend to shift away from potentially negative attitudes in cross-(sub)cultural interchanges, it is still necessary to be aware of and to recognise subtle attitudes both positive and negative, and to be alert for phenomena of metatransference and meta-countertransference.

Most chapters of Part 3 (about existential and cognitive aspects) are also applicable to a broad clientele, particularly the sections about the struggle for existential authenticity and intellectual integrity. This is so because these chapters treat aspects that are inherent to the process of spiritual awakening that in many cases precedes the seeking of a spiritual 'home'.

The chapters of Part 4 (about convergence and divergence between spiritual and therapeutic learning goals and about different types of spiritual relationships) apply only to forms of spirituality that are connected with the religions in which a personal Godhead is central. The only exception is the chapter on impersonal relationships, which in part also applies to people who orient themselves to an impersonal transcendent reality.

Thinking through the implications of this for a wider spiritually minded clientele (either 'personal Godhead oriented' or 'impersonal transcendent reality oriented'), requires *more information about the specific types of spiritual life* of the people you are in fact dealing with. This book offers a basic structure that allows you to select *which* information you need (otherwise you are in danger of drowning in the wealth of available information) and to decide *how* this more detailed information can be fitted in that basic structure. Please remember that the spiritual metaphors I have presented as organising principles for spiritual life are *systematisations*. They are emphatically *not* descriptions of differences *between* religions or spiritual traditions. For example, spiritual relationships that are strictly modelled as an analogy to a contract ('if I, human being, perform this or that religious duty, I have the right to expect from You, Divine Being, that you give me this or that favour') can be found *within* religions as widely varied as tribal worship to New Age spiritual movements to the major institutionalised world religions. Therefore you need to match the information about the particular spirituality of the person involved with the typology presented in this book.

Following is a list of recommended readings that can help you explore further the interplay between spirituality and psychotherapy. Each reference is selected for what I have found is its potential as background material to assist you as a therapist help those patients whose person is being enriched or impoverished (or perceived as being so) through his 'spiritual connection'.

Recommended titles
for further study

Psychology of religion

Hood Jr, R.W. (ed) (1995) *Handbook of Religious Experience*. Birmingham, AL: Religious Education Press.

This book covers: religious experience in Judaism, Catholicism, Islam, Buddhism and Hinduism; religious experience in the context of philosophy, sociology and phenomenology; religious experience and psychological theories (Freudian, Jungian, object relations, developmental, cognitive, affective, behavioural, role, attribution, attachment, transpersonal and feminist theory); religious experience and the body.

Spilka, B. and McIntosh, D.N. (eds) (1996) *The Psychology of Religion: Theoretical Approaches*. Boulder, CO: Westview Press.

Discussions of: functions of religion; social concerns; development of individual religiosity; influence of religion on worldview; experiential dimension of religion; original articles of renowned authors in the field.

Wulff, D.M. (1991) *Psychology of Religion: Classic and Contemporary Views*. New York: Wiley.

A comprehensive introduction to the psychology of religion, integrating theoretical, empirical and clinical literatures; biological foundations of religion; behavioural and comparative theories of religion; experimental and correlational approaches; the Freudian psychoanalytic perspective; object relations theory; Erikson; Jung; William James; phenomenological and interpretive psychologies; American humanistic and transpersonal psychology.

The interplay between religion/spirituality and psychotherapy

Benner, D. (1988) *Psychotherapy and the Spiritual Quest: Examining the Links between Psychological and Spiritual Health*. Grand Rapids, MI: Baker Book House, London: Hodder & Stoughton.

An examination of the religious roots of psychotherapy; views of spirituality found in the psychologies of Jung, Kierkegaard, May and others; the history and understanding of spirituality in a variety of Christian traditions; a model of personality as psychospiritual unity.

Bhugra, D. (ed) (1996) *Psychiatry and Religion: Context, Consensus and Controversies*. London and New York: Routledge.

A look at historical and theoretical issues; religions and psychiatry (Christianity, new African-American religious groups, Hinduism, Buddhism, new religions and Islam); articles on neurophysiology, psychopathology, guilt, pastoral counselling.

Fallot, R.D. (ed) (1998) *Spirituality and Religion in Recovery from Mental Illness*, New Directions for Mental Health Services no. 80. San Francisco, CA: Jossey-Bass.

Articles on spiritual and religious dimensions of mental illness recovery narratives; the assessment of spirituality and implications for service planning; the place of spirituality and religion in mental health services; the faith community as a support for people with mental illness; first-person accounts of the role of spirituality in the course of serious mental illness.

Jones, J.W. (1991) *Contemporary Psycho-Analysis and Religion: Transference and Transcendence*. New Haven, CT and London: Yale University Press.

Focus on the newer models of transference as the central category for researching and understanding religious experience; analysis of four cases shows connections between dynamics operative in individuals' transferences and their religious experiences before and during therapy; some important literature on the experience of the sacred (Rudolph Otto, Christopher Bollas, Paul Tillich and Martin Buber); a psychology of the sacred.

Koenig, H.G. (ed) (1998) *Handbook of Religion and Mental Health*. San Diego, CA: Academic Press.

Excellent articles about the connections between spirituality, religion, and physical and mental health. The book is divided into six sections: (1) historical background; (2) research; (3) religion and mental functioning; (4) religious perspectives on mental health (Protestant, Catholic, Mormon, Unity, Jewish, Buddhist, Hindu, Muslim); (5) clinical applications; (6) education of mental health professionals.

Lovinger, R.J. (1984) *Working with Religious Issues in Therapy.* New York and London: Jason Aronson.

Argues that therapists should appraise religious material as they would any other; such issues often characterise the quality of the patient's interpersonal relationships with others; it is vital to grasp the psychological implications of the patient's religious expressions; ethics, morals and values in psychotherapy; selected religious concepts; religion and personality organisation; implications for personality of Judaism, Catholicism, Protestantism and the American Moslem Mission; dealing with religious issues over the course of psychotherapy; translations and therapy; appendices with useful information on the Bible; appendix with information on Protestant denominations (Lutheranism, Presbyterian and Reformed, Protestant Episcopal, Baptist, Methodist, Holiness and Pentecostal, Salvation Army, Mennonite, Brethren, Quakers, Millenialism, Seventh-Day Adventist, Jehova's Witnesses, Church of Jesus Christ of Latter-Day Saints, Christian Science, Unitarian Universalist Association, Unionist).

Pargament, K.I. (1997) *The Psychology of Religion and Coping: Theory, Research, Practice.* New York and London: Guilford Press.

Clinically relevant discussion of religion as a resource for mental health; analysis of the many different functions that religion serves in the process of coping with tragedy and loss; develops theory based on first-hand accounts, clinical insight and empirical research.

Richards, P.S. and Bergin, A.E. (1997) *A Spiritual Strategy for Counseling and Psychotherapy.* Washington, DC: American Psychological Association.

Advice to psychotherapists to assess routinely the religious and spiritual system of their clients' lives to obtain a more accurate diagnostic picture; pointing out that spirituality is susceptible to scientific investigation; suggestions on how to integrate a theistic spiritual strategy into mainstream approaches to psychology and psychotherapy.

Schumaker, J.F. (ed) (1992) *Religion and Mental Health.* Oxford: Oxford University Press.

The introduction gives an overview of different opinions about the positive or negative influence of religion on mental health, of the problem of the many different definitions of 'religion' and 'mental health', each tending to select certain aspects of the overall phenomena, and of the most important reviews of the field. The four parts have excellent chapters on (1) historical perspectives, (2) religion in relation to different aspects of emotion and cognition, (3) religion and different dimensions of behaviour that involve both social and psychological elements, and (4) the interaction of religion and mental health in a wide cross-cultural context.

Shafranske, E. (ed) (1996a) *Religion and the Clinical Practice of Psychology*. Washington, DC: American Psychological Association Books.

Not a general psychology of religion, but a selection of concerns relevant to mental health and to the clinical practice of psychology; emphasis on integration of theory, findings derived from existing empirical data, and discussions of clinical approach and technique.

Shorto, R. (1999) *Saints and Madmen: Psychiatry Opens its Doors to Religion*. New York: Henry Holt.

The fascinating story, in journalistic style, of how psychiatry in the USA became aware of the importance of paying attention to religion and spirituality.

Theology and the major world religions

I have selected two unusual introductions to theology. They are unusual in that they do not explain or survey the various theologies, but rather show how everyday life confronts religious people with certain *kinds of questions and challenges*, and what *kind of thinking* goes into dealing with these questions and challenges. These books are meant for theology students, but are relevant for psychotherapists since these are the questions and cognitive activities religious patients are involved in, whether they realise it or not.

Ford, D. (1999) *Theology: A Very Short Introduction*. Oxford: Oxford University Press.

Considers how theological questions can grip all sorts of people, whether or not they identify with a particular religious tradition; defines theology as dealing with questions of meaning, truth, beauty, and practice raised in relation to religions and pursued through a range of academic disciplines; introduces theology by 'doing it' and inviting the reader to 'do it', mostly through Christian examples in a way that can inspire comparable thought in relation to other traditions.

Stone, H.W. and Duke, J.O. (1996) *How to Think Theologically*. Minneapolis, MN: Fortress Press.

A focus on *doing* theology distinguishes this book from most introductions and popular accounts of theology; discusses theological reflection as a vital, practical skill that all Christians need in order to make religious sense of real-life situations; treats the how and why of theological resources and reflection; case studies show how real-life situations are connected with major theological topics such as gospel, sin, salvation, vocation and ethical discernment.

For a first orientation to the Bible and the major world religions I recommend the titles mentioned below of the series A Very Short Introduction, published by Oxford University Press. Despite being introductions, these books strive to combine an awareness of contemporary diversity and theoretical problems with a succinct survey of classical approaches. Each volume concludes with suggestions for further reading that will assist you in selecting the specific information needed for a more in-depth study.

Cook, M. (2000) *The Koran: A Very Short Introduction.*
Keown, D. (1996) *Buddhism: A Very Short Introduction.*
Knott, K. (1998) *Hinduism: A Very Short Introduction.*
Riches, J. (2000) *The Bible: A Very Short Introduction.*
Ruthven, M. (1997) *Islam: A Very Short Introduction.*
Solomon, N. (1996) *Judaism: A Very Short Introduction.*

Spiritual development, mysticism and spiritual direction

Edwards, T. (1980) *Spiritual Friend: Reclaiming the Gift of Spiritual Direction*. New York: Paulist Press.

Theoretical and historical analysis of the practice of spiritual direction; practical considerations of what to look for in searching for a spiritual director; how to be a spiritual director for groups and individuals.

Jones, C., Wainwright, G. and Yarnold, E. (eds) (1986) *The Study of Spirituality*. London: SPCK.

Essays on: the theology of spirituality; history of the various Christian spiritual traditions from biblical and ancient Greek roots to twentieth century; other spiritual traditions (Judaism, Islam, Hinduism, Buddhism, African religion, Amerindian spirituality); current spirituality (Orthodoxy, Roman Catholicism, Protestantism, Anglicanism, ecumenical spirituality, Pentecostals and the

Charismatic Movement, and interplay with other religions); pastoral applications; types of spirituality.

Leech, K. (1977) *Soul Friend: A Study of Spirituality* (many reprints). London: Sheldon Press.

An examination of the Christian tradition of spiritual guidance and how this concept relates to the contemporary quest for spirituality.

Wakefield, G.S. (ed) (1983) *A Dictionary of Christian Spirituality*. London: SCM Press.

This book is useful if you want to read spiritual writings: all spiritual traditions have developed their own concepts and terminology, which often makes their literature difficult to read.

Woods, R. (ed) (1981) *Understanding Mysticism: Its Meaning, its Methodology, Interpretations in World Religions, Psychological Evaluations, Philosophical and Theological Appraisals*. London: Athlone Press.

Articles of renowned scholars and scientists (Underhill, Suzuki, James, Deikman, Ornstein and many others) on: description, analysis and methodological concerns; mysticism in world religions; scientific investigations; philosophical and aesthetic evaluations; theological appraisals.

Spiritual writings

I suggest you start by browsing through the books of Dag Hammarskjøld, Etty Hillesum, Thomas Merton, Henri Nouwen, Simone Weil, and Cardinal Basil Hume, to see if any of these writers appeal to you. They have all produced spiritual bestsellers that many booksellers have in stock. Some earlier spiritual writers whose work is still quite popular are Teresa of Avila, John of the Cross, Julian of Norwich, Meister Eckhardt, Thomas à Kempis, and the anonymous author of *The Cloud of Unknowing*.

Notes

Introduction

1   There are many studies and theories about the interplay of religious and psychiatric phenomena, particularly in the USA; see for example Fallot (1998); Shorto (1999).
2   *Diagnostic and Statistical Manual of Mental Disorders (DSM)*, (4th. ed. 1994); Lukoff, Lu and Turner (1998) p.24; Weaver *et al.* (1998a, 1998b,); see also the discussion of the American situation in Shafranske (1996b).
3   The study of Kerssemakers (1989) gives such a literature survey, as well as very illuminating in-depth research on therapists' religious countertransference. See also the research of Gartner *et al.* (1990) on the influence of ideological countertransference on clinical judgement.

Chapter 1

1   Campbell (2000) gives an amusing impression of how many different levels of interpretation are available for a group analyst to choose from in his search for the most effective intervention in a given situation.

Chapter 2

1   Hervormd Nederland, 13 June 1992, p.4.

Chapter 4

1   Kelsey (1978) pp.34–5; Winnicott (1988) p.78.
2   M. Romme, professor in social psychiatry at the University of Maastricht, in an interview published in *Trouw*, 20 May 1994. Cf. Romme (1996); Romme and Escher (1998).
3   The story is in 1 Samuel 3: 1–10.
4   See for example Shorto (1999) and its bibliography.
5   Karl Rahner (1963[1958]) provides an excellent description of the most important principles of evaluating visionary phenomena, both from a theological and a psychological point of view.
6   *Group* techniques have been introduced into the practice of spiritual direction only recently. Since the late Middle Ages spiritual direction has been offered nearly exclusively to individuals. Even when working with groups, as for example in Roman Catholic retreats, the participants were not allowed to talk to each other. They attended the services and listened to the lectures, but for the rest each one was supposed to meditate in isolation and to ask for an individual meeting with the retreat leader if he wanted to discuss anything. In the 1970s, when new group techniques were introduced for a great variety of purposes, group techniques were also introduced in spiritual direction. Schreurs (1990) investigates a

problem this raised, namely that group techniques are designed for purposes that are fundamentally different from the ones in spiritual direction. Some can be applied, some need to be adapted, some must be rejected, and for some purposes spiritual directors have to design their own techniques and exercises. Important books on group methodology in spiritual direction are G. May (1979); Edwards (1980, 1987).

7 1 Corinthians 12: 10.
8 G. May (1982a) p.125.
9 Foulkes 1948, p.29, as quoted in Pines (1983) p.271.

Chapter 5

1 Frankl 1967, ch. 6, p.73.
2 Some excellent writings in this field are Binswanger (1963); Frankl (1967); Yalom (1980); Van Deurzen-Smith (1988, 1997, 1999); Cohn (1997) has a 'recommended reading' list and a discussion of how group analysis fits into this approach. In chs. 13 and 14 of this book the existential view is discussed more extensively.
3 Quotations from Leo Tolstoy, *My Confession, 1879–82,* chs. 3, 4 and 9, trans. Leo Wiener.
4 For a more elaborate discussion, see G. May (1982a) pp.90–1.

Chapter 6

1 Freudenberger (1980) pp.105–7.
2 Fromm (1951) pp.123–4.
3 Benner (1988) ch. 6. For a view on idolatry (defined as psychic structures, forces, and images which masquerade as God) as the root of much pathology, see Jordan (1986).

Chapter 7

1 See Hauerwas' analysis of the unspoken plausibility structure of modern medicine in Hauerwas (1993, pp.62–3); also Bregman's (1999) survey of old and new 'language and imagery of death and grief'.
2 Yalom (1999) pp.24–30.
3 Berger (1980) ch. 1.
4 Dupré (1993).
5 An excellent study of the development of this break-up between spirituality and theology and its effects until this day is McIntosh (1998).
6 Cavell (1981) p.172.
7 Mauss (1938) is a still relevant and much quoted essay about the changes in the meaning of 'person' from antiquity till the twentieth century.
8 Exodus 3: 2ff.
9 Otto (1950[1924]), ch. 4 (on 'mysterium tremendum') and ch. 6 (on 'mysterium fascinans').
10 See Dupré (1976, 1972).
11 Berger 1980, pp.5–6; Myerson (2001); see also Graham (1999).

Chapter 8

1   Foulkes (1985) p.17; P. Schilder (1970); see also Belzen (1997).
2   Foulkes (1967) p.32; see also Roberts (1982); Brown and Zinkin (1994).
3   Foulkes and Anthony (1973) p.26.
4   Foulkes (1985) pp.17–18.
5   Foulkes (1964) p.292.
6   Foulkes and Anthony (1973) p.29.
7   Haubl (1995) pp.27–53 (This is my own free and somewhat shortened translation from German into Dutch into English); see Haans (1995) p.98.
8   For a discussion on the role played by the media and proliferating and changing forms of communication in the formulation of our identities and the constructions of self, see Grodin and Lindlof (1996).
9   See, for example, Dalal (1998) and Earl Hopper's (1996) systematisation of the mutual interaction between the 'social unconscious' and the group process.
10 Michel (1996).
11 De Boer (1994). A classic study of the clinician's concept of mental health is Broverman *et al.* (1970).

Chapter 9

1   Aristotle, *Poetics* 21, 1457b (in the revised Oxford translation (1984): vol. 2, pp. 2332 – 3).
2   See Barthes (1972[1953]); Schafer (1983) ch. 14, 'Narration in the Psycho-Analytic Dialogue' pp.212–39.
3   See Schafer (1983) ch. 16 'The Imprisoned Analysand.' pp.257–80.
4   Pepper (1942). There is an enormous amount of literature on the function of metaphors in people's lives and in the social and natural sciences. Some interesting studies about how metaphors shape human lives are, for example, Cochran (1986); Gibbs (1994), particularly ch. 4: 'Metaphor in Language and Thought'); Gregg (1991); Lakoff and Johnson (1980); Ricoeur (1975); Romanyshyn (1982); Stern (2000). For the efficacy of working with metaphors in the therapeutic interpretation, see Close (1998); Cox and Theilgaard (1987); Lyddon (1989); Lyddon and Adamson (1992); Reider (1972). For illness as a metaphor of cultural concerns, see Malson (1998) (anorexia); Sontag (1978) (TB, cancer); Sontag (1989) (Aids). For the role of root metaphors in religion, see Brümmer (1993); McFague (1983); Moulder (1987); Soskice (1987); Tracy (1981).
5   Abrams (1953).
6   Brümmer (1993) ch. 1.
7   Lyddon and Adamson (1992).
8   Douglas (1966; 1973).
9   Haans (1995) suggests that by restricting the analysis to this antithesis and its solution in this particular group, a much more fundamental change from anachronistic thinking in terms of 'nature' to modern thinking in terms of 'culture' has been hidden from view. I agree that indeed a more fundamental change has taken place in Haubl's group, but I do not think it is primarily the nature-nurture question that is the issue here. See also Erdheim (1995).
10 Watzlawick *et al.* (1973) ch. 7.

11 Jones (1991) discusses some interesting examples in his chs. 3 and 4.

12 Galatians 3: 28 (revised standard version).

13 Sutherland (1995) p.285.

Chapter 10

1   Landow (1982) p.70.

2   Landow (1982) p.16.

3   Borg (1994) pp.153ff.

4   See De Lubac 1998; see also ch. 7, section 6 of this book.

5   Hall (1993) characterises the psychological effects of seventy years of oppression on the Moscow population as analogous to the 'soul murder' of sexually abused children and interrogated prisoners.

6   Van der Kleij (1993) p.34.

7   Revelations 20: 1–5.

8   See Collins, McGinn and Stein (eds) (1998) *The Encyclopedia of Apocalypticism*. This is not so much an encyclopedia which seeks to cover key terms and ideas as it is a collection of essays on apocalypticism and on related themes. The second part of volume 3 (ed. S.J. Stein) treats the impact of apocalypticism on modern secularised (mainly Protestant North American) society. Also mainly limited to the USA is the excellent and very readable collection of essays in Robbins and Palmer's (1997) *Millennium, Messiahs and Mayhem*. A historical study of millenarian movements from their origins to contemporary New Age, ending with some speculations on how the myth may evolve in the future, is to be found in Grosso (1995). Chapter 4 of Anton van Harskamp's (2000) *Het nieuw-religieuze verlangen* discusses apocalypticism and millennialism in New Age and evangelical movements.

9   Patients who are convinced the death of their child is a punishment for their sins are sometimes also misled by another biblical passage, a story in which the death of a child is indeed connected with adultery, but not as a consequence of adultery. It is in the story of David and Bathseba in the book 2 Samuel 12: 1–25. To make it so is again an example of seeing a part and not its biblical whole. Were the *full* story about this particular child and the response of its father to its death known and understood it is clear the particular biblical message is not about punishment for adultery but about human repentance and God's forgiveness. This realisation would very likely bring significant relief to any patient who was responding to the part and not the whole. It would probably not take away guilt feelings, but would pave the way for breaking the vicious connection between religious guilt and the mourning process.

10 Augustine *Confessions* XII.14 (trans. M. Boulding (1999) p.321).

Chapter 11

1   F. Nietzsche, *Die Fröhliche Wissenschaft*, III, 124.

2   Landow (1982) pp.140ff.

3   Debats (1996) p.3; see Blocker (1974); Sartre (1943).

4   Yalom (1980).

5   Debats, Zika and Chamberlain (1992).

6   Debats (1996); Dunn (1994); Harlow *et al.* (1986); Silver *et al.* (1983); Schwartzberg (1993); Taylor *et al.* (1984); Somlai *et al.* (1996); Thompson (1991); Waisberg *et al.* (1994).
7   Fenn (1982) p.45.
8   Fenn (1982) pp.50–1.
9   Davies (1995); see also Baudrillard (1995).
10   Cochran (1986) ch. 4 'Position and Reenactment' pp.95–127, and ch. 6 'Dramatic Units' pp.153–81; Nixon (1962).

Chapter 12

1   Even then the implementation has also other demonstrable sources. The ascetic practice, for example, seems not originally Christian but to be adopted from Jewish, Neo-Platonic and gnostic sources.
2   Underhill (1960) p.300.
3   For example Groeschel (1984).
4   Kübler-Ross (1969).
5   Erikson (1963[1950]), (1982) and various other writings.
6   Both quotes are from Wakefield (1983) 'Ecclesiology and Spirituality', p.122.

Chapter 13

1   Frankl (1955a, 1955b, 1964[1946], 1967). Other 'Founding Fathers' are Binswanger (1963); Boss (1963[1957], 1979). Cf. also Van Deurzen-Smith (1988, 1997, 1999). An excellent overview of the history of existential thinking, its influence on psychology, its affinity to Eastern thinking, and its (often unrecognised) contributions to modern psychotherapy is to be found in Rollo May's 'The origins and significance of the existential movement in psychology' and 'Contributions of existential psychotherapy', both in R. May (1983, pp.37–59 and 91–171). Cohn (1997) includes Foulkes' relation to existential-phenomenological thinking.
2   Yalom (1975) pp.84–5.
3   Yalom (1980).
4   Yalom (1975) p.85. Cf. Combs (1989) who reviews research results on the similarities and differences between good and poor psychotherapists of various schools, showing not only that expert therapists from different schools were more alike in their thinking about therapy than were beginners and experts from the same school, but also that the basic belief systems of the expert therapists of different schools seem to be fundamentally alike. Combs has also literature references on these studies.
5   An interesting account of the history of the now so popular idea of the quest of a 'True Self' distinct from the everyday 'ego' can be found in Heisig (1997). As an example, he analyses how the concept is developed in the psychology of C.G. Jung.
6   Winnicott 1990/1960b, p.46.
7   Heidegger (1980) p.284 (1976, p.240). Martin Heidegger (1889–1976) had the most important, and also the most controversial, influence on modern European philosophy. Heidegger believed that Western philosophy had lost touch with the important questions of human existence, and gave an urgent account of human life as a search for its own

meaning and identity. His major work was *Being and Time* (1976[1927]), in which he presented a philosophical vision of 'man' as being 'thrown' into the world, and always in search of an 'authentic' identity. These ideas reached far wider than his own particular approach. Many important thinkers in such divergent fields as politics, ethics, religion and psychotherapy have developed his ideas further.

8 Cox (1988[1978]).
9 Van Deurzen-Smith (1988, 1997, 1999).
10 Winnicott (1990[1960a]) pp.144–5; Winnicott (1990[1959–64]) p.133; Winnicott (1988[1971]) p.67.
11 R. May (1983) pp.100–2.
12 Wolters (1986). A clear and concise explanation can be found in Benner (1988) pp.114ff. See also Benner (1998).
13 R. May (1983) p.91.

Chapter 14

1 Hammarskjøld (1964, p.180).
2 Otto (1958[1924]) chs. 4 and 6.
3 Moses: in Exodus 4: 10,13; Gideon: in Judges 6: 13; Samuel: in 1 Samuel 3: 10, Saul: in 1 Samuel 9: 21; Jesajah: in Jesajah 6: 8; Jeremiah: in Jeremiah 1: 6ff.
4 Pindar, Pythian Odes 2, 73 (my own translation of 'genoi' hoios essi mathoon').
5 An example is 'Ego regression and purgation', in Fauteux (1994) pp.14–31.
6 Dutch universities and colleges do not have a campus system *per se*, so most undergraduate students leave their homes, rent a room or a small appartment in town, and start their own housekeeping. This can lead to problems of loneliness.
7 Van Outsem (1991) pp. 397–8.
8 A critical discussion of the various theories on anorexia can be found in Malson (1998).
9 Barron (1989); Cheraskin and Ringsdorf (1974). An informative book on the history and practice of fasting in the Christian tradition is Ryan (1981); a study on the spiritual dimensions of eating problems among American girls and women is Lelwica (1999).
10 G. May (1982b) ch. 1.
11 G. May (1982b) p.6.

Chapter 15

1 Spero (1990) p.54.
2 Robinson (1977) pp.12–13.
3 As quoted in Benz (1969, p.93) : (dass sie) 'mit geistigen Auge durch das leibliche sahen.' (my own translation)
4 *Sancti Pachomii Vitae Graecae.* Vita A, Cap. 48 (ed Halkin). A. Veilleux (1980–1982) has translated the passage so: 'Tell us about one of your visions,' and I said to him, 'A sinner like me does not ask God to see visions. It is against God's will, and a mistake... But all the same, hear about a great vision. For what is greater than such a vision, to see the invisible God in a visible man, his temple?'
5 James (The Gifford Lectures 1901–02).

6 Greeley (1975); Hay and Morisy (1978).
7 Schlüter (1974) p.818.
8 Socrates in Xenophon, *Memorabilia* I.4 and IV.3.
9 Davis (1989). See also Gellman (1997).
10 Otto (1958[1924]).
11 Stace (1960).
12 'On March 18, 1958, Merton was in Louisville on an errand in connection with the printing of a new postulant's guide. Standing at the corner of Fourth and Walnut Streets, he had an experience which may well be described as 'mystical'. He saw the crowd of people hurrying about the shopping district and was overwhelmed with a realization that he loved all these people and that they were neither alien to nor separate from him. The experience challenged the concept of a separate 'holy' existence that made him, because he was a monk, different from all of them. He experienced the glorious destiny that comes simply from being a human person and from being united with, not separated from, the rest of the human race.' (Shannon 1987, p.xii)
13 Vernon (1968).
14 Watts and Williams' (1988) excellent book explains the psychological processes involved in arriving at religious knowledge; rejects the view that direct knowledge is impossible in religion, that only 'faith' is possible; argues that the ways in which people come to know other things, in particular how people arrive at personal insights, is close to how they arrive at religious insights; and points to analogies with cognitive processes in psychotherapy.
15 Grof and Grof (1989); see also Lukoff, Lu and Turner (1998); Shorto (1999).

Chapter 16

1 Kuhn (1970[1962], 2000[1979]), Brown (1991) and many others.
2 See Fisher (1967); Parsons (1998). Parsons (1999) is an important book on the Freud-Rolland correspondence about the 'oceanic feeling'. Contrary to the accepted view that Freud and the psychoanalytic tradition are entirely dismissive of mystical states of awareness, Parsons demonstrates that Freud implicitly held three views on mystical experience: the reductive view (reading the experience as regressive and delusional); the adaptive view (emphasising its therapeutic, artistic and adaptive features); and the transformational view (entertaining the possibility that at least some types of mystical modes of knowing may be engaging real cognitive ground).
3 Blumenberg (1983) pp.47–85; see also Scheler (1974) p.113, and Almaas (1989) p.207: 'When you are the personal, the universe that you see outside you is completely experienced as inside you, as if you become a miniature universe. When you are truly personal, you are not just merged with the universe, you are a child of the universe. You are the microcosm.'
4 2 Corinthians 12: 9–10.
5 Hopper (1997); Nitsun (1996).
6 See Sullivan (1953).
7 Van Baal (1985) vol. 1, p.448; (1996[1989]).
8 Weil (1950) Lettre IV (my own translation).
9 See Festinger (1971).

10 Two titles viewing such regularly recurrent doubts as indispensable for spiritual growth are Israel (1997) and McGrath (1990).

Introducing Part 4

1   In his *Categories* Aristotle defines 'substance' (Gr. 'ousia') as that which can neither be a predicate nor an aspect or an attribute of anything else (for example, 'Socrates' cannot be predicated of someone or something else than Socrates himself, and neither is Socrates an aspect or attribute of someone or something else). According to Aristotle, only 'substances' have an independent existence: all other things exist only indirectly, namely as attributes, aspects, qualities or relations of substances, or as kinds of substances. See also Brümmer (1993) pp.33–4.
2   Bowlby (1988).
3   Hassan (1998).

Chapter 17

1   Cohn (1997) ch. 5, p.45.
2   Rizzuto (1979); see also (1996), an excellent article from her on the complex trajectories of convergence and divergence between psychoanalytic psychotherapy and pastoral guidance, followed by four responses.
3   Garland (1982).
4   Some wellknown titles on the Jesus prayer are Gillet (pseud. 'A Monk of the Eastern Church') (1987); Chariton of Valamo (1997); Anonymous (1954).
5   Merton (1975) pp.16–17.
6   Jeffner (1996) p.150.
7   For a discussion of religious scrupulosity see Ciarrocchi (1995).
8   Pargament (1997). See also Pargament *et al.* (1999).
9   Cook and Wimberley (1983).
10 Smith (1968) pp.111ff.

Chapter 18

1   *Trouw* (a prominent Dutch newspaper) 3 May 1993.
2   An excellent article with an extensive bibliography is Lukoff, Lu and Turner (1998); see also Lukoff *et al.* (1992, 1995); Turner *et al.* (1995).
3   Weil (1950); Hillesum (1981).
4   Carretto (1971) Lettera 14 (trans. R.M. Hancock).
5   For 'spiritual emergency', see Lukoff *et al.* (1998); Grof and Grof (1989).
6   Fenton (1974); Schreurs (1996).
7   Manlowe (1995).
8   For 'second-order change' see Watzlawick *et al.* (1973) ch. 7.
9   James (1960[1902]) p.169; Pargament (1997) p.344, see also p.173.
10 Pargament (1997) p.251.
11 Matthew 18: 12–14; Luke 15: 4–7.

12 Brümmer (1993, see also 1999).
13 Brümmer (1984).

Chapter 19

1 Buckland (1970[1908]) is a standard work on this subject.
2 A readable account of this complicated matter is Pinnock (1994).
3 For 'double-bind' see Watzlawick *et al.* (1967) ch. 6.

Chapter 20

1 A. Schilder (1987).
2 Van Dantzig (1972); Dresselhuys (1996); Groen and Van Maanen (1977); Kalman (1977).
3 De Keizer (1998); Zondag (1999); see also Greenberg *et al.* (1986, 1991, 1997).
4 Pargament *et al.* (1999).
5 Braam (1999) ch. 4.

Chapter 21

1 Exodus 19: 5; 24: 8; John 3: 15ff.
2 Girard (1972, 1978, 1982, 1999).
3 Den Heyer (1998).
4 Brümmer (1993) p.194.
5 Ciarrocchi (1995).

Chapter 22

1 Some titles on the psychology of forgiveness are: Cox (1999); Enright *et al.* (1991); Freedman and Enright (1996); Klein (1975); Pingleton (1997); Worthington *et al.* (2000). Augsburger (1996) features various psychological theories in relation to their implications for the process of forgiveness. Jones (1995) explains the difference between what he calls 'therapeutic forgiveness' and 'forgiveness as Christians (ought to) understand it'.
2 See Scholtz (1992) pp.1386–7; Hillesum (1981) p.94.
3 Bondi (1993; see also 1995).

Bibliography

Abrams, M.H. (1953) *The Mirror and the Lamp: Romantic Theory and the Critical Tradition*. Oxford: Oxford University Press.

Almaas, A.H. (1989) *The Freedom To Be*. Berkeley, CA: Diamond Books.

American Psychiatric Association (APA) (1994) *Diagnostic and Statistical Manual of Mental Disorders* 4th edn. (DSM-IV). Washington, DC: APA.

Anonymous (1954) *The Way of a Pilgrim*, transl. R.M. French. London: SPCK.

Aristotle *Categoriae*. In *The Complete Works of Aristotle* (revised Oxford translation), ed. J. Barnes. Princeton, NJ: Princeton University Press (1984).

Aristotle *Poetica*. In *The Complete Works of Aristotle* (revised Oxford translation), ed. J. Barnes. Princeton, NJ: Princeton University Press (1984).

Augsburger, D.W. (1996) *Helping People Forgive*. Louisville, KY: Westminster Press.

Augustine *Confessiones* (*Confessions*, trans. M. Boulding. Villanova, PA: Augustine Heritage Institute (1997). (Another recent translation is by H. Chadwick, Oxford University Press, 1992.)

Baal, J. van (1985) *Ontglipt verleden*. Franeker: Wever.

Baal, J. van (1989) *Mysterie als openbaring*. Utrecht: ISOR (repr. Baarn: Ten Have, 1996).

Barron, E.P. (1989) 'Food for spirituality.' *Journal of Pastoral Care 43*, 2, 131–140.

Barthes, R. (1972[1953]) 'Par où commencer?' In *Nouveaux essais critiques*. Paris: Eds. Du Seuil, 145–55.

Baudrillard, J. (1995) *The Illusion of the End*. Oxford: Polity Press.

Belzen, J.A. (1997) 'Cultural psychology of religion synchronic and diachronic.' In Belzen, J.A. (Ed) (1997) *Hermeneutical Approaches in Psychology of Religion*. Amsterdam and Atlanta, GA: Rodopi.

Benner, D.G. (1988) *Psychotherapy and the Spiritual Quest: Examining the Links between Psychological and Spiritual Health*. Grand Rapids, MI: Baker Book House; London: Hodder and Stoughton.

Benner, D.G. (1998) *Care of Souls: Revisioning Christian Nurture and Counsel*. Grand Rapids, MI: Baker Books.

Benz, E. (1969) *Die Vision: Erfahrungsformen und Bilderwelt*. Stuttgart: Ernst Klett Verlag.

Berger, P. (1980) *The Heretical Imperative: Contemporary Possibilities of Religious Affirmation*. Garden City, NY: Anchor Press.

Bhugra, D. (ed) (1996) *Psychiatry and Religion: Context, Consensus and Controversies*. London and New York: Routledge.

Binswanger, L. (1963) *Being-in-the-world: Selected Papers*, trans. J. Needleman. New York: Basic Books.

Blocker, G. (1974) *The Meaning of Meaninglessness*. Den Haag: Martinus Nijhoff.

Blumenberg, H. (1983) *Die Lesbarkeit der Welt*, 2nd edn. Frankfurt am Main: Suhrkamp (*Legibility of the World*. Chicago: University of Chicago Press, 1990).

Boer, F. de (1994) *De interpretatie van het verschil: De vertaling van klachten van mannen en vrouwen in de RIAGG*. (The interpretation of the difference: The translation of complaints of men and women in ambulant mental health care.) Amsterdam: Spinhuis.

Bondi, R.C. (1993) 'Be not afraid: praying to God the Father.' *Modern Theology 9*, 3, 235–48.

Bondi, R.C. (1995) *Memories of God: Theological Reflections on a Life*. Nashville, TN: Abingdon Press.

Borg, M.J. (1994) *Meeting Jesus Again for the First Time: The Historical Jesus and the Heart of Contemporary Faith*. San Francisco, CA: Harper.

Boss, M. (1963[1957]) *Psychoanalysis and Daseinsanalysis*, trans. J.B. Lefebre. New York: Basic Books.

Boss, M. (1979) *Existential Foundations of Medicine and Psychology*, trans. S. Conway and A. Cleaves. New York: Jason Aronson.

Bowlby, J. (1988) *A Secure Base*. New York: Basic Books.

Braam, A.W. (1999) *Religion and Depression in Later Life: An Empirical Approach*. Amsterdam: Thela Thesis.

Bregman, L. (1999) *Beyond Silence and Denial*. Louisville, KY: Westminster John Knox Press.

Broverman, I.K., Broverman, D.M., Clarkson, F.E. *et al.* (1970) 'Sex-role stereotypes and clinical judgments of mental health.' *Journal of Consulting and Clinical Psychology 34*, 1, 1–7.

Brown, D.G. and Zinkin, L.M. (eds) (1994) *The Psyche and the Social World*. London: Routledge.

Brown, J.R. (1991) *The Laboratory of the Mind: Thought Experiments in the Natural Sciences*. London: Routledge and Kegan Paul.

Brümmer, V. (1984) *What Are We Doing When We Pray?* London: SCM Press.

Brümmer, V. (1993) *The Model of Love: A Study in Philosophical Theology*. Cambridge and New York: Cambridge University Press.

Brümmer, V. (1999) 'Bestowed fellowship: on the love of God.' In G. van den Brink and M. Sarot (eds) *Understanding the Attributes of God*. Frankfurt a/M: Peter Lang, Europäisches Verlag der Wissenschaften, 33–52.

Buckland, W.W. (1970[1908]) *The Roman Law of Slavery: The Condition of the Slave in Private Law from August to Justinian*. Cambridge: Cambridge University Press.

Campbell, J. (2000) 'The dangerous present: bridging past and future (a fictional account of two moments in a group).' *Group Analysis 33*, 2, 179–91; 'Die gefährliche Gegenwart: Brücke zwischen Vergangenheit und Zukunft.' *Gruppenanalyse 10*, 1, 7–18.

Carretto, C. (1971) *Lettere dal deserto* (18th edn) Brescia: La Scuola Editrice. *Letters from the Desert*, trans. R.M. Hancock. (8th edn) London: Darton, Longman and Todd, 1982.

Cavell, S. (1981) *Must We Mean What We Say?* Cambridge: Cambridge University Press.

Chariton of Valamo (1997) *The Art of Prayer: An Orthodox Anthology*, trans. E. Kadloubovsky and E.M. Palmer, with revised bibliography. London and Boston: Faber and Faber.

Cheraskin, E. and Ringsdorf, W.M. (1974) *Psychodietics: Food as the Key to Emotional Health*. New York: Bantam.

Ciarrocchi, J.W. (1995) *The Doubting Disease: Help for Scrupulosity and Religious Compulsions*. New York and Mahwah, NJ: Paulist Press.

Close, H.T. (1998) *Metaphor in Psychotherapy: Clinical Applications of Stories and Allegories*. San Luis Obisco, CA: Impact.

Cochran, L. (1986) *Portrait and Story: Dramaturgical Approaches to the Study of Persons*. New York: Greenwood Press.

Cohn, H.W. (1997) *Existential Thought and Therapeutic Practice: An Introduction to Existential Psychotherapy*. London: Sage.

Collins, J.J., McGinn, B. and Stein, S.J. (eds) (1998) *The Encyclopedia of Apocalypticism*. New York: Continuum.

Combs, A.W. (1989) *A Theory of Therapy: Guidelines for Counseling Practice*. Newbury Park, CA and London: Sage.

Cook, J.A. and Wimberley, D.W. (1983) *Dying and Grieving: Lifespan and Family Perspectives*. New York: Holt, Rinehart and Winston.

Cook, M. (2000) *The Koran: A Very Short Introduction*. Oxford: Oxford University Press.

Cox, M. (1988 [1978]) *Structuring the Therapeutic Process: Compromise with Chaos*. Oxford: Pergamon, repr. with new preface by Jessica Kingsley Publishers, London.

Cox, M. (Ed.) (1999) *Remorse and Reparation*. London and Philadelphia, PA: Jessica Kingsley Publishers.

Cox, M. and Theilgaard, A. (1987) *Mutative Metaphors in Psychotherapy: The Aeolian Mode*. London: Tavistock.

Dalal, F. (1998) *Taking the Group Seriously*. London and Philadelphia, PA: Jessica Kingsley Publishers.

Dantzig, A. van (1972) 'De tragedie der Puttenaren.' In A. van Dantzig, *Snippers*. Vinkeveen: Academic Press.

Davies, J. (1995) *The Christian Warrior in the Twentieth Century*. Oxford: Edwin Mellen Press.

Davis, C. Franks (1989) *The Evidential Force of Religious Experience*. Oxford: Clarendon Press.

Debats, D.L. (1996) *Meaning in Life: Psychometric, Clinical and Phenomenological Aspects*. Groningen: Rijksuniversiteit Groningen.

Debats, D.L., Zika, S. and Chamberlain, K. (1992) 'On the relation between meaning in life and psychological well-being.' *British Journal of Psychology 83*, 133–45.

Debats, D.L., Zika, S. and Chamberlain, K. (1996) 'Meaning in life: clinical relevance and predictive power.' *British Journal of Clinical Psychology 35*, 4, 503–16.

Deurzen-Smith, E. van (1988) *Existential Counselling in Practice.* London: Sage.

Deurzen-Smith, E. van (1997) *Everyday Mysteries: Existential Dimensions of Psychotherapy.* London and New York: Routledge.

Deurzen-Smith, E. van (1999) 'Existentialism and existential psychotherapy.' In C. Mace (ed) *Heart and Soul: The Therapeutic Face of Philosophy.* London and New York: Routledge.

Douglas, M. (1966) *Purity and Danger.* London: Routledge and Kegan Paul.

Douglas, M. (1973[1970]) *Natural Symbols.* New York: Random House.

Dresselhuys, C. (1996) 'Een relatie zonder aanpassen is onmogelijk.' *Opzij* 146–51.

Dunn, D.S. (1994) 'Positive meaning and illusions following disability.' *Journal of Social Behavior and Personality 5*, 123–38.

Dupré, L. (1972) *The Other Dimension: A Search for the Meaning of Religious Attitudes.* Garden City, NY: Doubleday.

Dupré, L. (1976) *Transcendent Selfhood: The Loss and Rediscovery of the Inner Life.* New York: Seabury Press.

Dupré, L. (1993) *Passage to Modernity: An Essay in the Hermeneutics of Nature and Culture.* New Haven, CT and London: Yale University Press.

Edwards, T. (1980) *Spiritual Friend: Reclaiming the Gift of Spiritual Direction.* New York: Paulist Press.

Edwards, T. (1987) *Living in the Presence: Disciplines for the Spiritual Heart.* San Francisco, CA: Harper and Row.

Enright, R.D. and the Human Development Study Group (1991) 'The moral development of forgiveness.' In W.M. Kurtines and J.L. Gewirtz (eds) *Handbook of Moral Behavior and Development*, vol. I, 123–52. Hillsdale, NJ: Lawrence Erlbaum.

Erdheim, M. (1995) 'Anachronizität und Unbewusztheit; Zum Problem der Reproduktion vergangener gesellschaftlicher Wirklichkeiten.' *Gruppenanalyse 5*, 9–27.

Erikson, Erik H. (1963[1950]) *Childhood and Society.* London: Norton.

Erikson, Erik H. (1982) *The Life Cycle Completed: A Review.* London: Norton.

Fallot, R.D. (ed) (1998) *Spirituality and Religion in Recovery from Mental Illness,* New Directions for Mental Health Services no. 80. San Francisco, CA: Jossey-Bass.

Fauteux, K. (1994) *The Recovery of Self: Regression and Redemption in Religious Experience.* New York and Mahwah, NJ: Paulist Press.

Fenn, R.K. (1982) *Liturgies and Trials: The Secularization of Religious Language.* Oxford: Blackwell.

Fenton, J.Y. (1974) 'Bodily theology.' In J.Y. Fenton (ed) *Theology and the Body* 127–45. Philadelphia, PA: Westminster Press.

Festinger, L. (1971) 'Cognitive dissonance.' In R.C. Atkinson (ed) *Contemporary Psychology.* San Francisco, CA: Freeman.

Fisher, D. (1967) 'Sigmund Freud and Romain Rolland.' *American Imago 33*, 1–59.

Ford, D. (1999) *Theology: A Very Short Introduction.* Oxford: Oxford University Press.

Foulkes, S.H. (1948) *Introduction to Group Analytic Psychotherapy: Studies in the Social Integration of Individuals and Groups.* London: Maresfield Reprints.

Foulkes, S.H. (1964) *Therapeutic Group Analysis.* London: Allen and Unwin.

Foulkes, S.H. (1967) Preliminary Issue of *Group Analysis.*

Foulkes, S.H. (1985) 'A short outline of the therapeutic processes in group-analytic psychotherapy.' In T.E. Lear (ed) *Spheres of Group Analysis.* London: Group Analytic Society Publications (first published in *Group Analysis 8* (1975), 63–9.)

Foulkes, S.H. and Anthony, E.J. (1973) *Group Psychotherapy: The Psychoanalytic Approach,* 2nd edn. Harmondsworth: Penguin.

Frankl, V.E. (1964[1946]) *Man's Search for Meaning.* London: Hodder and Stoughton.

Frankl, V.E. (1955a) *The Doctor and the Soul.* New York: Knopf.

Frankl, V.E. (1955b) 'The concept of man in psychotherapy.' *Pastoral Psychology 6,* 16–26.

Frankl, V.E. (1967) *Psychotherapy and Existentialism.* Harmondsworth: Penguin.

Freedman, S.R. and Enright, R.D. (1996) 'Forgiveness as an intervention goal with incest survivors.' *Journal of Consulting and Clinical Psychology 64,* 5, 983–92.

Freudenberger, H.J. (1980) *Burnout: The High Cost of High Achievement.* New York: Bantam.

Fromm, E. (1951) *Psychoanalysis and Religion.* London: Victor Gollancz.

Garland, C. (1982) 'Group-analysis: taking the non-problem seriously.' *Group Analysis 15,* 1, 4–14.

Gartner, J., Harmatz, M., Hohmann, A. *et al.* (1990) 'The effect of patient and clinician ideology on clinical judgment: a study of ideological countertransference.' *Psychotherapy 27,* 1, 98–106.

Gellman, J.I. (1997) *Experience of God and the Rationality of Theistic Belief.* Ithaca, NY and London: Cornell University Press.

Gibbs Jr, R.W. (1994) *The Poetics of Mind: Figurative Thought, Language, and Understanding.* Cambridge: Cambridge University Press.

Gillet, L. (psd. 'A Monk of the Eastern Church') (1987) *The Jesus Prayer,* rev. edn. with a foreword by Kallistos Ware, St Vladimir's Press. New York: Crestwood.

Girard, R. (1972) *La violence et le sacré.* Paris: Grasset. (*Violence and the Sacred.* Baltimore, MD: Johns Hopkins University Press, 1977.)

Girard, R. (1978) *Des choses cachées depuis la fondation du monde.* Paris: Grasset. (*Things Hidden since the Foundation of the World.* Stanford, CA: Stanford University Press, 1993.)

Girard, R. (1982) *Le bouc émissaire.* Paris: Grasset (*The Scapegoat.* Baltimore, MD: Johns Hopkins, 1989).

Girard, R. (1999) *Je vois Satan tomber comme l'éclair.* Paris: Grasset. (*I See Satan Fall Like Lightning.* Maryknoll, NY: Orbis, 2001.)

Graham, G. (1999) *The Internet: A Philosophical Inquiry.* London: Routledge.

Greeley, A.M. (1975) *The Sociology of the Paranormal: A Reconnaissance.* Sage Research Papers in the Social Sciences, vol. 3, series no. 90–023 (Studies in Religion and Ethnicity Series), Beverly Hills, CA: Sage.

Greenberg, J., Pyszczynski, T. and Solomon, S. (1986) 'The causes and consequences of a need for self-esteem.' In R.F. Baumeister (ed) *Public Self and Private Self.* New York: Springer Verlag.

Greenberg, J., Solomon, S. and Pyszczynski, T. (1991) 'A terror management theory of social behaviour.' In M.P. Zanna (ed) *Advances in Experimental Social Psychology 21*, 91–159. San Diego, CA: Academic Press.

Greenberg, J., Solomon, S. and Pyszczynski, T. (1997) 'Terror management theory of self-esteem and cultural worldviews.' In M.P. Zanna (ed) *Advances in Experimental Social Psychology 29*, 61–139.

Gregg, G.S. (1991) *Self-Representation: Life Narrative Studies in Identity and Ideology.* New York: Greenwood Press.

Grodin, D. and Lindlof, T.R. (eds) (1996) *Constructing the Self in a Mediated World.* London: Sage.

Groen, K. and Maanen, W. van (1977) *Putten op de Veluwe.* Zutphen: De Walburg Pers.

Groeschel, B.J. (1984) *Spiritual Passages: The Psychology of Spiritual Development.* New York: Crossroad.

Grof, S. and Grof, C. (eds) (1989) *Spiritual Emergencies: When Personal Transformation Becomes a Crisis.* Los Angeles, CA: Tarcher.

Grosso, M. (1995) *The Millennium Myth.* Newcastle: Quest Books.

Haans, A.H.M. (1995) 'Voortpeinzen.' *Groepstherapie 3*, 98–100.

Hall, Z. (1993) 'The Russian experience.' *Group Analysis 26*, 1, 96–7.

Hammarskjøld, D. (1964) *Markings*, trans. L. Sjøberg and W.H. Auden. New York: Ballantine.

Harlow, L.L., Newcomb, M.D. and Bentler, P.M. (1986) 'Depression, self-derogation, substance use, and suicide ideation: lack of purpose in life as a mediational factor.' *Journal of Clinical Psychology 42*, 1, 5–21.

Harskamp, A. van (2000) 'Nieuw-religieuze fascinatie voor het einde.' ('The New Age fascination with the end of the world.') In *Het nieuw-religieuze verlangen.* Kampen: Kok.

Hassan, J. (1998) 'Counselling with Holocaust survivors.' In C. Feltham (ed) *Witness and Vision of the Therapists.* London: Sage.

Haubl, R. (1995) 'Die Gesellschaftlichkeit der psychischen Realität. Über die gruppenanalytische Konstruktion multipler Wirklichkeiten.' *Gruppenanalyse 1*, 27–53.

Hauerwas, S. (1993) *Naming the Silences: God, Medicine, and the Problem of Suffering.* Edinburgh: T and T Clark.

Hay, D. and Morisy, A. (1978) 'Reports of ecstatic, paranormal, or religious experience in Great Britain and the United States: a comparison of trends.' *Journal for the Scientific Study of Religion 17*, 255–68.

Heidegger, M. (1976[1927]) *Sein und Zeit.* Tübingen: Max Niemeyer Verl. (*Being and Time*, transl. J. Macquarrie and E. Robinson. Oxford: Blackwell, 2000 (8th repr., first ed. 1962). This translation conveniently repeats the pagination of the German original.)

Heisig, J.W. (1997) 'The quest of the True Self: Jung's rediscovery of a modern invention.' *Journal of Religion 77*, 3, 252–67.

Heyer, C.J. den (1997) *Verzoening: Bijbelse notities bij een omstreden thema.* Kapen: Kok (*Jesus and the Doctrine of the Atonement: Biblical Notes on a Conversational Topic.* Harrisburg NJ: Trinity Press, 1998.)

Hillesum, Etty (1981) *Het verstoorde leven.* Haarlem: De Haan. (*Etty: A Diary 1941–1943*, introd. by J.G. Gaarlandt, trans. by Arnold J. Pomerans, London: Jonathan Cape, 1983.)

Hillesum, Etty (1991) *Etty. De nagelaten geschriften van Etty Hillesum 1941–1943*, derde herziene druk. Amsterdam: Uitgeverij Balans.

Hood Jr, R.W. (ed) (1995) *Handbook of Religious Experience.* Birmingham, AL: Religious Education Press.

Hopper, E. (1996) 'Das gesellschaftliche Unbewuszte in der klinischen Arbeit: Reflexionen über die "vollständige Deutung" und die "Quadratur des therapeutischen Dreiecks".' ('The social unconscious in clinical work.') *Gruppenanalyse 6*, 1, 67–113.

Hopper, E. (1997) 'Traumatic experience in the unconscious life of groups: a fourth basic assumption.' *Group Analysis 30*, 439–70.

Israel, M. (1997) *Doubt: The Way of Growth.* London and Oxford: Mowbray.

James, W. (1902) *The Varieties of Religious Experience: A Study in Human Nature.* The Gifford Lectures delivered at Edinburgh, 1901–2. (London and Glasgow: Collins, 1960; Cambridge, MA: Harvard University Press, 1985.)

Jeffner, A. (1996) 'Salvation in a secular world.' In V. Brümmer and M. Sarot (eds) *Happiness, Well-being and the Meaning of Life: A Dialogue of Social Science and Religion* pp.144–54. Kampen: Kok Pharos,

Jones, C., Wainwright, G. and Yarnold, E. (eds) (1986) *The Study of Spirituality.* London: SPCK.

Jones, G. (1995) *Embodying Forgiveness.* Grand Rapids, MI: Eerdmans.

Jones, J.W. (1991) *Contemporary Psycho-Analysis and Religion: Transference and Transcendence.* New Haven, CT and London: Yale University Press.

Jordan, M.R. (1986) *Taking on the Gods: The Task of the Pastoral Counsellor.* Nashville, TN: Abingdon Press.

Kalman, A. (1977) 'De kerk heeft de mensen weerloos gemaakt.' *Amersfoortse Courant,* 10 December.

Keizer, M. de (1998) *Putten: De razzia en de herinnering.* Amsterdam: Bert Bakker.

Kelsey, M. (1978) *Dreams: A Way to Listen to God.* New York and Mahwah, NJ: Paulist Press.

Keown, D. (1996) *Buddhism: A Very Short Introduction.* Oxford: Oxford University Press.

Kerssemakers, J.H.N. (1989) *Psychotherapeuten en religie: Een verkennend onderzoek naar tegenoverdracht bij religieuze problematiek.* Nijmegen: Katholiek Studiecentrum.

Kleij, G. van der (1993) 'Religion and Freud and groups.' *Group Analysis 26,* 1, 27–37.

Klein, Melanie (1975) *Love, Guilt and Reparation and Other Works 1921–1945.* New York: Delacorte Press.

Knott, K. (1998) *Hinduism: A Very Short Introduction.* Oxford: Oxford University Press.

Koenig, H.G. (ed) (1998) *Handbook of Religion and Mental Health.* San Diego, CA: Academic Press.

Kübler-Ross, E. (1969) *On Death and Dying.* New York: Macmillan.

Kuhn, T.S. (1970[1962]) *The Structure of Scientific Resolutions,* 2nd edn, enlarged. Chicago and London: The University of Chicago Press.

Kuhn, T.S. (2000[1979]) 'Metaphor in Science.' In T.S. Kuhn (2000) *The Road Since Structure: Philsophical Essays 1970–1993,* ed. J. Connant and J. Haugeland. Chicago and London: University of Chicago Press, 196–207. (Also found in A. Ortony (ed) (1979) *Metaphor and Thought.* Cambridge: Cambridge University Press.

Lakoff, G. and Johnson, M. (1980) *Metaphors We Live By.* Chicago: University of Chicago Press.

Landow, G.P. (1982) *Images of Crisis: Literary Iconology, 1750 to the Present.* Boston, MA and London: Routledge and Kegan Paul.

Leech, K. (1977) *Soul Friend: A Study of Spirituality.* London: Sheldon Press.

Lelwica, M.M. (1999) *Starving for Salvation: The Spiritual Dimensions of Eating Problems among American Girls and Women.* Oxford: Oxford University Press.

Lovinger, R.J. (1984) *Working with Religious Issues in Therapy.* New York and London: Jason Aronson.

Lovinger, R.J. (1996) 'Considering the religious dimension in assessment and treatment.' In E.P. Shafranske (ed) *Religion and Clinical Practice of Psychology.* Washington, DC: American Psychological Association, pp.327–63.

Lubac, Henri de (1998) *Medieval Exegesis, vol. 1: The Four Senses of Scripture.* Grand Rapids, MI: Wm B. Eerdmans.

Lukoff, D., Lu, F. and Turner, R. (1992) 'Toward a more culturally sensitive DSM-IV: psychoreligious and psychospiritual problems.' *Journal of Nervous and Mental Disease 180,* 11, 673–82.

Lukoff, D., Lu, F. and Turner, R. (1995) 'Cultural considerations in the assessment and treatment of religious and spiritual problems.' *Cultural Psychiatry 18,* 3, 467–85.

Lukoff, D., Lu, F. and Turner, R. (1998) 'From spiritual emergency to spiritual problem: the transpersonal roots of the new DSM-IV category.' *Journal of Humanistic Psychology 38,* 2, 21–50.

Lyddon, W.J. (1989) 'Root metaphor theory: a philosophical framework for counseling and psychotherapy.' *Journal of Counseling and Development 67,* 442–8.

Lyddon, W.J. and Adamson, L.A. (1992) 'Worldview and counseling preference: an analogue study.' *Journal of Counseling and Development 71,* 41–7.

McFague, S. (1983) *Metaphorical Theology: Models of God in Religious Language*. London: SCM Press.

McGrath, A.E. (1990) *Doubt: Handling It Honestly*. Leicester: Inter-Varsity.

McIntosh, M.A. (1998) *Mystical Theology*. Oxford: Blackwell.

Malson, H. (1998) *The Thin Woman: Feminism, Post-structuralism and the Social Psychology of Anorexia Nervosa*. London and New York: Routledge.

Manlowe, J.L. (1995) *Faith Born of Seduction: Sexual Trauma, Body Image and Religion*. New York and London: New York University Press.

Mauss, M. (1938) 'Une catégorie de l'esprit humain: la notion de personne celle de "Moi".' *Journal of the Royal Anthropological Institute 68* (Huxley Memorial Lecture, 1938) (Engl. trans. by B. Brewster in *Sociology and Psychology*. London: Routledge and Kegan Paul, 1979.)

May, G.G. (1979) *Pilgrimage Home*. New York: Paulist Press.

May, G.G. (1982a) *Care of Mind, Care of Spirit*. San Francisco, CA: Harper and Row.

May, G.G. (1982b) *Will and Spirit: A Contemplative Psychology*. San Francisco, CA: Harper and Row.

May, R. (1983) *The Discovery of Being: Writings in Existential Psychology*. New York: Norton.

Merton, T. (1975) *Spiritual Direction and Meditation*. Wheathampstead, Herts: Anthony Clarke.

Michel, L. (1996) 'The significance of the patient's and the therapist's cultural groups.' *Group Analysis 29*, 3, pp.393–402.

Moulder, J. (1987) 'Metaphors and models in religion and theology.' *South African Journal of Philosophy 6*, 1, 29–34.

Myerson, G. (2001) *Heidegger, Habermas and the Mobile Phone*. Cambridge: Icon Books.

Nietzsche, F. (1882) *Die Fröhliche Wissenschaft*. (*The Gay Science*, trans. Kaufmann, New York: Random House 1974.) The Complete Works of Friedrich Nietzsche, 20 vols, ed. Ernst Behler. Stanford, CA: Stanford University Press.

Nitsun, M. (1996) *The Anti-Group: The Destructive Forces in the Group and their Creative Potential*. London: Routledge.

Nixon, R. (1962) *Six Crises*. Garden City, NY: Doubleday.

Otto, R. (1924) *Das Heilige*. Gotha/Stuttgart: F.A. Perthes Verl. (*The Idea of the Holy: An Inquiry into the Non-Rational Factor in the Idea of the Divine and its Relation to the Rational*, trans. J.W. Harvey. Oxford and New York: Oxford University Press, 1958, 2nd edn.)

Outsem, R.E. van (1991) 'Anorexia nervosa in vier soorten.' *Maandblad voor Geestelijke Volksgezondheid 46*, 4, 394–406.

Pachomius (1932) *Sancti Pachomii Vitae Graecae*. Subsida Hagiographica 19, ed. F. Halkin. Brussels: Société des Bollandistes. (*Pachomian Koinonia: The Lives, Rules and Other Writings of Saint Pachomius and His Disciples*, trans. A. Veilleux. Kalamazoo: Cistercian Publications, 1980–1982.)

Pargament, K.I. (1997) *The Psychology of Religion and Coping: Theory, Research, Practice*. New York and London: Guilford Press.

Pargament, K.I., Smith, B.W., Koenig, H.G. *et al.* (1999) 'Patterns of positive and negative religious coping with major life stressors.' *Journal for the Scientific Study of Religion 37*, 4, 710–24.

Parsons, W.B. (1998) 'The oceanic feeling revisited.' *Journal of Religion 78*, 4, 501–23.

Parsons, W.B. (1999) *The Enigma of the Oceanic Feeling: Revisioning the Psychoanalytic Theory of Mysticism.* New York: Oxford University Press.

Pepper, S. (1942) *World Hypotheses.* Berkeley and Los Angeles: University of California Press.

Pindar (1994) *Pythionikoi. (Pythian Odes)* Herakleion: Bikelaia Demotike Bibliotheke.

Pines, M. (1983) 'The contribution of S.H. Foulkes to group therapy.' In M. Pines (ed.) *The Evolution of Group Analysis,* pp.265–85 London: Routledge and Kegan Paul.

Pingleton, J.P. (1997) 'Why we don't forgive: a biblical and object relations theoretical model for understanding failures in the forgiveness process.' *Journal of Psychology and Theology 25*, 4, 403–13.

Pinnock, C., Rice, C., Sanders, J. *et al.* (1994) *The Openness of God: A Biblical Challenge to the Traditional Understanding of God.* Downers Grove, IL: InterVarsity Press; Carlisle: Paternoster Press.

Rahner, K. (1958) *Visionen und Prophezeiungen.* Freiburg: Herder. (*Visions and Prophecies.* London: Burns and Oats, 1963.)

Reider, N. (1972) 'Metaphor as interpretation.' *International Journal of Psycho-Analysis 53*, 463–9.

Richards, P.S. and Bergin, A.E. (1997) *A Spiritual Strategy for Counseling and Psychotherapy.* Washington, DC: American Psychological Association.

Riches, J. (2000) *The Bible: A Very Short Introduction.* Oxford: Oxford University Press.

Ricoeur, P. (1975) *La métaphore vive.* Paris: Eds du Seuil. (*The Rule of Metaphor: Multi-Disciplinary Studies of the Creation of Meaning in Language,* trans. R. Czerny. Toronto: University of Toronto Press, 1977.)

Rizzuto, A-M. (1979) *Birth of the Living God: A Psychoanalytic Study.* Chicago: University of Chicago Press.

Rizzuto, A-M. (1996) 'Psychoanalytic psychotherapy and pastoral guidance.' *Tidsskrift for Sielesorg 2*, 95–107; repr. *Journal of Pastoral Care 52* (1998), 1, 69–78.

Robbins, T. and Palmer, S.J. (1997) *Millennium, Messiahs and Mayhem: Contemporary Apocalyptic Movements.* London: Routledge.

Roberts, J.P. (1982) 'Foulkes' concept of the matrix.' *Group Analysis 15*, 2, 111–26.

Robinson, E. (1977) *The Original Vision: A Study of the Religious Experience of Childhood.* Oxford: Religious Experience Research Unit.

Romanyshyn, R. (1982) *Psychological Life: From Science to Metaphor.* Austin, TX: University of Texas Press.

Romme, M.A.J. (ed) (1996) *Understanding Voices: Coping with Auditory Hallucinations and Confusing Realities.* Maastricht: Rijksuniversiteit Limburg, Dept of Psychiatry and Neuropsychology.

Romme, M.A.J. and Escher, A.D.M.A.C. (1998) *Stemmen horen accepteren: Verschillende manieren van omgaan met stemmen in je hoofd.* Baarn: Tirion.

Ruthven, M. (1997) *Islam: A Very Short Introduction.* Oxford: Oxford University Press.

Ryan, Th. (1981) *Fasting Rediscovered.* New York: Paulist Press.

Sartre, J.P. (1943) *L'être et le néant.* Paris: NRF. (*Being and Nothingness,* trans. H.E. Barnes. New York: Simon and Schuster, 1992/1956.)

Schafer, R. (1983) *The Analytic Attitude.* London: Hogarth Press.

Scheler, M. (1974 [1928]) *Wesen und Formen der Sympathie.* Bern and München: Francke (*The Nature of Sympathy.* Hamden, CT: Archon, 1970).

Schilder, A. (1987) *Hulpeloos maar schuldig: Het verband tussen een gereformeerde paradox en depressie.* Kampen: Kok.

Schilder, P. (1970) *The Image and Appearance of the Human Body.* New York: International Universities Press.

Schlüter, D. (1974) 'Gottesbeweis.' In J. Ritter and K. Gründer (eds) *Historisches Wörterbuch der Philosophie,* vol. 3, pp.818–30. Basel: Schwabe.

Scholtz, G. (1992) 'Schöner Geist, Schöngeist.' In J. Ritter and K. Gründer (eds) *Historisches Wörterbuch der Philosophie,* vol. 8, pp.1386–7. Basel: Schwabe.

Schreurs, A. (1990) *Spirituele begeleiding van groepen: Bijdrage tot een praktijktheorie voor geloofspractica.* (Group methods in spiritual direction.) Kampen: Kok.

Schreurs, A. (1996) 'Van zielige lijven en lijvige zielen: Op zoek naar een bruikbare spirituele antropologie.' ('Search for a workable theory of spiritual man'.) In B. Voorsluis (ed) *Geïnspireerd leven,* pp.100–19. Zoetermeer: Meinema.

Schumaker, J.F. (ed) (1992) *Religion and Mental Health.* Oxford: Oxford University Press.

Schwartzberg, S.S. (1993) 'Struggling for meaning: how HIV-positive gay men make sense of AIDS.' *Professional Psychology 24,* 483–90.

Shafranske, E. (ed) (1996a) *Religion and the Clinical Practice of Psychology.* Washington, DC: American Psychological Association Books.

Shafranske, E. (1996b) 'Religious beliefs, affiliations, and practices of clinical psychologists.' In E. Shafranske (ed) (1996a), pp.149–62.

Shannon, W.H. (1987) *Thomas Merton's Dark Path,* rev. edn. New York: Farrar, Straus, Giroux.

Shorto, R. (1999) *Saints and Madmen: Psychiatry Opens its Doors to Religion.* New York: Henry Holt.

Silver, R.L., Boon, C. and Stones, M.H. (1983) 'Searching for meaning in misfortune: making sense of incest.' *Journal of Social Issues 39,* 81–102.

Smith, J.E. (1968) *Experience and God.* Oxford: Oxford University Press.

Solomon, N. (1996) *Judaism: A Very Short Introduction.* Oxford: Oxford University Press.

Somlai, A.M., Kelly, J.A., Kalichman, S.C. *et al.* (1996) 'An empirical investigation of the relationship between spirituality, coping, and emotional distress in people living with HIV infection and AIDS.' *Journal of Pastoral Care 50,* 2, 181–91.

Sontag, S. (1978) *Illness as a Metaphor.* New York: Farrar, Strauss, Giroux.

Sontag, S. (1989) *Aids and its Metaphors*. New York: Farrar, Strauss, Giroux.

Soskice, J.M. (1987) *Metaphor and Religious Language*. Oxford: Clarendon Press.

Spero, M.H. (1990) 'Parallel dimensions of experience in psychoanalytic psychotherapy of the religious patient.' *Psychotherapy 27*, 1, 53–71.

Spilka, B. and McIntosh, D.N. (eds) (1996) *The Psychology of Religion: Theoretical Approaches*. Boulder, CO: Westview Press.

Stace, W.T. (1960) *Mysticism and Philosophy*. Philadelphia, PA: J.B. Lippincott.

Stern, J. (2000) *Metaphor in Context*. Cambridge, MA: The MIT Press.

Stone, H.W. and Duke, J.O. (1996) *How to Think Theologically*. Minneapolis, MN: Fortress Press.

Sullivan, H.S. (1953) *The Interpersonal Theory of Psychiatry*. New York: Norton.

Sutherland, A.V. (1995) 'Worldframes and God-talk in trauma and suffering.' *Journal of Pastoral Care 49*, 3, 280–92.

Taylor, S.E., Lichtman, R.R. and Wood, J.V. (1984) 'Attributions, beliefs about control, and adjustment to breast cancer.' *Journal of Personality and Social Psychology 46*, 489–502.

Thompson, S.C. (1991) 'Finding positive meaning in a stressful event and coping.' *Basic and Applied Social Psychology 1*, 81–96.

Tolstoy, L. (1884) *Ispoved 1879–82*. (many translations and reprints). The quotations are from *My Confession*, trans. Leo Wiener (1905). London: J.M. Dent & Sons.

Tracy, D. (1981) *The Analogical Imagination: Christian Theology and the Culture of Pluralism*. London: SCM Press.

Turner, R., Lukoff, D., Barnhouse, R.T. *et al.* (1995) 'Religious or spiritual problem: a cultural sensitive diagnostic category in the DSM-IV.' *Journal of Nervous and Mental Disease 183*, 7, 435–44.

Underhill, E. (1911, rev. edn 1930, many reprints) *Mysticism: A Study in the Nature and Development of Man's Spiritual Consciousness*. New York: E.P. Dutton.

Vernon, G.M. (1968) 'The religious "nones": a neglected category.' *Journal for the Scientific Study of Religion 2*, 219–29, quoted in J.F. Schumaker, 'Mental health consequences of irreligion.' In J.F. Schumaker (ed) 1992.

Waisberg, J.L., and Porter, J.E. (1994) 'Purpose in life and outcome of treatment for alcohol dependence.' *British Journal of Clinical Psychology 33*, 49–63.

Wakefield, G.S. (ed) (1983) *A Dictionary of Christian Spirituality*. London: SCM Press.

Watts, F. and Williams, M. (1988) *The Psychology of Religious Knowing*. London and New York: Geoffrey Chapman.

Watzlawick, P., Beavin, J. H. *et al.* (1967) *Pragmatics of Human Communications*. New York: Norton.

Watzlawick, P., Weakland, J.H. and Fisch, R. (1973) *Change: Principles of Problem Formation and Problem Resolution*. New York: Norton.

Weaver, A.J., Kline, A.E., Samford, J.A. *et al.* (1998a) 'Is religion taboo in psychology? A systematic analysis of research on religion in seven major American Psychological Association Journals: 1991–1994.' *Journal of Psychology and Christianity 17*, 3, 220–32.

Weaver, A.J., Samford, J.A., Larson, D.B. *et al.* (1998b) 'A systematic review of research on religion in four major psychiatric journals: 1991–1995.' *Journal of Nervous and Mental Disease 186*, 3, 187–9.

Weil, S. (1950) *Attente de Dieu*. Paris: La Colombe, Eds. du Vieux Colombier. (*Waiting for God*. San Francisco, CA: Harper and Row, 1973.)

Winnicott, D.W. (1990[1960a]) 'Ego distortion in terms of True and False Self.' (Repr. in *The Maturational Processes and the Facilitating Environment*. London: Karnac Books and the Institute of Psycho-Analysis.)

Winnicott, D.W. (1990[1960b]) 'The theory of the parent–infant relationship.' (Repr. in *The Maturational Processes and the Facilitating Environment*. London: Karnac Books and the Institute of Psycho-Analysis.)

Winnicott, D.W. (1990[1959–1964]) 'Classification: is there a psycho-analytic contribution to psychiatric classification?' (Repr. in *The Maturational Processes and the Facilitating Environment*. London: Karnac Books and the Institute of Psycho-Analysis.)

Winnicott, D.W. (1988[1971]) 'Playing: creative activity and the search for the Self.' In *Playing and Reality*. Harmondsworth: Penguin.

Wolters, A. (1986) *Creation Regained: A Transforming View of the World*. Leicester: IVP.

Woods, R. (ed) (1981) *Understanding Mysticism: Its Meaning, Its Methodology, Interpretations in World Religions, Psychological Evaluations, Philosophical and Theological Appraisals*. London: Athlone Press.

Worthington Jr, E.L., Kurusu, T.A., Collins, W. *et al.* (2000) 'Forgiving usually takes time: a lesson learned by studying interventions to promote forgiveness.' *Journal of Psychology and Theology 28*, 1, 3-20.

Wulff, D.M. (1991) *Psychology of Religion: Classic and Contemporary Views*. New York: Wiley.

Xenophon, *Memorabilia*. In Xenophontis Opera Omnia tomus II, ed. E. Marchant, Oxford: Oxford University Press (1901, repr. 1955).

Yalom, I.D. (1975) *The Theory and Practice of Group Psychotherapy*, 2nd edn. New York: Basic Books.

Yalom, I.D. (1980) *Existential Psychotherapy*. New York: Basic Books.

Yalom, I.D. (1999) *Momma and the Meaning of Life: Tales of Psychotherapy*. New York: Basic Books.

Zondag, H. (1999) 'De herinnering aan "Putten". Een cultuurpsychologisch perspectief op de verwerking van leed.' *Psyche en Geloof 10*, 2, 129–42.

Vignettes index

Author Index

Subject Index